HOW CREATIVITY

RULES THE WORLD

THE ART AND BUSINESS OF TURNING

YOUR IDEAS INTO GOLD

■

MARIA BRITO

HarperCollins
Leadership

An Imprint of HarperCollins

Published by HarperCollins Leadership, an imprint of HarperCollins Focus LLC.

Any internet addresses, phone numbers, or company or product information printed in this book are offered as a resource and are not intended in any way to be or to imply an endorsement by HarperCollins Leadership, nor does HarperCollins Leadership vouch for the existence, content, or services of these sites, phone numbers, companies, or products beyond the life of this book.

ISBN 978-1-4002-3539-1 (eBook)
ISBN 978-1-4002-3538-4 (HC)

Library of Congress Cataloging-in-Publication Data
Library of Congress Cataloging-in-Publication application has been submitted.

Printed in Canada
22 23 24 25 26 LSC 10 9 8 7 6 5 4 3 2 1

*To Enrique, who taught me with actions what being creative really means,
and to all of you whose creativity will rule the world.*

Contents

PART III: **TOOLS OF THE TRADE**

PART IV: **THE WAY FORWARD**

Introduction

TODAY EVERYTHING AND everyone competes for our attention. We live in a world that constantly drowns all of our senses. It is not enough to do something well; it is necessary to stand out, to be different, to be creative. Mastering this skill will not only benefit your career but also have a ripple effect in all you do. This book will teach you how to do that, for life.

Businesses need to get noticed, marketers want to sell more, artists long to create impact, entrepreneurs look for ways to surprise and delight their customers with every new turn. But most people fail at these endeavors because they don't know how to.

The good news is that you possess a never-ending and always-renewable source you can use to make money, reinvent yourself, pivot your business, or create products or services that your clients will love and will keep them coming back. It's called creativity. No matter what the issue, you can discover ways that disrupt and shake, allow you to make noise and gain influence, get your practice noticed or your big idea materialized.

Every breakthrough in every industry and field comes from people who used their creativity to think differently. Developing your unique ability to express your ideas while generating value to your clients, your audience, or the people you serve will take you far.

Whether you are an entrepreneur, an artist, or an employee, your creativity will help you turn the mundane into the extraordinary. This is the most crucial skill to have on your path toward success. Creative people come up with solutions that are relevant and novel for today's world. For years you've been told that to be like them you had to come to this world with a special God-given talent, that there's something inside these visionaries that sets them apart and which nobody else can emulate. However, that is not true. Nearly everything that you've been told about creativity is a lie. Don't believe the myth that creativity is only for the few chosen ones or that it is genetic. It's false to think that you either have it or you don't, that it can't be taught or learned. Trust me; you were not born with a deficit in your creative abilities. Whoever said only artists are creative or that only scientists, engineers, and tech people innovate was dead wrong. Creativity is not about arts and crafts and cutouts or technical wizardry. Creativity is about fostering specific habits, making associations, and standing behind the ideas that come out of them.

The old adage *think outside the box* doesn't cut it anymore. The most creative people in the world have a bag of tricks that help them nurture and grow their best ideas. This book gives you timeless strategies and tools that have been used time and time again by people from all walks of life throughout history.

Creativity also is not one single thing. It is an amalgamation of habits and mindsets nurtured by will and design. Creativity is what allows artists and entrepreneurs to move, shake, invent, disrupt, and transition as often as needed to meet today's challenges and tomorrow's, in our convoluted world where change is the only constant. The way to survive and thrive in this environment is by using our creativity to keep us relevant and ahead of the curve.

What do Leonardo da Vinci, Elon Musk, and Shonda Rhimes have in common? They are creative entrepreneurs. Successful entrepreneurs and artists are very similar; they imagine radical new possibilities without constraints or limitations and depend on their creativity to achieve their goals. As you'll see from the examples in this book, they share every trait that sparks the genius of their creative minds—their most important resource, which allowed them to forge their unique paths. Many of the examples in this book point at brilliant and creative tech entrepreneurs, but it is a mistake to think that creativity and innovation can only spur out of people dedicated to technology or science. It is also a mistake to think that only artists can be creative.

I once was a miserable corporate attorney working at a big law firm in New York City, confined by restrictive rules and surroundings. After much soul-searching, I left that well-paid and stable job to start my own business in a completely unrelated industry, with no connections, no clients, no previous training, and no formal education in the business of art. Had I not learned how to develop my own creativity, I wouldn't have made it this far. It's been thirteen years of tremendous joy, entrepreneurial effort, and hard work, but mostly my ability to generate thousands of ideas and relentlessly pursue and execute the most original ones.

In this book, you'll discover how to do all of the following:

- Turn your business around
- Invent something new
- Get unstuck
- Adopt habits and teach your brain to see things that others miss
- Make associations that you never thought about before
- Materialize your best ideas

I know it can be done because I have not only been my own guinea pig, but also taught hundreds of others—executives, entrepreneurs, freelancers, managers, business owners, artists, and many more—in person and online to do it. But you must put in the time needed to understand that creativity is a series of actions that bring about desired results. The operative word is *action*—creativity eludes those who sit down and wait for it to come. Your ability to respond swiftly to changes and come up with novel ideas that can be realized will determine your long-term survival and success in any endeavor.

Right after I quit my job as an attorney, I opened an art advisory company that helps people and companies acquire, curate, develop, and display art and gain the financial, emotional, and aesthetic value that comes from collecting. By slowly learning how to use my dormant creativity and disrupt models that existed before I entered the business, I later branched out into creative design, product design in collaboration with artists, app development, gallery exhibitions, consulting, online classes, content creation, and TV hosting.

With novel ideas and a fresh point of view, I helped build the art collections of hip-hop moguls, Oscar- and Emmy-winning actors,

Grammy-winning musicians, CEOs of Fortune 500 companies, Broadway producers, world-renowned physicians, law firm partners, fashion designers, bankers, and many more.

More important, in the past thirteen years, I have had the opportunity to observe, befriend, interview, write about, and work in many different capacities with more than 450 contemporary artists, which allowed me to witness their creative process from start to finish. In working with many businesspeople and entrepreneurs, I noticed that the most creative and innovative ones shared with successful artists the same creative habits and patterns of behavior.

Even science has proven that the creative process for people in areas as far apart as math, engineering, and the arts is the same. After examining 2,277 university students in Germany, researchers from Maastricht University and the University of South Australia concluded that creative thinking doesn't differ much across domains and disciplines. While it is true that CEOs, programmers, and artists create different kinds of work with diverse intentions and outcomes, the skills and attitudes they use to get there are very similar.

You may have noticed that I haven't talked about talent. Talent is a complicated issue. I know plenty of successful contemporary artists with not that much artistic talent but loads of innovative ideas that they can execute with the right team and the creative vision to achieve them. I also know many wealthy and accomplished entrepreneurs, Jacks and Jills of all trades, who are not particularly talented at one thing, but they surf their own never-ending wave of creative ideas and they know with whom to associate to reach success. Of course, I am not saying that talent isn't needed. It is a wonderful thing, especially if you were born with it, but talent without creativity is like pedaling a tricycle down the information superhighway—it will take you only so far.

Companies and organizations are aware of the importance of creativity in the workplace and beyond, yet they struggle with the unorthodox idea that creativity can be taught and learned. For example, IBM conducted a survey of more than fifteen hundred CEOs from sixty countries and thirty-three industries worldwide. Sixty percent of those CEOs answered that successfully navigating our complex world requires creativity over other qualities such as rigor, management, discipline, or integrity. Creativity is the number one quality they look for when they are hiring people and also when deciding whom to keep employed.

For many years, LinkedIn has been scanning the information shared in the network by roughly 660 million professionals, searching for the skills that were most in demand in relation to its supply. The number one in-demand skill turns out to be creativity. During the pandemic, the World Economic Forum called creativity "the one skill that will future-proof you for the job market." Interestingly, Adobe also interviewed five thousand adults in the United States, United Kingdom, Germany, France, and Japan, which showed that only one in four people believed they were living up to their creative potential and four in ten said that they didn't have the tools or access to the tools they needed to become creative.

This creativity gap between what industries, companies, and societies are clamoring for and what people believe they can contribute is plain wrong. Everyone is and can be creative. The tools aren't hard to find or expensive to get. They already belong to each one of us. To reap the benefits that come with revitalizing your creativity, you need the presence of mind and the openness of spirit to practice your creative skills. Knowing that you will be dealing with ambiguities and being willing to experiment will take you far.

You will need to be original, distinct, and sometimes even radically different than you were. As you incorporate the habits and use the tools you learn here, you will be able to adjust to the inevitable changes that occur. Your shifts and reinventions will happen easily, almost organically, because your mind and intuition will alert you to the right time to do so.

In this book, I draw from the fields of art, history, business, entrepreneurship, psychology, and neuroscience, but my day-to-day observations of artists over the past thirteen years are key to finding the core of the creative process. Most of the artists I've worked with can't explain how they reach their creativity, but having observed them closely for over a decade, I've unearthed the patterns and categories that I present in these pages. You may have heard of some of the artists named in this book; others may be completely new to you. But what's important is that I've distilled what I learned from them so that you, too, can achieve your optimal flow of creative ideas.

Artists are some of the most creative people not because they have a special set of superpowers, but because they aren't bound by content restrictions or subject matter rules. Even the biggest challenges with materials cannot stop them. Their job is to imagine other worlds and envision many possibilities. Their art doesn't have to conform to the limits of reality or societal conventions. I found the same characteristics in the most innovative and disruptive entrepreneurs. They see how far their ideas can get and they push until they see them materialize. That is pure creative alchemy.

In this book, I will show you how to access your ideas, how to materialize them, how to shift, and how to innovate in the same way that artists and entrepreneurs do. By weaving six hundred years of art history with concrete examples of modern entrepreneurs, in areas ranging from cosmetics to entertainment, as well as my own experiences and personal anecdotes, you will learn how to ignite your creative mind. Some of these stories highlight controversial artists or entrepreneurs. They upset the status quo. They are eccentric. They marry, divorce, and marry again. We may not always like or agree with them or how they behave, but these are the habits that have helped them climb the ladder in their creative endeavors. Their success gives us clues, and I'm glad we can pick them up, analyze them, and take what worked to make ourselves more creative.

If you are creative and know how to execute your ideas and bring them to the market, you should be compensated for that. The myth of the starving artist who died in abject poverty is mostly that: a myth. In every field and in every profession, there are people who succeed and make it big and there are people who can barely make ends meet, artists or not. The majority of the artists I talk about make a very good living. Some possess considerable wealth; some died extremely wealthy. My hope for you is that, after applying what you learn in this book, you can turn your great ideas into gold.

I structure this book in four parts:

Part I: The Intersection of Creativity, Art, and Business contains the history of creativity, explains why artists have been the original creators and innovators, tells the story of how I turned my life around, and dispels the myths and lies that we have been taught about creativity, all backed up with scientific research.

Part II: Habits of the Mind is about the qualities that artists and entrepreneurs nurture and cultivate in order to arrive at those amazing "aha" moments that turn their worlds (and ours) around.

Part III: Tools of the Trade offers a series of practical methods that can be used to form creative ideas, concepts, and processes in a more concrete way.

Part IV: The Way Forward explains how to put together what you've learned in parts I, II, and III and how to keep moving forward with your ideas to the point where you can easily spot opportunities, connect invisible dots, and invent the future at will.

I believe that your ideas can be turned into gold, and at the end of each chapter is an Alchemy Lab. These are practical invitations to explore and apply what you learned in that chapter. If you want to reap abundant ideas, I urge you to dive into these sections with pen and paper. Yes, I prefer analog methods (their benefits far outweigh those of a computer; see why in chapter 20).

Since we seem to live in an era where we go from one crisis to the next, I think we can start by understanding why crises are also gold mines of creativity.

PART I

THE INTERSECTION OF CREATIVITY,

ART, AND BUSINESS

■

For the past two millennia, the history and evolution of the concept of creativity have been surrounded by fables and mysteries, erroneous beliefs, and misconceptions. The truth is that creativity is the most vital and necessary skill in any occupation or field. It is an exclusively human amalgamation of attitudes and habits, not replicated by any other species. In the following chapters, I explain the connection between creativity and artists, shed a light on how throughout history humans have evaluated their own creations, and how science has debunked, one by one, the myths that have kept creativity elusive and sacrosanct.

1

Creativity and Crisis

IT WAS MY fifty-fourth day on lockdown during the coronavirus pandemic. I was pondering what this new crisis would mean for creativity, innovation, and invention in every imaginable field, including fields that we don't even know about but will soon exist. I had just reopened my online course on creative thinking applied to business and entrepreneurship and couldn't shake these thoughts.

After forty-four years, the first half in Venezuela, I survived two failed coups d'état, tear gas day in and day out, and lootings and shootings. In the second half, living in New York City, I lived through 9/11, the financial crisis of 2008, Hurricane Sandy, fights between political extremists, Black Lives Matter protests, and other vicissitudes. But I never imagined that in the era of technology, we would face such an unprecedented opponent. In the blink of an eye, we went from the optimism of welcoming a new decade to protagonists in a sci-fi movie.

I had been pressing ahead nonstop, immersed in work. I traveled from one continent to another, from one city to the next, curating an exhibition in Beirut, visiting clients in Los Angeles, attending the opening of the Venice Biennale, going to Miami for Art Basel, supervising an art installation in East Hampton, moderating a talk in Charlotte, and on and on. Our modern way of living was ensnaring and numbing us with piles of work, and I was no exception. On top of that, every week, I would also see at least twenty art shows in Manhattan, attend dinners and openings, benefits, and auctions, and meet and correspond with hundreds of people ranging from clients to art dealers. That merry-go-round spun continuously with no chance to get off to take a sip of water.

That Wednesday night in the beginning of May, I had to allow myself to feel my feelings because there was no way to escape them. I had nowhere else to go. For the first time in many years, I felt nostalgic for Caracas, the city where I was born and grew up, and which I hadn't visited in fifteen years. After Hugo Chávez and then his appointed successor, Nicolás Maduro, amended the Venezuelan Constitution and carried out electoral fraud, perpetuating themselves in power and committing the most atrocious crimes against Venezuelans and democracy, I decided to never return. I let myself drift in my memories and feelings, remembering my childhood and that city I left behind, which many have told me is completely unrecognizable nowadays.

I thought of my maternal grandfather, Enrique Dao, who passed away one month after my wedding day in 2004. That was the last time I saw him. I'm grateful it was a joyous day surrounded by the people I love the most, as that framed what would be my last interaction with him. I was back in New York when he had another heart attack he couldn't survive. There were no goodbyes, no dramas, no soap-operatic Latino funerals. I'm glad it was this way. We were extremely close; Enrique was not only my favorite grandparent but also one of my favorite people in the world and the embodiment of what it means to be a creative, resourceful human being. I wanted to preserve in my heart his warm, energetic, loving image, and not the one of a cold body inside a coffin.

EMOTION: THE BRIDGE BETWEEN CRISIS AND CREATIVITY

That night in May of 2020, I did something quite unusual, particularly in connection with someone who had been dead for sixteen years and had almost no relationship with the internet. I googled my grandfather's name, and the first hit after I pressed "search" was a link to a Reuters webpage containing a three-minute video of the exact moment on March 6, 1971, that my grandfather arrived at his house after spending almost a month in a dense tropical rain forest atop a mountain after being kidnapped by the Venezuelan guerrillas. I was stunned with my discovery.

I hadn't been born yet, but this event was so devastating for my mother's family that it changed their lives forever. In my childhood and teenage years, I heard the story many times, from my parents, other family members, and, of course, my grandfather, who abhorred being the center of attention.

Before 2020, I had never seen these images before. Never. Who would want to preserve clips or memories of being kidnapped? And, even if they wanted to, how could my grandparents, or my mother, who was twenty at that time, have stored any of these files back in the 1970s?

The first time I saw that Reuters video, it hit home, literally. It starts with a shot outside of the 1960s modernist house in which I practically grew up; I spent so much time with my grandparents as a child. About twenty-five policemen, ten members of the military, and one hundred journalists and reporters with cameras and recording devices were waiting for my grandfather.

Another camera shows the moment my grandfather arrives at his house after twenty-four anguishing days in the jungle. He came walking from the direction where the Ávila mountain is. He had called my grandmother from a pay phone, she had warned the police, and they were waiting for him in Caracas to take him to the precinct first. After his testimony and physical exam, the police drove him to his house. He was wearing a white button-down shirt (he never wore anything other than white shirts) and dark sunglasses and looked a lot tanner and a lot thinner than normal.

He was escorted by someone I believe was the congressman who had negotiated his release; the man was giving directions with his hands and trying to protect my grandfather from the hordes of journalists, onlookers, family members, and policemen who swarmed around him. This was the moment when I cried. And I cried and cried. To see Enrique, alive, sixteen years after his passing, simultaneously burst open every emotion. I missed my grandfather; remembered the generosity, love, and humility with which he treated everyone; mourned the loss of the country I was born in and where my parents still live; and was nostalgic for my entire family, which is scattered all over the world. I longed for the fractured piece of history, the one that links my ancestors to me and my children.

Slowly, my grandfather tries to catch his breath. He is evidently exhausted, but he has the mannerisms and expressions I so vividly remember. I can read his lips telling a journalist, "Easy, easy, I will answer soon." There is a quick jump cut, and then the second camera inside the house shows my grandfather, still wearing dark sunglasses, sitting on that memorable antique baroque settee next to his older brother, Aníbal.

In a semicircle around my grandfather and his brother, the journalists looked agitated and gesticulated in desperation to get their answers so they could complete their assignments and send their recordings to all the news agencies and TV stations around the world. They had been waiting for hours to have the press conference with my grandfather and were eager to leave. That marked the end of the video and the beginning of this book.

THE PIVOT FROM CRISIS TO CREATIVE REINVENTION

My grandfather had an incredible life filled with creativity that allowed him to experience remarkable reinvention. Even though I didn't know it back then, he was my first example of what being creative can do for people's lives and their fulfillment. I have often wondered what made my grandfather so creative. Was it his curiosity? Was it his open mind? Or was it his ability to change swiftly without getting stuck in the past? He was, from his early years, a brilliant, creative, and inquisitive person. He developed so many abilities and interests including painting, music, and languages. I am certain that the fuel that drove his creativity was the curiosity to never settle in one area; he was always looking to expand, and he wanted to learn as many disciplines as possible.

Enrique was born on a coastal city in Venezuela called Puerto Cabello, one of eight children of Lebanese immigrants. He moved to Caracas in the early 1940s to attend medical school where he graduated with honors, specializing as an ob-gyn. He had a stellar career, met and married my grandmother, became the director of the Red Cross, and had four children, including my mother, his firstborn. In his midforties he suffered a small accident and had the humility to acknowledge that he wasn't as dexterous as he had been, and decided to quit his career as a physician to work for his family's bank.

This might have been a crisis, but he reinvented himself spectacularly. Reclaiming his love for painting, on weekends he sat with his easel and many tubes of oil paint on his patio to create magic landscapes and lush still lifes of gorgeous vases filled with colorful tropical flowers. He also became an avid art collector. My grandfather was so brilliant that, within a few years, he became one of the top three executives running his family's financial institution. He had found a new passion and career. The combination of backgrounds and interests made him creative and original in his ideas and their execution. Then he was kidnapped.

The 1970s in Venezuela were marked by social unrest, particularly from Marxist extreme-left antigovernment guerrilla forces that operated in remote rural areas far from the main cities. Some of these men had been trained by Fidel Castro in the Sierra Maestra in Cuba, where the dense vegetation and the difficult topography presented the best conditions for clandestine operations. There was no better place to hide.

Enrique was the perfect target for the guerrillas who were against the government's land reform and its economic, fiscal, and international policies. They wanted to drive Venezuela toward an "anti-imperial" socialism: and here was Enrique, a high-profile, bright forty-seven-year-old, second in command of an important national bank. His captors followed all his moves for months, and on February 10, 1971, they intercepted his car when he was driving to work. Three men with guns blindfolded him, tied his hands behind his back, made him lie down in the back of a station wagon, and then drove for hours.

In those first minutes as a kidnapped man, a million thoughts raced through his mind, particularly of his wife and kids. His pulse accelerated, and he began to sweat profusely, but as a physician who had operated and carried out thousands of procedures, he also knew how to compose himself and breathe until the panic had subsided. That is what he did, that day and for the twenty-three days after.

The men drove my grandfather through rocky grounds and arrived at their destination in the afternoon. They barely spoke to him while they exchanged his blindfold for duct tape and gave him a straitjacket that they tied tightly behind his back, then told him to rest in a hammock. He slept like that every day while in captivity.

During those interminable twenty-four days, he sent five letters to my grandmother, as proof of life, while the kidnappers also sent letters asking for ransom, identifying themselves as a cell of a national liberation force. That's how the negotiations with my grandmother, my grandfather's brother, and a congressman-negotiator took place.

He prayed; he was patient. It had been the only time in his life where thoughts and feelings, padded with infinite silence, were his only undertakings. I remember an impactful line in his narration: "I don't hold grudges. They fed me, and they didn't kill me."

On March 6, 1971, at dawn, they told him he was free to go. They removed the duct tape from around his eyes and gave him dark sunglasses. They never allowed him to see them. The men pointed him in a specific direction, always with his back at them, and told him to walk all the way down the mountain.

Payment of his ransom is surrounded by many parallel accounts, even today. There were too many people involved in crafting a pact with the kidnappers: the government, my great-uncle Aníbal, the top management and directors of the bank where he worked, and my grandmother. The actual number is anywhere from $500,000 to $1,000,000, and that was half a century ago. What is undeniably true is that all the money that my grandparents had went to paying that ransom. They had gone from glitz to nothing.

None of that could deter my grandfather from pursuing other ventures, and what came after was his second reinvention, starting with a new entrepreneurial path. He bought a printing company that made everything from books to posters, business cards to lithographs, and anything in between. He served everyone with love and attention and kept his employees happy and his family always close. He continued acquiring art and at times also selling it and trading it.

He had such a level of dignity and respect for work, people, and life in general. It was a joy to be around him. He took all his crises as opportunities to better himself and adjusted his course every time he realized that what once worked wouldn't do it anymore.

HOW CALAMITY FUELS CREATIVITY

It is fair to say that creativity and crisis are related. The biggest human developments, major industrial advances, greatest inventions, and most important art movements have happened after big crises. Art was being created even before the idea or the word *creativity* existed. The Italian Renaissance followed on the heels of the Black Death in the late 1300s. The Bauhaus, modernism, surrealism, and art deco movements came in the 1920s right after the Spanish flu ravaged the world and the devastation of World War I was felt in every corner of the planet. We wouldn't have Picasso's *Guernica*, painted in 1937, had it not been for the Spanish Civil War. The Great Depression brought Franklin Delano Roosevelt's "New Deal" between 1933 and 1939 and with it the creation of several agencies that engaged artists in public art projects all over the United States. The era of "content creators," the propagation of digital images and videos, leveraged by the social media revolution, came after the economic collapse of 2008. When we find ourselves with limited resources, when we confront harsh conditions, or need to figure out how to react to difficulty, creativity thrives.

The word *crisis* comes from the ancient Greek *krisis*, which means "to make a decision." For the Greeks it also meant "the turning point of a disease," where it either got worse or got better. *Creativity* comes from the Latin term *creō*, "to create, make," and back then it did not have the same meaning and connotation it has today. Remarkably, *creativity* was a word associated with the divine. It was only after Darwin's evolutionary theory highlighted that man and nature could be "creative" without appealing to God that the word and concept of creativity took a new turn. Even then, for more than seventy-five years, Americans didn't use the word *creativity* in their day-to-day vocabularies.

In 1955, MGM released a movie called *Blackboard Jungle,* based on a novel of the same name written by Evan Hunter. The revolutionary film, directed by Richard Brooks and starring the great Sidney Poitier, exposed the cracks and deficiencies in public education in the United States and sent shock waves everywhere. It made people wonder if formal education alone could prepare

men and women, whose "creativity" was necessary to keep the economy going
and allow America to retain its competitive edge. This was the beginning of
a collective appreciation for what creativity, an exclusively human trait, could
do when people applied it to whatever their industry may be.

In 1959, in the middle of the Cold War, the United States started to get
serious about the ideas of "creativity" and "free thinking" to differentiate
itself from the totalitarianism of the Soviet Union. Between the 1950s and
the 1960s, the Central Intelligence Agency used abstract expressionism as a
weapon in the Cold War. The CIA was imitating the strategy of the Medicis,
the infamous Florentine family, art collectors extraordinaire, and patrons of
Sandro Botticelli, Michelangelo Buonarroti, and Leonardo da Vinci, among
many other luminaries of the Renaissance. By financing abstract expressionism, the United States would show the world that this new movement
was the quintessential expression of the creativity, intellectual freedom,
and cultural power of this country. Russian art, stifled and communist,
didn't stand a chance next to the exuberance, energy, and dynamism of its
American counterpart.

The US government went to great lengths to ensure that the exhibition
called *The New American Painting*, which included the works of Jackson
Pollock, Robert Motherwell, Willem de Kooning, and Mark Rothko, among
many other abstract expressionists, toured the globe visiting some of the
best museums in the world. It debuted in Basel, then went to Milan, continued in Madrid, followed by Berlin, Amsterdam, Brussels, Paris, then
London. It triumphantly retuned to America with a massive show at the
Museum of Modern Art in New York in 1959. The many hundreds of thousands of dollars needed to pay for these exhibition costs came—in secret—
from US taxpayers.

SCIENTIFIC PROOF OF THE RELATIONSHIP
BETWEEN CREATIVITY AND CRISIS

Marie Forgeard, an American psychologist, conducted the first empirical
study (of 373 participants) proving that there are increased levels of creativity

in people who have faced crises and adversity. Forgeard calls these spikes in creativity resulting from severe challenges "posttraumatic growth." That doesn't mean adversity is needed for creativity. You don't have to suffer to become creative, but if you find yourself in the middle of a crisis, know that it can be a catalyst for progress and originality.

History and science have demonstrated that in moments of crisis, creativity flourishes. These definitive events push humans to the edge, and those who know how to use a crisis as a springboard for creativity reap the biggest rewards. It is easy to conclude that creativity abhors complacency.

It was in the middle of the pandemic crisis that I found myself the most vulnerable and most creative. So many parallels connected me during that time to the story of my grandfather's kidnapping: the isolation, the days of silence, the nostalgia for what once was, the uncertainty, the introspection, the austerity, paring myself down to the minimum, and having more time to think than I ever imagined. When would this be over? What would the future look like? How many times will this happen again? Do I really need all the stuff that surrounds me? Why did I buy so many shoes?

The memories I have of my grandfather are those of resilience and creativity. Of happiness and tolerance. Of reinvention and renewal. He always had a solution for everything; resourcefulness was another one of his many skills. Up until his death, people called him "the banker-doctor." He still correctly diagnosed everyone in the family, no matter the size or origin of the malady, and he could analyze balance sheets and stock market charts with the most acute eye. He was never just one thing; that would have been unthinkable for someone with the richness of his inner world. He didn't live to witness my own reinvention, even though I learned so much from him, including the fine art of adaptation and pliability. Enrique was, in his own right, the ultimate Renaissance man. He had creativity in its most bountiful and valuable form, and his most brilliant ideas came after the most severe calamities.

ALCHEMY LAB

- *If you experience any type of crisis,* take an inventory of your skills, connections, resources, and knowledge. You may have more than you think you do. Use your answers as a foundation either to start something new or tweak what you have been doing.

- *Look closely for opportunities to use your skills* to solve problems that (1) you survived during your crisis or (2) that the crisis generated.

- *Use the crisis to your advantage* to create opportunities; for example, where certain rules have been relaxed or perhaps even eliminated. During trying times, people find the courage to reach out to different collaborators or find new clients they previously hadn't thought about or shied away from. Resources can get pooled in ways that weren't considered before. This is where creativity and innovation shine.

2

Creativity and Artists: A Brief History

My LOVE AFFAIR with the Greeks started in fifth grade, when I had to read Homer's *The Iliad* and *The Odyssey*. I was very young for such a complex work, yet that was what the educational system in my school demanded from us in the last two years of elementary school. This was a time in my life when I was hungry to discover new things and explore the meaning of culture: Why have the Greeks given us so many contributions to culture and society? Why not the Egyptians or the Etruscans? Why did they write poetry? How did they sculpt those marble bodies so perfectly? I had so many questions and was so curious about everything, especially about the meaning of art, and desired to time-travel to a distant past and faraway lands. I wanted to meet different people and hear their stories. As an only child, I spent too much of my time daydreaming and having a million internal dialogues in my brain. I was craving to see the world.

THE MUSE AND ME

The sheer volume of each book was daunting, but once I had them in my hands, I couldn't stop turning the pages. This was the first time I came across the term *muse*. *The Iliad* starts with an invocation to "the Muse," in reference to one of nine goddesses, the daughters of Zeus and Mnemosyne. These goddesses had the enormous responsibility of bringing inspiration to poets, musicians, storytellers, dancers, and artisans. Depending on the translation, Homer asks the muse of poetry, Calliope, either to sing to him the rage of Achilles, or to sing it *through* him. In the sequel, *The Odyssey*, Homer wrote "all men owe honor to the poets, *because they are dearest to the muse*." More than 2,700 years ago, "inspiration" was something believed to be granted to poets from outside sources, and what sprang out of that inspiration was the creativity to write enthralling epic poems.

Paradoxically, while Homer called upon the goddesses of creativity for himself, he gave his characters full creative autonomy: he described Odysseus as "the master of invention," whose imagination was able to create the most ingenious pieces of carpentry, including the legendary Trojan Horse. These were the first recorded attempts in history to categorize the creative power that exists in humans.

Oh, so the Greeks needed a fairy to come and inspire them, my elementary-school self thought, recognizing that the concept of creativity ignited by external forces was indeed foreign to me. By the time I was eight, I had written long stories and books. I mostly shared them with my grandfather, one of my most patient and loyal fans. I also painted canvases without asking for or expecting anyone to tell me how to express myself. I even planned my birthday party and asked guests to wear costumes. I thought regular outfits would have been too ordinary for me and for them.

By the time I was eleven, I already felt pressured by teachers to conform to a way of thinking or doing things, which I despised. I abhorred processes and rules; I always got to the right answer, but not by using their methodology. I became suspicious of formal education. I thought of it as "indoctrination." I figured that the only way "out" was to get deeply "in," so I became a voracious reader, a fast learner, and an unchallengeable student and rule breaker. Much to my parents' discomfort, they were called to the principal's office several times to discuss my "rebellion." Sister Rodríguez, a nun born and raised in Madrid, who was in her forties, told my parents, "Your daughter has the ability to learn all the subjects at great speed, yet insists on doing things her way and is constantly asking provocative questions to disrupt the classroom." It wasn't enough that that obsolete Catholic school system avoided teaching creative thinking; if anyone expressed it, they wanted to crush it.

CREATIVE OWNERSHIP DURING THE RENAISSANCE

For my fifteenth birthday, my parents gave me a monthlong trip to Europe. I went with a group of other girls who were also celebrating their quinceañeras (a term used in Latin America to denote a rite of passage from girlhood into adulthood). Our chaperones were a group of middle-aged women who spent their afternoons drinking cheap wine and flirting with the tour guides. This was the first time I had so much freedom—most important, the intellectual freedom to form my own ideas and debate them with people of different backgrounds. I had long chats with our tour guides and locals I befriended over gelato in squares. In Florence I felt that everything was different—the art looked "alive."

The magnificent corridors of Galleria degli Uffizi, with its checkerboard marble floors and rows and rows of beamed ceilings covered in frescoes painted by Alessandro Allori, stunned me. His truly fun, saturated colors; the animals, angels, mythical and humorous figures; their instruments and the garlands made it feel like scenes from one big party. I had never seen anything like that. Our guide, Filippo, a short Italian man in his mid-fifties with a thick singsong accent and even thicker glasses, told us that before the fourteenth century it was rare that writers, architects, artists, or scientists claimed authorship to their creation. They felt that their work was a collaborative effort among artisans. With the Italian Renaissance, which started in Florence, individual authorship and creativity blossomed in a prolific and impactful way.

THE REBIRTH OF CREATIVITY

The Medicis of Florence established a Platonic Academy on their country estate. Their goal was to make Florence as important as Athens once was. They also were obsessed with becoming cultivated and, for this reason, became the ultimate patrons of the arts. The director of that Platonic Academy, Marsilio Ficino, wrote the first complete translation of Plato. One of his most important conclusions was that "the power of the human person almost resembles that of God's nature." That sentence changed the Medicis' view of individual creators and led them to propel the spectacular rebirth that was the Italian Renaissance.

This is the moment after the Dark Ages and the Black Death, when artists, architects, poets, and writers were free to rediscover the ideas of the ancient Greeks. The humanists were encouraged to go back to the sources. They imitated and reimagined what the ancient Greeks created, making their own versions, and changing, enhancing, and adapting the classics where they saw room for improvement. Thus began creativity as we know it: the evolution of an idea that already existed, understanding that true originality isn't really possible.

Artists, architects, scientists, and writers now had one eye on the past and their hands, hearts, and minds firmly grounded in the present, in the act of the creation. Sandro Botticelli couldn't have painted *The Birth of Venus* had it not been for the Greek mythology that had already created Aphrodite, the goddess of love, beauty, passion, and procreation. Anonymous Greek sculptors immortalized Aphrodite in statues carved out of marble that were later copied by the Romans, who changed her name to Venus. Botticelli gave a new spin to existing works and even got inspiration from a contemporary poem by Angelo Poliziano.

Turning the myth of Aphrodite's birth into Botticelli's sublime colorful canvas was a joyful act of pure creativity. The goddess's long blonde hair covering her naked body; the "Winds" flying on her right copied from a Hellenistic-period work; and spring's extraordinary colors, ranging from seafoam green to soft turquoise, from deep mulberry to muted violet, embody this evolution combining past and present.

Botticelli's innovations in the *Birth of Venus* ranged from it being the first large-scale life-sized nude anyone had seen in Europe in one thousand years, the first large-scale Florentine work to be painted on canvas, and the first time a painter added fat to the pigments mixed in the egg tempera to achieve his extraordinary and long-lasting colors. For 550 years, this painting has inspired artists, from entire Versace runway collections, to re-creations by Andy Warhol, to Beyoncé announcing the birth of her twins.

Standing in front of *Venus* for the first time in 1991 gave me goose bumps all over my body. Five hundred years collapsed in seconds in front of me. Her expression is so pure and so demure; did he merge Virgin Mary's face into Venus's body? What was going on in his life? What was he thinking about every time he picked up his brush to complete a piece?

CREATIVITY'S RENAISSANCE ROCK STARS

The Renaissance gave us the rock stars of creativity, who, more than five centuries after their deaths, are still known by one name: Michelangelo, Donatello, Raphael, and Leonardo, among many, many others. This was the precise time that artists were encouraged to experiment even further. As a result, their creations took more time and were more complex and ambitious. Artists became more skilled and retained more and more ownership of their works. Almost every Renaissance creative, regardless of their area of expertise or discipline, had a deep desire to improve the present and leave something of substance for the future. By the end of the sixteenth century, important authors and innovators were well established, and explicit ownership of their creations became the norm. It was the curiosity, skill, and the power of making their thoughts visible that connected the Athenians and the Florentines. The Medicis accomplished what they had set out to do. From that moment on and for the next three hundred years, the word *creativity* became almost exclusively associated with art and poetry.

HUMANS BECOME CREATIVE

By the end of the nineteenth century, because of the novelty of Darwin's evolutionary theory, along with the Industrial Revolution, and the fast advances in technology, the domain of creativity grew to include people outside of the "traditional" arts. Curiously, the invention and development of photography in the early and mid-1800s transformed people's perceptions of creativity and bridged the gap between art and technology. The machine could imitate and reproduce whatever was in front of the lens, but photographers could improve on what they saw through those dark boxes. The advent of photography caused painting to change dramatically. If the camera could produce an image so real, there was no need to paint realistically.

The impressionists realized that painting as close as possible to reality was exhausted and attempted a new color symbolism to represent the changing effects of light. They swiftly moved from their predecessors' perfect portraiture and realistic landscapes and focused on formulating new methods. Monet and Renoir invented the broken-color technique, placing small patches of different colors side by side instead of completely blending them, leaving the viewer's eyes to merge the colors. The impressionists enforced full autonomy over their creativity, immersed themselves in nature, and successfully changed the question from "Is it realistic?" to "Is it new? Is it creative?"

At this point the challenge for artists was to figure out issues connected with creating new techniques that would take them beyond realism, while photographers were preoccupied with aesthetics. Both groups were quite intent on coming up with "the new." The confluence of these events culminated with the word *creativity*, which appeared for the first time in the English language in 1875. Its invention is attributed to a London historian, Adolphus William Ward, who wrote that Shakespeare was a "creative genius" whose "poetic creativity" encompassed many abilities in many different areas, not just those of being a writer.

In parallel, the 1880s saw a resurgence of the study of Leonardo da Vinci. His notebooks, first published in 1881, introduced the genius inventor to the world, demonstrating that his discoveries were as important as his paintings.

MODERN CREATIVITY: ART AND INNOVATION

After World War II, prompted by America's obsession with having a competitive advantage over other superpowers and looking to expand "creativity" over any realm, the term appeared in the *Webster's New World Dictionary* under *creative* as a noun. Since then, the concept spread like wildfire.

Based on its history, it is easy to see why creativity was so closely intertwined with artists. It took more than 2,500 years of artistic endeavors to finally come up with the term we now know. Artists were the first creatives and the most skilled alchemists; they came up with something out of nothing, and their work inspired, moved, engaged, created controversy, and taught. First, they sparked their minds by asking the muses, then by imitating nature, next igniting their own imaginations, and finally finding their creativity within themselves.

Artists depend 100 percent on their ingenuity. It is a profession that always requires being inventive. Artists are also the ultimate entrepreneurs. They develop a unique style that becomes their brand. They must find galleries, fabricators, collectors, financial backers, public art foundations, museum directors, and engage in myriad inventive activities to succeed, both financially and creatively.

Today, my favorite definition of *creativity* is the one that is sufficiently open and inclusive so that everyone can partake of it. I like to make the barriers to entry low because, for too long, the concept of creativity has been misinterpreted by many and monopolized by some. To me, creativity is the use of known or old information and ideas to produce something relevant and new. It is the "fun engine" of imagination, and it applies to all industries, including technology, advertising, science, banking, fashion, education, and, of course, art.

Innovation is a concept related to creativity, although newer in history and a bit more specific. I view innovation as the application of the creative process to existing products or services, or the combination of different extant variables to create something original that brings value to a group of people. Innovation happens only if the creation offers a novel solution to meaningful problems, and it is a much more concrete concept than just creativity. Unfortunately, for too long, tech people and scientists hijacked the concept, making people outside of those circles shy away from innovating. Paradoxically, the word *innovation* stems from the Latin *innovatus*, which means "to renew or change," and dates back to 1540, long before we modeled our faces with Snapchat's filters and played *Fortnite* until our fingers were numb.

THE VIEW FROM THE CAVE: PREHISTORIC INVENTION

Artists have been innovating for almost 44,000 years. Scientists and archeologists working on the island of Sulawesi in Central Indonesia reported the discovery of a painting, estimated to be at least 43,900 years old, on the walls of the Maros-Pangkep cave. They concluded that the finding was "the oldest pictorial record of storytelling and the earliest figurative artwork in the world." There is a complex narrative in the scene in which eight figures approach wild pigs and dwarf buffalo. They are surrounded by thin lines that may represent ropes or spears. One of the creatures has a large beak; another, a tail. In the archaeologists' interpretation, these were not only representations of human hunters, they were a mix of people and animals, or "animal spirit helpers," which are common in shamanic beliefs. Furthermore, the scene is probably a representation of a hunting strategy that shows how to guide animals toward an ambush. Talk about innovation! These artists were storytellers whose red-pigment cave paintings explained how to solve a problem, most likely related to their source of survival, and, by including mythological symbols, perhaps their source of protection.

EMERGING FROM THE DARK AGES

Due to a glitch that I allowed to happen in my own wiring, I went from being a tremendously creative girl to a miserable corporate attorney as an adult. Throughout my teenage years, I had wanted to be a singer. I auditioned, and wherever I went I got a yes, whether it was the school play or a touring band. However, I had to say no with bitter tears, because my mother adamantly insisted that singing was a job for hookers. If I wanted to pursue it, I had to pick up my things, move out, and never come back. I gave up on my artistic pursuits and chose a more certain path. Since I was persuasive and loved to read and write, becoming a lawyer would, theoretically, fit me to a T and please my parents. Maybe I fantasized about those scenes in John Grisham's movies. *The Firm* had just been released and showed an exciting world inside law firms and courtrooms. Little did I know that being a lawyer in New York City was nothing like that.

By the mid-aughts, at the age of thirty, I was hitting the mid-six figures, had great insurance, a 401(k), a car service that took me home every night, and other perks that enslave and envelop people like barbed-wire safety nets.

The thought of going back to that building on Pine Street, walking from the Wall Street 2/3 subway station through those bleak, joyless, sunless narrow streets in the Financial District, still makes me recoil. Every day, as soon as I emerged from underground, the first thing I saw were dozens of interchangeable white men in dark suits, sporting the same haircut, sunken eyes, and blank stares; I couldn't tell them apart.

Looking through the window in my office, from which all I could see was a sliver of the East River framed by concrete buildings, the job felt tedious and endless. Each billion-dollar deal had hundreds and hundreds of pieces, and each piece required thousands of documents. There was a style manual that prescribed how each document should look. The days were ceaseless and the nights interminable. My coworkers felt proud when they pulled all-nighters. Some women partners didn't see their kids for weeks. It was a lifestyle I wanted absolutely nothing to do with. I label this period in my life as my very own dark ages.

One day in January of 2009, I told my husband, "I can't do this law firm anymore. I can't pretend I'm a happy attorney; I'm not even a happy person." He was supportive but hesitant, perhaps thinking I was still experiencing postpartum depression. After all, it was only about eight months since my firstborn, Daniel, was born. I couldn't stop thinking about the baby I had left at home at 9:30 a.m., whom I wouldn't see again until the next morning. (I came home too late at night to take him out of his crib to hold or feed him.) An even more devastating thought was that I would be a role model to this baby, and what would not quitting teach him? That I was someone who sold out her dream of living a creative life, on making an impact in the world, on sharing my real gifts just to follow a lucrative but predictable path set out by my parents? Hell no.

After days and nights banging my head against the wall, thinking about what to do next, exploring options that were not viable, I asked God for help. I buried my head in my hands and humbly invited an answer. What was my gift? What could I do?

It then hit me. A few months prior, my husband and I had sold an apartment in Midtown 35 percent above the price we had paid two years before. "It is because of the way you decorated it and the art you put on the walls," the real estate broker told me. "You have an incredible sense of aesthetics; you are extremely creative. Use that," she added.

My whole life flashed in front of me: my childhood days visiting museums with my dad, the days that I spent painting with my grandfather, my trips around the world, the incipient art collection I formed since moving to New York City in 2000, and the outings to galleries and art fairs that I attended in my very, very few spare moments.

That winter, at the age of thirty-three, I left my dark ages behind and I have never looked back. Not only did I build a creative business and pursue every creative project I wanted to, but what came after that January of 2009 has been the most delicious, most successful, most pleasurable, most liberating, most creative period of my life. I wouldn't change anything about it.

CREATIVITY AND THE ENTREPRENEURIAL VISION

Ever since I opened my company in 2009, I have been in search of ways to constantly develop my own creativity. I knew that in order to be successful and take my business off the ground, I had to be resourceful, authentic, unique, and bring something new to an old industry, especially since I was an outsider. Even though I knew that the value of creativity in business is temporary, I was also keenly aware that creativity is a never-ending renewable human resource. Cultivating and working on my creativity would allow me to adjust along the way. Also, and more important, since my choice of business had to do with art and artists, curation of spaces, and everything that a creative director does, I had little alternative but to be innovative.

The decision to start a new career saved my internal life and brought back my creativity. Harnessing the magic that comes with creating and placing my efforts into opening the world of art and artists to others saved me from living with regrets.

The more I hung out with artists, the more I grew my company, the more I saw the parallels between artists and entrepreneurs. I realized, even if artists didn't say it, that for them it was about 70 percent creativity and 30 percent execution of that creative vision. I also grasped that I had been applying a lot of these artists' habits and techniques in my own business, and the result was an open stream of original ideas.

Entrepreneurship is a visionary act of creativity that must positively impact those who are served much in the same way that art enhances, challenges, or enriches the lives of those who experience it. Every artist starts with an idea and then a blank canvas, a clean page, or the cursor blinking on an empty document.

Entrepreneurs, no matter the industry, the background, or the idea, start with zero, as I did. By "zero" I mean actually launching the business itself: the idea hasn't been proven yet, there are no customers, and nobody can vouch for it. This is the entrepreneurs' blank slate, whether or not they have angel investors, a multimillion-dollar trust fund, or invested their savings in an act of faith.

JUMP-STARTING THINGS

In 2019, I launched an online creativity class for anyone who felt stuck or unmotivated and needed to boost their creative thinking. I called it Jumpstart. I discussed my objectives with the CEO of a consulting company, who had sold several training businesses and knew what company executives were looking for when they enrolled in personal development courses. He was confused about my concept and premise. How could I teach creativity, much less innovation? He told me, "That is reserved for those who could really make a change, improve systems, processes, services, develop faster algorithms, disrupt markets."

"Huh?" I replied, incredulous. "Is that what people think? Have we disconnected so much from our true sources of ideas that now creativity and innovation belong only to engineers? I need to launch that class even more now!" And so I did.

I designed four prerecorded core modules broken down into smaller video lessons and a weekly Zoom group call over the course of four weeks to discuss the materials live with my participants. With a social media campaign, I recruited my first group of students, who were based in five continents and came from all sorts of backgrounds. There was a real estate broker, a serial entrepreneur, several visual artists, an e-commerce shop owner, the CEO of a management consulting company, a business school professor, and many more. Some of them got up in the middle of the night to be present at the virtual meetings. Many had incredible breakthroughs in their businesses.

Within two or three weeks, my students started seeing opportunities they had missed before. One participant said that my program was the mother of all other courses she had taken because, thanks to what she learned in it, she knew she'd never run out of executable business ideas. Others told me that they had restructured their businesses to do things differently from their competitors and were reaping the rewards.

In early 2020, I called an entrepreneur friend to ask her opinion about turning the course into a book. When I mentioned the word *creativity*, she asked, "Like arts and crafts? Will people have to paint and draw and make cutouts?" Still another misconception about creativity. I pondered why.

The answer came after much research and intuitive nudges. In the era of technology, which evolves and multiplies at the speed of light, for that CEO who told me I had no business teaching creativity, the world is only moving forward as long as there are cutting-edge advances and disruptive innovations. He hadn't had a chance to observe art or artists or to fully understand where creativity comes from. My friend had the same misconception, although her perspective was different: many parts of the arts seem obsolete. What could anyone learn from artists that they could apply to their businesses today?

The answer, I'm happy to say, is life-altering.

ALCHEMY LAB

- *Own your creativity.* Like the artists of the Renaissance, claim ownership over your past inventions and improvements. The first step on

the road to creative recovery is to acknowledge that you can produce new and relevant ideas, regardless of how small they are.

- *List the turning points in your life* where you've come up with creative solutions to big and medium challenges. The objective is to establish confidence in your ideas.

- *Focus on the general idea and avoid getting stuck in details.* Visual thinking can bring a problem down to its essence, because sometimes language doesn't have all the answers. Try practicing with pen and paper; all you need is an ability to create basic diagrams with figures, boxes, and arrows.

- *Choose an artist, ideally one who has inspired you in your business or career* (if not any artist). Study his or her life and incorporate their ideas, giving them your own spin, to inspire your creativity.

3

Dispelling Myths About Creativity

MANY PEOPLE, AS they become adults and get settled in a job or in a particular lifestyle, ask themselves a similar question to the one I pondered: *If I was such a creative and curious child who formed independent conclusions, could I recover from the decades of educational rigidity and years in law firms?*

When I quit that job, it never occurred to me that it wasn't possible to build a creative career and make money doing something I really loved. On the contrary, the first thing that crossed my mind is that I had the ability to use my dormant creativity to serve others and positively affect their lives. Until then, I bottled everything up inside of me; it was only waiting to erupt. I had the wholehearted willingness to start a creative business. I was determined to leave behind and "unlearn" the years of Catholic school indoctrination and education that began when I was four and continued all the way through nine years of corporate law practice. My journey into living a creative life, and making a living from it, started with a decision to make personal meaning out of my life, to give my heart and soul to what mattered to me.

MYTH NUMBER 1: ONLY SOME ARE BORN CREATIVE

In 1968, an Arizona scientist and researcher, Dr. George Land, along with his partner and wife, Dr. Beth Jarman, conducted a research study to test the creativity of 1,600 children ranging from three to five years old who were enrolled in a Head Start program. They developed the original creativity test at the request of NASA, who wanted to select the most innovative engineers and scientists and assign them to their most difficult problems.

The assessment worked so well that Land and Jarman saw an opportunity to try it on children. The test consisted of looking at a problem and coming up with new, different, innovative ideas. Ninety-eight percent of the five-year-olds scored at the highest level of creativity. Land and Jarman retested the same children at age ten, and again at age fifteen. The results were quite different; only 30 percent of the ten-year-olds and merely 12 percent of the fifteen-year-olds scored at the highest level of creativity. When they gave the same test to 280,000 adults whose average age was thirty, only 2 percent scored as highly creative.

The findings of these studies were and continue to be astounding. According to Land, the issue stemmed from educational systems around the world that push children toward *what* to think rather than *how* to think. Land proved that creativity is a normal part of every human being that is suppressed as we learn more rules, facts, and "unquestionable" theories, as well as by standardized tests that insist on only one correct answer for each of the questions. Based on Land's conclusions, the way back to our five-year-old selves is by respecting and nurturing our fertile imaginations, our dreams, the ideas that seem silly and outlandish, and allowing them to come to the surface and become concrete creations.

That's what I did that winter of 2009: I took all the crazy ideas that had been bubbling up inside of me and allowed them to surface. I took inventory of my copious gifts, passions, likes and dislikes, strengths and weaknesses. I started paying attention to the repeated voices of friends and strangers who had praised my eye for aesthetics. I also looked back on the informal recommendations I gave to others about buying emerging artists at a time when Instagram didn't exist and I had to spend time physically going from one gallery to another and from one art fair to the next to find the best talents. I decided to take the risky decision to start a company in the world of art. I had no clients, no art degree, no on-the-job training at a gallery, museum, auction house, or anything similar. I was somewhat of a blank canvas.

MYTH NUMBER 2: CREATIVITY "HAPPENS" TO A HANDFUL OF LUCKY ONES

One of the most dangerous myths perpetuated for centuries is that creativity comes on its own, without any effort on our part, in a sudden flash of insight, or when some capricious Greek muse shows up unexpectedly to inspire. We may still call on the muses sometimes, but we now know that creativity lives inside each one of us, and in order to express it to the fullest, we must work at it. What leads to those "aha" moments is doing the work and being sufficiently attuned to recognize our intuitive flashes as creative pieces of a bigger puzzle.

Creativity is a "do," a series of actions; it is a muscle that either gets stronger or atrophies depending on how much we use it. After years and years of observing artists showing up to do the work, day in and day out, I know their creativity improves the more dedicated they are to doing it. That's how creativity grows, when people hone their craft with passion, persistence, and discipline. Most of my painter friends paint every single day. Some are extremely meticulous, their brushstrokes are flat and almost perfect, and they take several weeks to complete a composition. Others use raw and visceral strokes and tackle their canvases in a gestural way, finishing a painting a day. Regardless of the technique they choose, accomplished artists evolve their styles by working at them, finding that sweet spot where the work is a commercial success that both charms collectors and wins critical acclaim that pleases museum curators, critics, and the press.

To create something new, people have to act, test different ideas, and provide novel solutions. That's how cubism, the most influential art movement of the twentieth century, was born. We all think of Pablo Picasso when we think about cubism, but Georges Braque's cubist construction sculpture preceded his own and Picasso's cubist works on paper and paintings. Braque had been drawing and painting since childhood and started working as a full-time artist in 1901, initially taking on impressionism as his style, then switching to fauvism in 1905, and later becoming the inventor of cubism along with Picasso, whom he met in 1907. From then on and for the next six years, the two artists became inseparable. In the fall of 1912, Braque, while wandering the streets of Avignon, spotted something in a store window that caught his attention. It was a roll of *faux bois* wallpaper that simulated oak paneling.

Seeing the wallpaper made him think about questions like how to bring dimensionality to paintings so they would not appear flat and how to break with the past and invent something new. A week later, Braque went back to the store, bought it, and, once in his studio, started cutting it into different shapes. He then glued the fragments onto one of his charcoal drawings, which depicted words, a glass bowl, pears, and grapes. After that he drew and painted over the fake wood paper and mounted it on a mix of sand and gesso. That brought texture and even more dimension to the composition. In doing this, Braque invented the art medium of collage—a brand-new creative form that other cubist artists, Dadaists, surrealists, and others quickly adopted.

Although it may seem like a "eureka" moment, it took Braque years of embracing different styles, experimenting, and thinking about solutions to his artistic problems to come up with a true innovation. Braque later said, "After having made the *papier collé*, I felt a great shock and it was even a greater shock to Picasso when I showed it to him." Modern collage, as Braque invented it, was the precursor of decoupage, photomontage, Photoshop, the mood board, and Pinterest, a company whose stock is publicly traded in the New York Stock Exchange with a value in 2021 of almost $37 billion.

MYTH NUMBER 3: CREATIVITY IS ONLY FOR ARTISTS

Art history is deeply interwoven with the concept of creativity. I can see why my friend asked me if my book would be about "arts and crafts," but creativity doesn't belong to artists alone. Creativity is not and should not be confused with artistic talent. Artists are the perfect examples to emulate when trying to spark our best ideas, but carving the *Pietà* out of a block of marble or making the *Mona Lisa*'s eyes follow you wherever you move are the results of innate skills and many years of training.

It is true that artists depend heavily (although not exclusively) on their creativity and their artistic ability, but creativity is applicable to every facet of life and to every business regardless of the industry. Even if you don't have any artistic talent, creativity is still yours for the taking. Thomas Alva Edison, one of the most creative minds in history, invented the phonograph, the rechargeable battery, the motion picture camera, and the electric bulb. This was not because of artistic ability but due to a sheer desire to use his creativity to challenge the status quo for the betterment of humanity.

Whether using their intuition, or intentionally being aware of how creativity works, inventors and entrepreneurs are no different from artists. They know that to get to that creative breakthrough, all those "muscles" must be exercised daily. Creativity develops in those who put the work in, even in the unlikeliest suitors.

Anybody can be creative in business regardless of their background or industry if they work at it. Proof is in the story of a French Benedictine monk called Pierre Pérignon who, in 1668, was sent to the Abbey of Saint-Pierre d'Hautvillers, near Rheims, where he was appointed administrator and cellar master. One hundred years prior, the abbey had been looted and was completely abandoned. In 1603, rebuilding began, and the vineyards were replanted. When Dom (Father) Pérignon arrived, they gave him the task of quickly boosting Hautvillers's revenues to continue funding the restoration. He could do that, he decided, by improving the quality of the wines they produced and increasing the price per bottle. Dom Pérignon set out to make "the best wine in the world." Day after day, Pérignon visited the cellars, monitored the barrels, observed every activity in the vineyards, took liberal notes, and kept an eye on the details that others thought insignificant. Everything interested him. He questioned every method and turned every bottle upside down until he found what worked, eliminated what didn't, and experimented with new things.

A Benedictine monk might seem like an odd candidate for creativity and innovation, particularly as an inventor of what became a luxury product associated with the royals and their lavishness, excesses, and debaucheries. But this man, who followed a regimen of prayer, study, and manual labor, was given a problem to solve: to make more money to fund the abbey's restoration. He improved the quality of the wines with his inventive new techniques, including picking only the best grapes and using corks instead of wooden sticks, an innovation never before seen in the entire region.

You would think that the monk's creativity was limited to the improvement of the product, but Pérignon was also an innovative marketer. He became aware that Louis XIV, the Sun King, drank almost exclusively sparkling wine and knew that everything the king did became a social trend in France. Pérignon decided to send several bottles of his wine to Versailles. Not only did Louis XIV love Pérignon's wine, he declared that it was the best in France. The French nobility took heed. From then on, Champagne's reputation as a region for excellent winemaking skyrocketed as quickly as the demand for its wine. After forty-seven years at Hautvillers, where he died, Dom Pérignon made the region of Champagne famous everywhere in France and was largely responsible for perfecting winemaking methods still used today.

Creativity is the willingness to challenge the status quo and come up with better solutions than those that exist, as Braque, Thomas Edison, and Dom Pérignon did. Each of them possessed vastly different skills and abilities, yet what they had in common was an immense reservoir of creativity. Creativity is an inexhaustible resource; the more you work at it, the more it reproduces.

MYTH NUMBER 4: CREATIVITY IS A ONCE-IN-A-BLUE-MOON SPARK

The other fable tightly knitted with the "sudden and miraculous spark of creativity" is that artists have no discipline and no structure, that they follow no rules and just "go wild" until an idea comes to them. This is a long-held, romanticized view of bohemian life, where artists work when the mood strikes and just hang out with other artists and have fun the rest of the time. Yes, artists have fun, friends, family, and vacations, but the most successful ones prioritize their work around structure and routine.

We can look at Picasso's life and learn from him. It is no coincidence that he still holds first place, certified by *Guinness World Records*, as history's most prolific visual artist: 13,500 paintings and designs; 100,000 prints and engravings; 34,000 book illustrations, and 300 sculptures and ceramics. What was his secret? He worked every day, obsessively, and pursued the solitary aim of his art to the exclusion of practically everything else.

At the age of twenty-six, Picasso and his girlfriend, Fernande Olivier, lived together in an apartment on the Boulevard de Clichy in Paris in which he had his studio. Every day, including weekends, he woke up late, locked himself in the studio starting at 2:00 p.m., and worked there until dusk. He ate little and avoided guests. Because of Fernande's loneliness, she asked him if they could have Sundays "at home," an idea she had borrowed from Gertrude Stein and Alice B. Toklas. Picasso agreed, and Sundays became the only day they would see all their friends, at home.

Years later, in November 1918, when Picasso was married to Olga Khokhlova, they settled into a large apartment on the second floor of 23 Rue de la Boétie in Paris. The Picassos divided the spacious floor into his-and-hers quarters. Picasso's half was his workspace—filled with paintbrushes, pots of paint, oil tubes flattened on the floor, and canvases propped against the walls—in which he maintained a similarly intense routine as in years prior. Around that time, he bought a large property called Boisgeloup, one hour outside of Paris, in the village of Gisors in Normandy. He wanted a house in which he could have a second studio for the summer and utilize the space to make large sculptures, which was impossible to do in his Parisian apartment.

His friend and photographer Brassaï recalled that on a visit to the countryside property, when the night fell, to continue working, Picasso lit a large oil lamp. There was no electricity in the shed, and it reminded him of his childhood when he drew by the light of a candle inserted into the neck of a bottle. Such was Picasso's obsession with his work.

Later, after separating from Olga, Picasso got a studio at 7 Rue des Grands Augustins, into which he eventually also moved. The place was messy and filled with art supplies and canvases, reams of paper, sculpture models, and books. Dust covered everything. Picasso sometimes said it "preserved things." He could tell something had been moved by his driver or his cleaning lady because the spot would be dustless. At this studio, Brassaï asked him, "Where do you get so many ideas?" Picasso answered, "Ideas are simply starting points. . . . As soon as I start to work, others well up in my pen. To know what you're going to draw, you have to begin drawing." Picasso, one of the greatest geniuses of history, painted one and sometimes two canvases a day and told his friend, in his own words, that creativity is a "do."

When Picasso died in 1973 at the age of ninety-one, he had an estimated net worth of $500 million although some say that it was higher than that. Adjusted for inflation, that is $2.9 billion today. Marc Blondeau, former head of Sotheby's France, told *Vanity Fair* that "if Picasso were alive today, he would be one of the ten wealthiest men in the world." Not bad for those who think that artists are a bunch of hippies sitting down on a square waiting for inspiration.

In case you are wondering, Picasso was born into a family of modest means in Málaga in the south of Spain; his father was an art teacher and his mother a housewife. He didn't inherit his wealth from his parents; he built it on his own, with his creativity and his art.

Joan Miró also had a strict routine. Beginning in the early 1930s, he woke up at 6:00 a.m. every day, including weekends, drank a cup of coffee, and ate toast; at 7:00 a.m. he was in his studio working straight until noon when he would exercise for an hour. If he was in Paris, he'd box; if in Barcelona, he'd either jump rope or do gymnastics, or run and swim on the beach. At 1:00 p.m. he had a light lunch and then five minutes of what he called "Mediterranean yoga," or what today we call a power nap. At 2:00 p.m. he'd see friends or take care of business matters, maybe write some letters, and at 3:00 p.m. he was back in the studio, which he left at 8:00 p.m. for dinner with his family.

Not only did he make more than two thousand paintings, one thousand lithographs, and ten thousand drawings and collages, but there was also no medium that he ever shied away from. His other work included giant public sculptures, tapestries and textiles, ceramics, murals, and even books that he produced himself. Maybe we don't have the luxury to go swimming on the beach in the middle of the day, but Miró shows us that creativity requires rules, parameters, and a strong work ethic.

Most of the contemporary artists I've worked with have daily routines and rituals that they follow religiously. Paradoxically, this structure keeps them unstuck and flowing creatively. If any of them ever experiences a creative block, their simple solution is to keep working diligently. The discipline to stick with a routine sparks creativity and materializes breakthroughs.

MYTH NUMBER 5: CREATIVITY IS GENETIC

What about genetics? Is creativity inherited? Does it come packaged in our DNA sequence from the moment of conception? As I collected and read a dozen different studies about genes and creativity, all of them inconclusive, I stumbled upon the findings of Baptiste Barbot, an assistant professor in psychology at Pace University and an adjunct assistant professor at the Child Study Center at Yale University. After many years studying the human genome, he concluded that creativity is a dynamic concept, based on many factors like risk-taking, personality, interests, and associative thinking, and that *genes play no role*.

Dr. Elkhonon Goldberg, an active researcher in the field of cognitive neuroscience, clinical professor of neurology at New York University, and author of several books on subjects related to the brain, determined after many years of research and observation that creativity is an amalgamation of traits not related to each person's genetic makeup.

It seems that blaming our DNA architecture for our lack of creativity isn't only inaccurate but also takes all our creative power away from us. The things we do best as humans are learning, adapting, creating, and making culture. Creativity and culture aren't affected by our genes and can't be genetically passed onto our descendants; everyone is creative or can be.

MYTH NUMBER 6: CREATIVITY IS FOR THE RIGHT-BRAINED

A most persistent myth comes from those who insist on calling themselves or labeling others as either left-brained (analytical, good at math, and logical) or right-brained (artistic, intuitive, and imaginative).

Eric Kandel, an Austrian-born, New York–based physician and scientist, won the Nobel Prize in Physiology in 2000 for his research on how the brain works. He concluded that both the right and the left sides of the brain need each other; the creative couldn't function without the analytical and vice versa. The brain's right hemisphere does not work in isolation from the left one. Similarly, it is incorrect to conclude that the left brain is uncreative. Creative ideas come from both sides of our brain. Our brain is complex and the interactions between the hemispheres are necessary and cannot be simply compartmentalized.

British-Hungarian novelist and journalist Arthur Koestler said it best in his 1964 book, *The Act of Creation*: "Creative activity is a type of learning process where the teacher and pupil are located in the same individual." Everything we need to be creative is already inside of us.

MYTH NUMBER 7: CREATIVITY CAN'T BE TAUGHT AND CAN'T BE LEARNED

But you don't understand! I was wired this way! I am not creative! I have heard this multiple times from many people. I always respond, "Maybe you feel this way right now, but you can learn to be creative and your brain isn't wired just one way."

Michael Merzenich, professor emeritus and a neuroscientist at the University of California, San Francisco, made the enormous discovery of neuroplasticity after years of studying patients and conducting rigorous studies. That means the brain not only grows, but also changes, well after adulthood. His extensive data indicates that the more we willingly engage in something continuously and challenge ourselves, the more the brain rewires itself.

The magic word is *willingly*; you have to want to become creative. Using your experiences and your intelligence to come up with creative ideas of value has to be meaningful to you. Learning to be creative, by diligently applying all the exercises that you will learn in this book, can rewire your brain to become more creative.

When you learn something new like a foreign language, or how to play a video game, your brain physically changes. In addition, every time you have a new experience, your neural mapping is altered, and those new structures and maps result in more connections between concepts. This is how we form new ideas. Only you can create these connections and bridge your experiences with concepts that you have learned, which are the foundations of creativity. Applying daily habits that increase your observation, intuition, and ability to build connections can rewire your brain into a more creative one.

A study published in the *European Journal of Social Psychology* by Phillippa Lally, a health psychology researcher at University College London, and her team, examined the habits of ninety-six people over a twelve-week period. Each person chose to perform one new habit for twelve weeks and reported each day on whether they did it and how automatic it felt. At the end of the twelve weeks, the researchers analyzed the data to determine how long it took each person to go from starting a new behavior to automatically doing it. On average it took sixty-six days for new habits to become natural and for the brain to rewire itself.

Diana, one of my course participants, told me that throughout her life she believed that creativity was one of those things "that you either have, or you don't." Could I really teach her how to become creative, she asked. She was skeptical. She saw no way to be innovative in the real estate industry, due to how inflexible and boxed in most of her colleagues were. After completing the four-week course and using the techniques I shared in the course and will share with you, she devised and implemented an entirely different marketing plan for her and her team members and felt confident enough to break the rules of an outdated system. Her first step was to take the decision to become creative and dispel the myth that creativity couldn't be taught or learned.

We are living on the front lines of unpredictable change. The avalanche of technology coupled with social, political, economic, and cultural upheavals that we face demand creative solutions to big and small business problems every day. Continuous use of our creativity and willingness to innovate is the only solution that we have to get ahead of these dramatic shifts. Creativity is available to anyone who wants to develop it. Claim this reality for yourself and don't let anybody diminish you because you aren't finding the cure to cancer (or maybe you are, and that is fantastic!). We can learn to be more creative. We can learn to innovate. We can challenge the status quo.

ALCHEMY LAB

- *Do the opposite of any of the seven myths about creativity in this chapter* that most hangs you up for at least sixty-six days.

- *Design a daily routine that works for you.* Write down how you will spend your time every day. Create structures around you, regardless of the job you do. What's the best time to answer emails? When is the time to make phone calls? When should you work out? Allocate time to think in silence and to read every day. If you want to switch careers, dedicate time to research that new field. If you are the CEO of a company, make sure to spend time talking and listening to your clients, employees, and vendors every day.

- *Try to learn something new* and carve out at least thirty minutes daily to practice it: another language, a new game, a hobby. You'd be amazed at the amount of expertise you can accumulate over the course of a few months, and even more amazed at how your commitment and consistency helps you experience creative breakthroughs.

PART II

HABITS OF THE MIND

■

Creativity takes work and discipline. In the following chapters, I explain the habits and mindsets that artists and entrepreneurs most commonly cultivated—either by will, design, or inherent in their personalities—that led to breakthroughs, masterpieces, discoveries, and developments in the past six hundred years. My hope is that you will stack, replicate, and repeat these habits until they become second nature. The more of these habits you nurture, the more your creativity expands.

4

Beyond 20/20: Your Vision,

Your Creativity, Your Success

Having a vision is an act of faith. One never really knows how a creative project will turn out or if it will ever happen the way one envisioned it. Nevertheless, we push ourselves every day to see our vision come to fruition. This is why artists and entrepreneurs are so good at living with ambiguities and seeing challenges as solvable problems and not death blows. Whether artistic or business-oriented, creative visions have to be ambitious. You are setting out to do something that hasn't been done before. Having a vision requires patience, commitment, and resilience.

A creative vision is the specific way an artist articulates their world. It is the way they see and think, and it references the moment long before it becomes a reality when they can envision that goal materialized. As artists develop their vision, it becomes a two-way street. On one side is what the artist sees and on the other side what the audience perceives. Artistic vision is, in this sense, inexhaustible and evergreen. Once the work is out in the world, the number of interpretations and emotions around it are as varied as what each spectator sees and feels.

Artists create because they want to express their vision. Humans are a meaning-making species, and artists make sense of their internal space, their identity, and the world around them by creating art. Often, the vision of an artist comes from skill and experience mixed with intuition and observation.

Innovators and entrepreneurs are also visionaries. We see things in our minds that others don't. Having a vision is what keeps us going in our businesses. It's what engages us, revitalizes us in moments of doubt, and maintains our sense of persistence even when everything around us may push us to stop. We go boldly into unchartered territories, in the same way that great artists do. This unique vision, no matter if you are a business founder or an artist, is what determines your style, your brand, and your business culture.

CREATIVITY AND AMBITION

Michelangelo Buonarroti's vision was to be the greatest artist of his time. He wanted to do this by moving his audience to their core with his creations' grandeur and excellence. His vision inspired him to paint one of the greatest landmarks of humanity, the Sistine Chapel.

Michelangelo was wildly ambitious, and he wasn't afraid of going after big things. After all, he was aware that he was both in the business of making great works of art and of becoming history. I vividly remember visiting the Vatican, first when I was fifteen and again at thirty-nine, and crossing the small doorway that led me into this fantastic space. The ceiling rises sixty-eight feet above the ground and covers an area of almost 5,900 square feet, half the size of a professional soccer field. The *Last Judgment*, which extends over the wall of the altar, is almost forty-five feet high and forty feet wide, engulfing the viewer in a rhapsody of blue skies, muscular bodies, biblical scenes, and mythical creatures. Goethe had it right when he said, "Without having seen the Sistine Chapel, one can form no appreciable idea of what one man is capable of achieving."

The central composition of Michelangelo's ceiling, *The Creation of Adam*, gave me my first idea when I was four years old of what God might look like. I saw, on the cover of a religion textbook, Michelangelo's buff man with thick, wavy gray hair and beard energizing Adam, touching his finger, a spark of light coming from the Creator to infuse his creature with life.

Michelangelo at first refused the commission to paint the chapel. After spending fifteen months in Bologna casting a large bronze statue of Pope

Julius II, he was called by the pontiff again, this time to Rome, and told point-blank that his new commission was to paint the ceiling of the Sistine Chapel. Michelangelo replied, "Painting is not my art." He thought of himself as a sculptor. But the pope insisted, and Michelangelo grudgingly agreed. However, as the visionary he was, he had a flash of intuition about what completing this ceiling would mean for his career. It was this vision of doing something bigger than anything done before that convinced Michelangelo to throw himself fully into this undertaking.

He was only thirty-three when he began painting the frescoes, and had great doubts about the outcome, but his vision had more power.

Keep in mind that big visions require collaborators; nobody can do anything meaningful alone. Even though Giorgio Vasari, Michelangelo's friend and biographer, wrote that he worked alone since none of his painter friends were up to par, that is simply not true. We know this because Michelangelo left records of how much he paid whom, when, and for which tasks, week after week. At any given time, he had at least twelve people involved in the Sistine Chapel project. He knew that the larger the vision, the more people he needed to work with to see it come true.

Furthermore, to carry out a big vision, you need to know how its different parts work. That's why Michelangelo had his hand in every aspect and detail of the great enterprise he was to manage and execute. He designed his own scaffolding, built on poles that didn't touch the walls in order to avoid ropes attached to the ceiling that would have left unsightly holes. He ordered the best azurite pigment from Florence to make the deepest blue paint, worked on sketches depicting his ideas for each section of the ceiling, and then translated them on *cartones* (cartoons), monumental chalk drawings composed of multiple sheets glued together to provide guidance for scale.

You must always remember that the path toward completing a large-scale vision will be riddled with challenges, and the Sistine Chapel was no exception. After much testing, Michelangelo decided to paint standing on top of the scaffolding with his head bent backward, and not lying on his back, as some have suggested. Although extremely uncomfortable for his neck and his eyesight, his vision superseded all the difficulties he faced.

We know much irritated him in the process, from the irregularities of the ceiling, the mold that accumulated in certain spots over the winter, the paint that dripped on his face, and the pope's insistence that he and his closest advisors see the progress, often showing up unannounced. Nevertheless, Michelangelo persevered, using his vision as a sounding board in moments when he wanted to give up.

The desire to see his progress, coupled with all of his years of training, as well as his studies, technical knowledge of materials and architecture, and the experience he had gained from carving his sculptures gave him the confidence he needed, reinvigorated his vision, and allowed him to go above and beyond what was then possible. Michelangelo's vision of the chapel was an unparalleled feat of artistic genius against which few can compare.

VISION = AMBITION

Creative visions can't stand being small; they thrive on greatness. I can't think of a better contemporary example than the maverick couple formed by Bulgarian-born Christo and his wife, the French Jeanne-Claude. They lived together in New York City for over four decades until she died in 2009, and where he continued working until his passing in May 2020.

They were the embodiment of what it is to be an ambitious artistic visionary. They were always dreaming about and pursuing spectacular monumental art projects, which they executed in ways that had never been done before. Christo and Jeanne-Claude had a specific style, and their "brand" relied on using common elements, which they repeated in all of their large-scale outdoor projects. They used millions of yards of fabric in bright colors to intervene and drape around man-made structures or nature. Nothing was off limits. Lakes, mountains, bays, and islands were part of their vision and later their reality.

By design, each project was ephemeral; none lasted more than a few weeks. Each was set in public spaces, allowing their work to interact directly with anybody who encountered them. Bringing their vision to fruition involved gaining the approval of dozens of communities and constituencies.

Above all, to avoid restrictions on their work, each project was self-financed; they never accepted sponsorships or government money.

Christo said that his projects were about "physical pleasure and also the angst I feel as an artist, the fight to make something that pleases me first. . . . Every project is a struggle, but I need contact with other people and physicality in my life."

I had been living in New York City for five years when Christo and Jeanne-Claude unveiled their most ambitious project in Central Park in the winter of 2005: *The Gates*, 7,503 saffron-colored fabric panels on steel gateways built along twenty-three miles of walkways. My husband and I lived on the Upper East Side, a few blocks away from the park, and walking through the gates was magic and monumental like nothing I had ever experienced before. It took the artists twenty-six years to see the fulfillment of their vision of *The Gates*. The local administration and various community boards turned down their earlier proposals. Mayor Michael Bloomberg finally ended their quest and agreed it could go forward.

A combination of sales of their own preparatory drawings and collages and bank loans allowed Christo and Jeanne-Claude to finance *The Gates*, which cost approximately $21 million. They bought all the materials, paid engineers for all the plans and specifications, ordered the fabrication of the parts, and paid six hundred workers to install the gates and an additional three hundred to monitor the work during the installation, duration, and removal of the project. It all started with the vision, then preparatory drawings and technical renderings to see how the fabric moved with the wind, research into what type of steel structure was needed, the design of the grid of steel gates around the walkways of the park, and various studies of the technical equipment that best suited the project.

The artists never compromised their vision, but found ways to make it happen. *The Gates* was up for only two weeks, but it made history. To date, it is the only art project of its kind to have taken over Central Park. Christo and Jeanne-Claude's vision about pioneering spectacular art projects and their connection and involvement with communities remained strong for over sixty years, up to their last project—the wrapping of the Arc de Triomphe in Paris—which was unveiled posthumously in September 2021.

WHERE VISIONS ARE BORN

The Sistine Chapel and *The Gates* were incredible in scale and vision, but you don't have to have Michelangelo's skill or wait twenty-six years to see your project materialize. Every one of your experiences, interests, and ideas makes you a unique person with a point of view that nobody else has. Everyone can have a grand vision.

The English word *vision* has its roots in the Latin *videre*, which means "to see," and the old French *vision*, defined as "something seen in the imagination or in the supernatural." That's exactly what having a vision requires, planning the future with imagination, oftentimes thinking about the impossible. Having a vision is central to any entrepreneurial dream.

SOMETIMES YOU NEED A REALITY DISTORTION FIELD

It is hard to use the word *visionary* and not think about Steve Jobs. The "supernatural" was part of Jobs's vision. He conceived his inventions in his mind without knowing how to make them or what his team might need to bring them to reality.

After changing and refining his vision during his first years at Apple, Jobs dreamed of designing and manufacturing millions of personal computers with an easy interface. With the passage of time, and accomplishing each "impossible" feat, his vision expanded to creating the iPod, iPhone, iPad, and the high-tech, seamlessly designed Apple stores. With these achievements, Jobs cemented his status as one of the greatest visionaries of all time. Many of his close associates remember that he either promised to people or required from people things that seemed unreasonable and out of the question.

They called this strange habit Steve's "reality distortion field." This distorted field, however, is what allowed Jobs to change the course of computer history without the resources that competing companies had. If creative visions don't seem impossible at first, then they aren't good enough visions. Jobs always quoted and lived by the maxim of Alan Key, a computer scientist and inventor, who said, "The best way to predict the future is to invent it."

EXPAND YOUR RANGE

The backbone of everything in my business, since the day I began, is contemporary art. I wanted to create a company that made contemporary art fun and meaningful and to integrate it unpretentiously into my clients' lives. While visiting art fairs and gallery openings, I noticed that art advisors were stern and snobbish, didn't display much passion for the art or their clients, and had a very zero-sum, transactional approach to what they did—the client buys, the advisor gets paid, repeat. They seemed, in a way, "the lawyers of the art world." They didn't care about making art more democratic or sharing their knowledge with a larger audience. All they wanted, it seemed to me, was to perpetuate an arcane structure. There wasn't much innovation or creativity in what they did.

Similarly, I noticed that interior designers featured in glossy magazines favored mostly beige furniture, copied themselves and each other time and again, and had little knowledge of contemporary art. They either worked with art advisors or made mediocre art choices for their clients, sometimes even selling them sculptures or paintings fabricated and private-labeled for the designer.

Something was missing on both sides. Nobody did fresh, colorful, and original interiors incorporating the work of contemporary artists with something to say, whose messages were deeper than the aesthetics alone. Contemporary art goes beyond the surface, always tells a story, has meaning, educates, and/or comments on things, ranging anywhere from social issues to history. That was what fascinated me most about it and still does. It isn't decorative; it is a living narrative providing context on how we can process the now.

My vision was to serve hundreds of private clients, building their art collections, expanding their points of view through art, and making them full participants, not mere bystanders, in the cultural conversation.

I had other visions as well. I wanted to reach millions of people. My premise was to demystify the art world and make it accessible. I created a plan for how to do this mainly by using the tools that then existed: rudimentary blogging platforms, Facebook, and Twitter. The art world was obscure to most people, and galleries in Chelsea felt snobbish, stuffy, and impenetrable. If, as I believed, artists were creating so much that was beautiful, generating ideas, and desiring to educate people with their unique points of view, why did the system insist on keeping their work hermetically sealed? I had a vision to develop an extraordinary client base while simultaneously marrying fine art with larger audiences who couldn't normally have access to galleries, artists, and art fairs the way I did.

My first blog post in December of 2009 was about my experience at the preview of Art Basel Miami Beach. I had attended the fair in years prior as a collector and art enthusiast. This time, as an art advisor, I had a very different mission. I was six months pregnant with my second child; it seems that my business creativity wasn't the only thing fertile!

Some dealers and gallerists who knew me were surprised by the pregnancy and confused by my career shift: "Are you an advisor now?" they asked. "Not only that," I answered, "but I'm also writing about art and demystifying the art world!" At that time, art publications and magazines were incomprehensible to the layperson, furthering the idea that contemporary art was just for the elite. I was following my vision, blazing my own trail, and ignoring the naysayers. I wrote on diverse topics, exhibitions, and artists, and kept the tone casual, approachable, and easygoing.

WHEN OPPORTUNITY KNOCKS, OPEN THE DOOR

A year and a half after my first blog post, through an entrepreneurs' organization I joined, I had an opportunity to write a straightforward article about art collecting for Forbes.com. That gave me some momentum. Around the same time, I met Gwyneth Paltrow; we had a friend in common. She also had started a new project, a weekly email newsletter called "Goop," and she sometimes allowed contributors to write about topics that were "mysterious," "taboo," or not commonly discussed.

I boldly told Gwyneth what I did and what my vision was, and later that week sent her some material about my company together with a copy of the Forbes.com article. A few weeks later, Gwyneth had left me a voicemail: "Hi, Maria, it's Gwyneth Paltrow. Thank you for what you sent me. I hadn't been in New York for many weeks, but as soon as I saw your envelope, I wanted to call you to invite you to collaborate with Goop and write a piece about demystifying contemporary art for us." I couldn't believe it. I immediately called her back, ecstatic. I said I'd work on it and have it to her within a week.

I wrote an unpretentious but comprehensive six-page article on collecting and living with contemporary art, on how to navigate and understand the ecosystem that existed between the artists, galleries, art fairs, auction houses, and novel websites that sold art online. I included information about the differences between prints, editions, and one-of-a-kind artworks. When that newsletter was sent out on a Thursday morning in September 2011, my life changed forever. My article for Goop was so successful that when Gwyneth graced the cover of *InStyle*'s October 2012 issue and was asked about Goop's ten biggest stories among hundreds that had been published, she mentioned mine and said, "It's just so fabulous, the idea that you can have an art collection at any price and that no one should be priced out of art and anyone can live with vibrant, creative, imaginative, inspirational pieces in their homes."

This pivotal moment in my new career not only opened up the path for my "demystification" project in a much bigger way than what I had been able to do, but it also got me a deal for my first book, a coffee-table monograph called *Out There*, published in 2013 by Pointed Leaf Press.

Since that first blog post, I have written more than 150 articles and essays, some of them published in the *Huffington Post*, others in *W* magazine, a few on Elle.com, a couple in *Vogue Brazil*, many in *Cultured Magazine*, and a handful in books and literary journals. I kept the same tone, and no matter what artist's studio I visited, whom I interviewed, or what exhibition I covered, I kept my vision intact—to enable more and more people to have access to the artists' minds, their private and sacred spaces, their ideas and feelings, and the reason they create what they do.

In January 2014, I started playing with another medium, video. I had a sense that I could use film to get my message across to more people. Instagram was allowing fifteen-second videos, which had a great response from users, and YouTube was gaining traction and on its way to becoming the most populated social media platform. I began collaborating with Peter Koloff, a videographer who had just moved from Los Angeles to New

York. He found me on Instagram and loved contemporary art. What I did intrigued him and he needed new material to build his New York clientele.

I asked Peter if he could film me interviewing photographer David LaChapelle, who had agreed to do the shoot while installing his exhibition *Land Scape* at Paul Kasmin Gallery in Chelsea. David had quite a long and high-profile career. His unique style and aesthetic gained him hundreds of thousands of fans and followers. He photographed a fantasy world of celebrities dressed in pop-saturated colors set in outlandish situations. He re-created biblical scenes such as the Last Supper, in which his version of Jesus, wearing a red sweatshirt and an electric-blue toga, was surrounded by multiracial "disciples" covered in tattoos and sporting sweats.

This new exhibition was a departure from all that. David had other preoccupations. He lived in both Los Angeles and Maui and wanted to address global warming and the indiscriminate exploitation of natural resources. With that in mind, he built small models of gas stations and refineries, painted them in his characteristic saturated hues, and shot them in the rain forest of Maui and in the expansive deserts and majestic coastlines of California. None of his fans or collectors had seen this body of work. While Peter was filming, I asked him all the questions: Why did he go in that direction? What did global warming mean to him? Was he going to continue photographing models and celebrities? What did he expect the audience's takeaway to be when they left the show?

After the interview, Peter and I ran to edit the footage; we condensed the highlights into a two-minute video and uploaded it to YouTube. I also gave it to the *Huffington Post* and reposted it on my own blog. Even though the result was far from perfect and the audio was iffy, David's fans loved having access to information they wouldn't normally have. Several emailed and messaged me to thank me for providing more about their favorite artist than they could have found in newspapers or magazines.

It took me another three years to figure out how to refine and better channel my use of video. In 2017, while on vacation, I realized I needed to go deeper with the artists and discuss important sociocultural issues that impacted all of us. With art as the entry point, the complexity of the topics discussed would be more palatable to viewers. By then, Instagram supported one-minute videos, and I had this burning desire to create. When I landed in New York, I immediately called Peter and told him that we were going to film the "C Files." C for *culture*, but also for *classified* information that people didn't know much about or were afraid to discuss.

I selected artists whose work and careers reflected and covered specific themes that interested me: race, gender, inequalities, the income gap, immigration, online dating, body image, and much more. When shooting, my conversations with the artists were casual. We filmed in their studios, parks, and the galleries in which they were exhibiting. As we walked, we talked in an extremely open way. Nothing was posed, we weren't looking straight at the camera, and nobody ever felt nervous or uncomfortable. I selected the B-roll and the music, which had the perfect vibe for the topic we were discussing, and coedited the footage with Peter. The videos were a success and lived in different formats: long for my website, shorter versions for social media. I also licensed to *Cultured Magazine*, which posted them on their website and promoted them on social media. Over the course of eighteen months, we created more than twenty videos.

In the winter of 2019, a friend who worked at the New York PBS station reached out to me: "We are launching a very cool TV/streaming/digital platform called All Arts. I think your videos could become a TV series; may I connect you with the executives in charge?" Six months after my first meeting with PBS, we shot four episodes of *The "C" Files with Maria Brito.* Each one required two full days of filming, a crew of six people, and a handful of postproduction editors. I had absolute freedom. I selected all the artists based on the specific issues I thought we needed to address and added other voices and personalities so that the series felt dynamic. I chose hip-hop and electronic music for the background tracks. My goal was to keep it as natural as my incipient online version and to engage the artists in difficult conversations with compassion and empathy.

We shot the first episode in Sanford Biggers's Harlem studio. Sanford is an African American multimedia artist who has dedicated an important part of his career to addressing racial tensions in America, the aftermath of slavery, and modern-day police brutality. He is also a musician and his performance band, Moon Medicin, fuses jazz, reggae, and rock-and-roll. He immerses the audience in giant screens that project imagery from visual art, sci-fi, new media, and film noir. We balanced the heaviness of the issues that he confronts in his work with the enjoyable memories and footage of his performances. We walked from his studio to the Apollo Theater, a place where he and his band had performed. To add color and perspective, I also interviewed Sanford's friends, including jazz musician Jason Moran and chef Marcus Samuelsson.

My show premiered on cable TV and online in October 2019, and it was the first time in the history of American television that a series focused on sociocultural issues through the lens of contemporary art. Prior to *The "C" Files*, there were art programs that shot artists talking alone in front of the camera, played classical music in the background, and put heavy emphasis on process and brushstrokes. There were news anchors, late-night hosts, and personalities who occasionally interviewed famous artists about their social justice agendas. But none like *The "C" Files*. Having a unique creative vision allowed me to dare to go beyond what already existed.

ALCHEMY LAB

Creative visions are powered by ambition. Follow these steps to form yours:

1. *Visualize what your end goal looks like* without worrying how you are going to get there. Working from the end is an exceptionally good way to engage with your vision. It lets you see the big picture, the materialization of what you want to achieve. Michelangelo envisioned the result of his work before and during its execution; you can too.

2. *Make a list of each of the goals you need to accomplish* to realize your vision. Write them down as they come to mind. Don't stop

to edit them; rely on your stream of consciousness to avoid any self-censorship.

3. *Rank your goals* from the most important to the least. Focus on the top three. This is like building your scaffolding to the ceiling of the Sistine Chapel. You need a sound structure that allows you to get to the finish line.

4. *Break each goal down to create subgoals and objectives.* Add each of the steps you need to accomplish to reach each objective.

5. *Consider the challenges that may come and their potential solutions.* This objective step is designed to help you hedge your bets. You will encounter stumbling blocks on your way to achieving your big vision, but accounting for them from the get-go will better equip you to deal with them. For Christo and Jeanne-Claude, the obstacles were always related to obtaining the permits and the sources they could tap into for self-financing. They knew these two issues required as much creative thinking as the artistic vision itself and tackled them head-on from the start of each project.

6. *Create a diagram or an outline of goals, subgoals, and smaller steps.* This will be your own personal vision map and the blueprint or rough outline that will guide you to start any creative project. Your ideas will flow a lot easier once you have them in front of you. This is exactly the way artists, innovators, and entrepreneurs break down their big projects. Keep this document in front of you, refer to it often, and don't be afraid to adjust, refine, and change goals, subgoals, and steps as you move forward, as Steve Jobs did.

5

Daring Convention:

Creativity and Autonomy

BACK IN 1610, women weren't autonomous. They were expected to marry young and bear children. Women who wanted to become artists could not study anatomy or life drawing. As a young girl, Artemisia Gentileschi learned how to draw, mix color, and paint. Her father, Orazio, was an accomplished Roman painter. He encouraged her artistic talent and let her play in his studio and hang out with other artists.

One of those artists was a bad boy whose emotions ran high. He was a provocateur known for getting into brawls. Everyone called him Caravaggio, after the town he'd been born in. As an artist, he had a stunning reputation that extended across Europe for breaking decisively with the Late Renaissance and introducing the key elements of a new style, eventually called baroque. He used dark backgrounds and created emotional intensity by employing a heightened chiaroscuro technique (called tenebrism), which created dramatic contrast of light and shade. It rendered his subjects in a way that made them look like real human beings, not the perfect and idealized figures of Renaissance art. When most artists were still painting celestial apparitions and plump cherubs, Caravaggio employed live models (some of whom were prostitutes) and portrayed them as everyday people, warts and all, even in religious scenes.

Caravaggio died in 1610 after years fleeing from one city to the next for killing a man in a street fight in Rome. He left raving fans everywhere. That included Artemisia, who considered him her biggest influence. He instilled in her his maxim that art and life are the same thing.

In that year, seventeen-year-old Artemisia finished her first major work, *Susanna and the Elders*, a scene from the book of Daniel in the Old Testament. The narrative of the painting shows a young woman in her garden taking a bath harassed by two old lascivious men. As the biblical story goes, they threaten to tarnish her reputation by saying she was unfaithful, unless she agreed to have sex with them. The Bible tells us that Susanna refuses, is then arrested, judged, and about to be killed, when a young man, Daniel, interrupts the trial shouting that the old men are lying and should be questioned, turning Susanna's fate around and exposing the truth about the corrupt men.

This painting, showing Artemisia's phenomenal talent, prompted her father to hire another painter, Agostino Tassi, to privately tutor his daughter. As if the painting was a prophecy, Tassi raped her and, with the false promise of marriage, lured her into a continuing sexual relationship. Artemisia eventually told her dad, who pressed charges against Tassi. In a public and humiliating trial, nineteen-year-old Artemisia was tortured with thumbscrews (a barbaric precursor of a lie detector test) to assess the veracity of her testimony. Tassi was convicted, although he never served his sentence.

After all that Artemisia had gone through, she didn't hide or resign herself to a life of misery. She married an older man, moved to Florence, had four children, and pursued her ambition to become a famous and well-paid artist. She never again painted a woman looking like Susanna, a victim of men. Artemisia determined she would be thought the equal or better than any of her male counterparts. Her creativity soared in tandem with her skill and fame.

Most of Artemisia's works have women protagonists. Her painting style as well as her own life became bold and defiant. Following the trial, she produced one of her masterpieces, *Judith Slaying Holofernes*, another biblical scene, this time fully influenced by Caravaggio's dark backgrounds and his use of light and shadows. The book of Judith narrates the story of a Jewish woman who seduces Holofernes, an Assyrian general, who wanted to attack the city of Bethulia. She gets him drunk, then decapitates him with his own sword, saving her town.

Artemisia portrays Judith as strong. Her countenance is calm and reflects absolute conviction; her rolled-up sleeves show muscular forearms. With her left hand pulling his hair, she holds the almost-lifeless head of her victim; while the sword in her right one is deep inside his neck, rendering him powerless. Blood is streaming down the white mattress on which he lies. Before this painting of Judith, no male artist had captured a scene with such intensity, drama, and naturalism.

Years after she completed the painting in 1613, Artemisia revisited this passage and other variations a few more times. In an era where such acts of defiance were unheard of, she asserted her independent vision and communicated her autonomy through her art and in how she lived her life. While she remained married, she was always the main breadwinner. Throughout her forty-year career, she painted many heroic women nude or in sumptuous dresses that revealed ample décolletages and tight cleavages, including Cleopatra, Venus, Danaë, and Mary Magdalene, charged with eroticism and orgasmic facial expressions.

She became friends with influential people like Galileo Galilei; took commissions from princes, kings, cardinals, and dukes; traveled to different cities in and outside Italy; and became the first woman accepted as a member of the prestigious Accademia del Disegno in Florence. She was the headliner, the earner, and the leader in control. Had Artemisia been alive today, her life might look like a Quentin Tarantino movie: an avenging heroine marked by crime and violence, absurd situations, dark humor, wittiness, and, ultimately, triumph.

BE A CONTRARIAN

Every creative leader possesses autonomy, which is the quality of being self-governing, self-directing, and independent. It is an essential trait that every successful artist, innovator, and entrepreneur must develop and cultivate. Autonomy is at the heart of an artist's practice and that of an innovative entrepreneurial venture. It is the conviction that each of us must have to stand by our ideas, to back them up with our actions, and to not only be willing, but also eager to go against common beliefs.

Leadership, critical thinking, and autonomy are intertwined concepts in both business and art. Autonomy has many facets; for example, when creative leaders embrace self-direction, they have the confidence to know they can solve any problem that comes their way. They don't have to take what life throws at them; they can find ways around business's and life's circumstances if they are creative enough. Developing creative autonomy begets action; you don't wait around for things to happen; you take the initiative because you know your success or failure depends on what you do or don't do.

Autonomous people assert themselves against the status quo. They don't accept the prevailing opinion just because it's the one given to them. Nothing creative has ever come from taking things at face value. No one exemplifies this more than China's most relevant and daring artist, Ai Weiwei. For more than three decades, he has merged art and activism in his own life. He is a sharp critic of the authoritarian Chinese government, its archaic institutions, lack of transparency, and precarious position on human rights. He dreams of social transformation and always uses his autonomy to express how China should be, to bring awareness about a regime that masks and hides crucial information that endangers its citizens' and the world's well-being. With a practice that incorporates photography, sculpture, ceramics, installation, film, assemblages, performance, and more, Weiwei's thread as a dissident is not only part and parcel in his art, but also a vital form of communication.

In 2008, a massive earthquake in the city of Sichuan, China, killed eighty thousand people. Of special concern to Weiwei were the children who succumbed under the unsafe and poorly built public school structures. The Chinese government never released the official number of deaths, but Weiwei used his blog to make an open call enlisting the help of citizen investigators. They went about Sichuan asking parents, visiting the ruins, and knocking on every door to gather the names and ages of the deceased children. After one year, his team collected 5,219 names. Weiwei published all their names and ages on his blog, which was promptly shut down by the government because too many people were reading and following him on social media. That didn't deter him.

In 2009, the Haus der Kunst in Munich presented Weiwei's solo exhibition entitled *So Sorry*. One of the works was an installation created from nine thousand backpacks in multiple colors that covered the façade of the museum. Together they formed a sentence written in Chinese that said, "All I want is to let the world remember she had been living happily for seven years," a direct quote from the mother of a girl who died trapped under one of the school buildings. Accompanying captions and printed pamphlets translated the quote and explained where it came from. The installation, called *Remembering,* sent shock waves around the world; pictures were shared on social media and newspapers wrote about it, solidifying Weiwei's reputation as a dangerous enemy of the Chinese government.

In 2011, the Chinese government arrested Weiwei and charged him with tax evasion. He was held in police custody, incommunicado for eighty-one days, and then released with a $2.4 million fine but never formally charged of any crime. The Chinese authorities used this event as an opportunity to confiscate Weiwei's passport and place him under modified house arrest, preventing him from leaving Beijing. He never stopped producing art and exhibiting it in museums, art fairs, and galleries worldwide, even if he couldn't be physically present.

WHEN EVERYONE ZIGS, YOU ZAG

In December of 2013, a client asked me to contact Weiwei's studio to commission a special sculpture. Such a task wasn't easy. He was still under house arrest, his email was monitored, and his galleries wouldn't share contact information. I knew my client wouldn't take no for an answer, so I dug and dug, asked people, and scoured my contacts. I finally found the email address of an American businessman who lived in Hong Kong and sometimes worked as Weiwei's manager. I contacted him, explaining what my client wanted, and after weeks of back-and-forth communications, Weiwei agreed to fabricate the sculpture for my client.

Serendipitously, three months after I started communicating with Weiwei's business manager, the social media department of the Brooklyn Museum reached out to me. They were looking for creative ways to promote their exhibitions and events, including an upcoming gala honoring Ai Weiwei and the opening of *According to What?*, a survey of some of his most important works of the last twenty years of his career.

"Obviously, doing anything with Weiwei would be impossible," the museum's representative said. "Maybe you'd want to come the day the museum is closed to the public and take pictures? Feel free to create any content, just please send us something at least five days before the gala."

Taking pictures around the museum per se for a project that involved Weiwei's exhibition didn't interest me. On the other hand, this was an opportunity to come full circle with my creative vision to work with extraordinary private clients building relevant art collections and offering free access to something hundreds of thousands of people would normally be unable to attend. The timing was perfect.

I went against the status quo and focused on figuring out how to interview this high-profile artist who lived under house arrest. First, I had to get Weiwei to agree. I wasn't sure he'd be amenable to granting me an interview. Second, I had all sorts of logistical and technical challenges in front of me. I could not go to China. Emailing questions was not the same as a firsthand account of what Weiwei had to say. Recording a phone conversation would have been impossible. I thought about FaceTiming; I was sure he had an iPhone, but FaceTime calls also couldn't be recorded. Neither Zoom nor Instagram Live existed in 2014. What I was attempting to do seemed quite complicated. At last, I got it: I would use Skype for a video call, split the screen in two, and record the conversation. Then I would give the file to Peter, my videographer, to smooth it out so we could upload it to YouTube. After that, I would embed it in a *Huffington Post* article, on my blog, and also promote it on social media.

I emailed my request to my Hong Kong contact and was thrilled when Weiwei's Beijing studio manager granted me the interview.

I was worried that the technology would fail us, that the Chinese government would block Skype, or that the recording would disappear. None of that happened, and at 9:00 p.m. local time in New York City and 9:00 a.m. local time in Beijing, Ai Weiwei and I connected on video via Skype and were able to talk for more than fifteen minutes.

He walked around his backyard wearing headphones, the camera pointing below his face, a lag of nanoseconds separating the image and the voice.
He told me how happy he was to have a solo show at the Brooklyn Museum,
after having lived in New York City in the 1980s. This big honor, he said,
validated his constant quest to protect freedom of speech, especially for
artists, writers, and thinkers who questioned authority. I pointedly told
him how ingenious he was in his use of social media, and he replied, "It's
a powerful tool that allows humans to communicate freely. It feels like a
miracle that occurred to human society; the response is so fast and so direct
regardless of who the user is: politicians, kids, artists, leaders. . . . Without
social media, I would never have reached the point where I am today. Of
course, it also puts me in danger, but it is a beautiful way for me to communicate with the world, especially with young people, because it gives them
hope and strength; it makes them think that things are possible."

The Brooklyn Museum got the content a week before the gala. My client received his sculpture a couple of months later, and the audience got so
much more. I consider this interview, using technology that wasn't yet com-
monplace, a triumph of creativity and the meeting of two willful, autonomous people expressing their minds. In case you are wondering, Weiwei
got his passport back in 2015, moved to Berlin, and in 2019 relocated again
to Cambridge, England, and in 2021 to the outskirts of Lisbon in Portugal.

Entrepreneurs express their autonomy both as an extension of their own
identities and in their willingness to explore the ideas that come into their
minds and those that others bring to their tables.

CREATIVITY THRIVES ON PUSHBACKS

Given the circumstances of her life, I can't think of a more autonomous
and independent entrepreneur than Madam C. J. Walker, whose creativity and innovation took her from extreme poverty to substantial wealth.
Born Sarah Breedlove in 1867 in Delta, Louisiana, to slave parents who
worked in cotton fields, she was lucky enough to have come into this world
after the Emancipation Proclamation. Nevertheless, she still faced enormous obstacles as a Black woman living in America. As a teenager, she

first worked as a washerwoman. She moved to different states looking for better opportunities, finally settling in Denver, Colorado. Against all odds, she started building a business of her own: selling a restorative formula for Black women who suffer from hair loss.

As many rural Americans in the late nineteenth century did, Madam grew up without indoor plumbing and proper hair hygiene. Consequently, she started going bald and always covered her head with a wrap. She was adamant about finding a solution, and eventually formulated a product that she said "came to her in a dream." She was married to a man named C. J. Walker who encouraged her to use his name for her brand. The moniker *Madam C. J. Walker*, as she became known, was imprinted on the metal cans that contained her "wonderful hair grower." As soon as she made some money, she reinvested it in newspaper ads with her own "before and after" pictures, which helped her build a mail-order business. She added shampoo and a pressed oil to her product offerings, and opened a parlor to demonstrate the benefits of her mixes. Madam had almost no formal education, but her gift was palpable. She realized that she could train others and recruit them as commissioned sales agents of her products, thus expanding her reach and sales exponentially.

In 1910, when Denver proved too small, she uprooted her family and business operations against the advice of many of her advisors and settled in Indianapolis, buying office spaces and a building that would be turned into a factory—an impressive feat for a woman in those days, let alone a descendant of slaves. She networked relentlessly with pastors, members of the church, and Black community organizers. She realized she had to do this all over the country, and embarked on long tours that involved meeting Baptist church leaders, churchgoers, and anyone else who could spread the word about her transformational hair treatments. In 1913, she purchased a large townhouse and opened a salon in Harlem when it was becoming the center of African American culture. She decided to move to New York, to a mansion that she restored in Irvington-on-Hudson, twenty miles north of Manhattan, near John D. Rockefeller's estate.

Her best and most creative business strategy was to autonomously do what she thought best, even in the face of cultural and racial pushback. She recruited and trained twenty thousand sales agents throughout the two decades she was at the helm of her company, and the novel way in which she organized them set her and her business apart. She instilled principles of corporate responsibility, social betterment, and racial justice in her agents and offered people who might otherwise not stand a chance an opportunity to make a good living. That Walker diploma helped the agents use the money it earned them to improve their living standard and pay for the education of their children and grandchildren. By the time of her death in 1919, Madam's personal net worth was close to $600,000, which translates to almost $9 million as of this writing.

The trick of successful artists and entrepreneurs is to know how to self-regulate, maintaining that fine balance of autonomy with the discipline to get things done. Excessive freedom leads to lack of attention and repeated effort that dilutes concentration and focus. Parameters, structures, and routines counterbalance autonomy.

ALCHEMY LAB

Being autonomous doesn't mean working in isolation or disconnecting from the rest of the world. Practice independent thinking and foster your autonomy by following these steps:

1. *Question the status quo, processes, products, systems, authoritarian models, and/or information* coming from media sources that don't offer an alternative point of view.

2. *Hold an internal debate with yourself on a divisive topic.* Balance all the options, benefits, and disadvantages that might come from choosing an unusual idea that you believe in.

3. *Take the road less traveled.* Creativity and innovation don't spurt out of "business as usual." When everyone zigs, you zag.

4. *Ask for opinions, advice, and feedback from others you trust.* This is to get perspective, not approval.

5. *Take a step forward with that unpopular or untested idea* in your business, studio, or marketplace. Assess the results objectively. For example: launch a survey on Instagram, release an early prototype and let your best customers play with it in exchange for feedback, call your closest friends or business advisors, present your ideas and listen to them, weighing their opinions carefully.

6

Bringing the Inside Out:

Creativity and Authenticity

THE MOST CREATIVE ideas are always the most personal. Most artists I know have an uncanny ability to experience deep feelings. Most of the time those feelings are tied to their own narratives. Artists are usually authentic, sensible people. When artists create, there is no right or wrong. It's based on their aesthetic values and personal meaning. All other judgments, whether from the marketplace or the press, are subjective.

Having such an ample sphere of action provides artists with the latitude to make mistakes. Often, they incorporate them as part of their work. Many artists get past the idea of perfection. They don't need to attain it to be happy with the results of their work.

The expression of authenticity in artists comes with the openness to accept that making art means sharing a piece of themselves with the world. Not everyone will understand it, like it, or relate to it, so it takes a lot of courage to do that. Artists can't blame anybody but themselves if a particular body of work, a project, or an exhibition isn't a commercial success or well received by critics. At the end of the day, no matter how many people they employ in their studios, the art they produce comes with their signature imprinted on it.

When I was seven, my parents took me to New York City for the first time. That crucial trip informed my visual understanding of modern and contemporary art. The impressive, dizzying Guggenheim Museum kept me wandering up and down the ramp during that frigid month of April 1983. The graffiti on the subway trains mesmerized me, and the pace of people walking on the streets enthralled me.

The most magical moment was our visit to the Grey Art Gallery and Study Center of New York University to see the exhibition of "an artist who was married to Diego Rivera," according to what my father said. That exhibition, called *Frida Kahlo and Tina Modotti,* contained works by two women challengers of the conventional standards of "macho" high art. Modotti was a photographer and, many say, Frida's lover. Frida wasn't yet the celebrity she has now become, even though almost thirty years had passed since her death.

There were sixty paintings by Kahlo in that show. Each spoke to me in a language that I had never heard or seen before. They were raw, intense, colorful, and sometimes frightening. They had convoluted narratives, but I somehow connected with them. Kahlo painted motifs that reminded me of my own tropical life: watermelons, parakeets, flowers, folk items, religious iconography, Indian masks. In most of her canvases, she painted herself, in all her glory, pain, vulnerability, and authenticity. She wore flamboyant clothes, her black hair braided up with colorful yarn or worn down and parted in the middle. In one, she painted her own legs and feet; her toenails were colored a deep scarlet. She seemed both sophisticated and friendly, worldly and accessible.

The paintings were relatively small, creating a complicit relationship between them and the viewer. In one, she painted herself as a baby, but with her adult face and long hair, being breastfed in the arms of a Native Indian wet nurse wearing a pre-Columbian mask. Baby Frida seemed disconnected and aloof. Another one showed a scary scene: Frida lying on a hospital bed holding red cords attached to a floating fetus. I was too young to understand that it depicted one of her miscarriages, but I was intuitive enough to know that Frida had left her life story in those paintings.

NOBODY SEES IT LIKE YOU DO

The mental and emotional space in which we allow ourselves to be ourselves, no matter the job or the industry, is ripe with opportunities to create, disrupt, and have big breakthroughs. Hiding ourselves, pretending to be someone else, and avoiding mistakes stifles creativity. Those who are afraid of revealing their true stories, personalities, and feelings either end up depleted or burn out. They miss the great opportunity to share their true gifts with the world. On the other hand, for those who aim for perfection, the work is never done. There are always flaws and faults, which ensnare the perfectionist in a never-ending loop. For the perfectionist, there is never personal fulfillment or professional satisfaction.

I created my own business after becoming a mom, an experience that opened me up to showing my real self. Motherhood changed me more than I could have ever imagined it would. The tenderness, sweetness, and innocence of my kids moved me, and still does, to the core. Being a mother opened a path for me to explore my authenticity and vulnerability and, with it, my more creative ideas. After all those many years in law firms, showing my softer, nurturing side wasn't really my forte. Before having my firstborn, while I still was practicing law, I was stoic and disconnected from who I truly was. It took me some time to regain my balance. When I found myself free from the emotional masks that I had worn to protect myself, I developed the guts to go to places I hadn't dared before.

In the fall of 2010, when my youngest boy was seven months old and my oldest two years old, I envisioned, designed, and launched an app for kids telling the story of Frida Kahlo. It was an homage to one of my favorite artists and a tribute to what I consider my best creation: my children. Inspired by their purity, laughter, spontaneity, and loving gaze, I was excited to make my curious toddler and other kids engage with art, and learn about artists' lives in a way that would keep their attention.

I wrote a very accessible biography of Frida and split the twelve most important events of her life into chapters of one paragraph each. I recounted how close she was to her father as a child, her bus accident, painting while bedridden, meeting Diego Rivera, moving to the United States, and so on. I hired a children's illustrator and met with her several times, reviewing photographs of Frida and all her paintings. I asked her to paint Frida's life in a positive and enlightening way, nothing creepy, nothing bloody. The audience was to be from two to seven years old. The illustrator created spectacular watercolors that were photographed and digitalized.

It then occurred to me that the story should also be in Spanish, so I translated it. I found a phenomenal app developer, who loved the project and helped me add music, narration (I read the Spanish version myself), animation, and even a digital coloring book. We created an interactive app for kids. It ticked off all the boxes. It was fun and dynamic. Users could go back and forth between the Spanish and English versions to teach children language skills. They had the option to listen to the voice-over or read the book with the sound muted. Kids could use their motor skills to "paint" on the screen and make their own "art."

The app told the story of a woman whose strength helped her overcome many adversities and whose authenticity turned her into one of the most celebrated female artists of all time. It went live in December 2010 and ranked high in both the children and educational categories of the App Store for more than a year. It became a success and was an innovation in an area where, despite thousands of existing apps, nothing like it existed before.

It is easy for people to accept their own insidious thoughts, which kill their ideas before they see the light of day and block their creative flow, because they convince themselves their ideas have no value. Building the courage to express one's authenticity isn't easy and can sometimes be quite emotionally painful. The pain of not doing so is a lot worse.

CREATIVITY FROM PAIN

Even artists sometimes struggle with their own personal narratives. However, when they are able to confront them, magical things happen. Caledonia Curry is a classically trained fine artist, who is widely known as the first woman to gain large-scale recognition in the male-dominated world of street art, where she got her moniker of Swoon.

Swoon is an extraordinary draftsman and her work highlights the humanity of her subjects, whether on the 1,300-square-foot wall on Bowery in Lower Manhattan or on the walls of the Tate Modern in London.

I followed Swoon's trajectory from the time I stumbled upon one of her wheat-pasted murals in Brooklyn in 2002 to the time I got lost in an immersive installation she created for the Brooklyn Museum in the spring of 2014.

At that Brooklyn show, I felt that something in Swoon's work had dramatically shifted. There was so much energy, love, and audacity in the fantastical installation called *Submerged Motherlands*. She constructed it in the museum's upper floor rotunda, which included a seventy-two-foot-tall dome, and mixed architecture and drawings that whimsically wove reality and mythology. At the top was a giant portrait of a beautiful woman breastfeeding her baby in the most loving way. Lower and closer to the floor was an older female figure, with an exposed bony thorax and an oxygen tube around her nose. Farther down was a younger and healthier version of the same ill woman, holding a cute baby in her arms. The world Swoon created blew me away.

It wasn't until 2019 that Swoon and I connected personally. She had been traveling around the world with projects and exhibitions. I invited her to be a guest on one of the episodes of my TV series, where we would talk about her and her work. She told me then that *Submerged Motherlands* was a turning point in her career. Her mother, a heroin addict, had passed away. Swoon had had to face the years of shame and anguish of growing up with "junkie parents" as she cared for her dying mother during the last three months of her life. She drew her as her frail body was disintegrating, and she also drew her young and happy, holding Swoon in her loving arms. Shortly after, her father died too.

Swoon told me she escaped from her childhood by hiding and running away from it. She never told anybody about her parents' addiction until she realized that the anger breeding inside of herself was keeping her stuck in a never-ending cycle of blame and shame. She had chosen to reject her own life story, and the results were hindering her art.

By risking being authentic and embracing her story, she incorporated first her mother, then her father in her work. This marked the beginning of her healing path. It gave her the freedom to share her story openly with the world. Ever since, she has not only produced her best work, but through her nonprofit organization, the Heliotrope Foundation, she sponsors, among other projects, a long-term community revitalization program for drug addicts in rehab in Braddock, Pennsylvania. Thanks to Swoon's efforts, people who otherwise are condemned by society now have access to work, training, and a supportive environment. Being honest with herself about her family and her past opened up a world of possibilities for Swoon. Her skills are the same. Her cheerful personality is there. Her work and her heart, however, are only getting better.

CREATIVITY FROM WAR

Holding tightly on to the "stuff" about ourselves we don't ever want to revisit is a sure way to never reach our full potential. Once we are able to look the "stuff" in the eye, dissect it, and deal with it, our creativity, like floodgates, opens. During a trip to Beirut, Lebanon, in the spring of 2019, I visited the studio of Serwan Baran. I knew nothing about him, but my hosts took me and a small group of friends to meet with local artists.

When Serwan greeted us, he seemed both sad and strong and immediately gave me the impression of someone who had unburdened himself of something quite heavy. My jaw dropped when I saw the scale and subject of the paintings he was working on. Several canvases were close to ten feet tall and twenty feet long. They were propped against the walls, and some were covering the floor. They depicted hundreds of soldiers wearing green uniforms, piled on top of each other, holding on to their rifles, their lifeless faces blurred and conveying the horror and chaos of war. The whole studio felt cinematic.

For forty-five years, Serwan lived in his native Iraq during continuous war. He escaped Baghdad in 2003. He made it to Beirut after having served as a soldier in the Iran-Iraq War and as a "war artist" in the First Gulf War, forced to record, for government propaganda purposes, the "glory" of the Iraqi army. Day in and day out, all he saw was death and devastation. For fifteen years after arriving in Lebanon, he never tackled the subject in his paintings, choosing to adapt to a new life in a different country and not reopen that wound.

But in 2018, two curators contacted Serwan. They told him a private foundation had chosen him to be the first solo artist representing Iraq at the Venice Biennale, one of the most prestigious, celebrated, and internationally attended events in the art world. "It was time to meet the beast again," he told me. "I was looking for myself in those paintings." While he was reliving the battles, he also had to face his own internal battlefield and the emotional scarring and PTSD that those years had left him. It was without doubt the best work he ever produced.

Two months later, I visited Iraq's pavilion in Venice. In an interesting parallel to Swoon naming her climactic installation *Submerged Motherlands*, Serwan called his pivotal pavilion *Fatherland* as a profound critique of the masculine and paternalistic dimension of the political culture of Iraq and the region, acknowledging that he believed only men pursue war.

These concepts of authenticity and openness may seem daunting when the subject is business, but it's important that you tackle them. Take, for example, ideas like those shared by Ray Dalio, the billionaire and philanthropist founder of the hedge fund Bridgewater Associates in Westport, Connecticut. In his book *Principles*, he talks about the underlying tenets he used to build his business. One of them, Dalio says, is that "pain plus reflection equals progress." With this simple sentence, he encourages his team—and himself—to look for growth through honesty and curiosity about each person's strengths and weaknesses. He says that once the ego is removed, you can see yourself and your work from a higher perspective, which allows the best and most creative business decisions to come to the surface.

If you think that authenticity and emotions don't belong in business, think again. A group of researchers from the University of Maryland, Wharton Business School, Merrimack College, and the London School of Economics decided to study the link between creativity and emotions after visiting a global tech company. They noticed that the reason why it was lagging behind its competitors in innovation was because there was no authentic expression of emotions in the company's teams.

That was the impetus to start investigating. Through two field studies and two lab-based experiments, the researchers focused on the ability of each team member to authentically express opinions and emotions, whether positive or negative. When people felt they could open up, particularly in the early stages of the creative process when ideas are more intuitive and rely more on feelings and emotions than on logical explanations, there was a greater generation and evaluation of diverse points of view. But when emotional expression was killed altogether, all other information processing died with it and suppressed the most creative outcomes too.

What this study has confirmed is that companies that want to boost creativity and innovation should focus on cultivating more authenticity in their teams' emotional climates.

These implications are profound for the business world and for our personal lives: we become better creative thinkers when we become more authentic and feel emotionally safe to express our minds.

Authenticity and openness in business, with proper boundaries, is crucial for success. Having honest conversations with clients, team members, and even with competitors can reveal hidden gems. They may help us solve problems in ways not considered before, unearth new sources of revenues, bring new clients, or propel us closer to the breakthroughs we have been looking to experience.

The point of authenticity is not to overshare one's personal life or intimacies, which aren't relevant to the business, but to lead with so much conviction about who we really are that people can't help but notice our uniqueness and creativity. Our minds will never go to places if the heart hasn't been there before.

ALCHEMY LAB

Honor your authenticity. There's nobody else with your exact point of view and experiences. Write down the answers to these questions:

1. What do you enjoy most in your life?

2. What are your strengths?

3. What are your weaknesses?

4. What unique characteristics and gifts do you alone have?

5. How could you bring the aspects of these four things to the job you do?

6. What are you most afraid of as it relates to your occupation?

7. What is the likelihood of this fear materializing?

Taking the Outside In:

Creativity and Empathy

Empathy is the key to thinking differently, a cornerstone of creativity in entrepreneurship and elsewhere. Fostering diversity in companies, teams, and partnerships and developing multiangle perspectives is essential to creativity, and it all starts with empathy.

We cannot feel exactly how another person feels, but we can try as much as possible to be on their wavelength and imagine what they might be experiencing. Empathy is the ability to put ourselves in someone else's shoes. If authenticity is a habit nurtured from the inside out, empathy begs us to take the outside in.

It's almost unfeasible to be creative and innovative without experiencing a good amount of empathy. Art is one of the mediums of communication that most evokes it. We love to watch movies and TV shows that take us into other worlds and let us experience someone else's inner perspective. Long before movies and TV, artists and writers did the same—with storytelling that spoke to our emotions. They invited us, through their creativity, to explore other points of view and outlooks.

INSURRECTION AND INNOVATION

The French monarchy wasn't particularly empathic. Throughout their reign, they never seemed to get it. By not listening to, connecting with, or understanding their own people, they ultimately lost the throne, their riches, their palaces, and even their heads. Between 1792 and 1848, the French witnessed three revolutions and profound changes in their socio-political structure and experienced long periods of severe social unrest. Into this France the painter Eugène Delacroix was born. This is where he developed his career during the last years of the Age of Enlightenment.

Delacroix was one of the originators of a new artistic era, Romanticism, which responded to political upheaval by rebelling against the establish-ment. Like all Romantics, Delacroix, who became the leader of that move-ment, emphasized the emotions of his subjects, including their terror and awe. He rejected the calm compositions of his neoclassical predecessors, favoring chaos, movement, and color to convey feeling. His canvases, some of which were as big as thirteen feet tall and almost seventeen feet wide, provided his viewers with a realistic and dramatic feel for the events they depicted.

OUT OF CHAOS: AN EMPATHIC MASTERPIECE

Understanding the emotions of others certainly inspired Delacroix. When he was thirty-two, he painted one of the world's most recognizable pictures, *Liberty Leading the People*. As a painter and gifted artist, Delacroix straddled two worlds. One was the world of ordinary people. He felt a kinship with craftsmen and factory workers who used their hands to make things. On the other side, he forged connections with the intellectual elite who com-missioned his paintings and supported his work.

By 1830, the French were once again fed up with their monarch. Charles X, another tone-deaf king, imposed more taxes, repressed election laws, and violated the new constitution's provision for freedom of religion by restoring the established church. The French were not having it, and after three days of fighting on the streets of Paris, on July 29, 1839, Charles X was deposed. Delacroix watched these events unfold. He saw people fighting and dying. He saw the insurgents building barricades. He saw them raise the French flag in front of the cathedral of Notre-Dame, a scene that deeply stirred him and stayed vivid in his mind.

Although he had not carried guns or stones or mounted the barricades, he was fully aware of the social and political realities of France. He had witnessed, firsthand, the pain and suffering of his compatriots, and a couple of months after the July Revolution, Delacroix began painting what would become his masterpiece. In October 1830, he wrote his brother, "I have undertaken a modern subject, a barricade, and although I may not have fought for my country, at least I shall have painted for her."

Rather than highlighting the idea of victory and freedom, he focused on the uniqueness and diversity of the people. He gave each of the subjects in this painting their own characteristics. He wanted contemporary viewers to believe that they could all be revolutionaries and that everyone in France contributed to bringing forth much-longed-for change.

The revolutionaries in *Liberty Leading the People* represented many social classes and backgrounds. There was a young student holding a pistol in each hand, wearing a black velvet beret, with a cartridge pouch crossing his body. The expression on his face conveys the adrenaline rush of the moment. He is shouting for freedom.

A factory worker sports a white shirt and an apron while wielding a sable. A bourgeois young man wearing a tailored black coat, top hat, vest, and cravat around his neck is armed with a hunting shotgun. Another boy, or gamin, from the street, probably an orphan, is crouching, holding a stone in one hand and a spade in the other, his head covered with a green bonnet that was associated with Napoleon's army.

Intellectuals, street kids, and working-class people all became rebels, guided by an allegorical figure, "Liberty." She is half nude, her round breasts exposed; her right arm, waving the French flag, is muscular and strong; the left holds a bayonet; her yellow dress is stained.

Delacroix made her alive, assertive, and relatable. She's not flying above, she's not a supernatural goddess, she's in the middle of the action, getting down and dirty with the insurgents. Far in the background, amid clouds of smoke, he painted the towers of Notre-Dame completing the scene he had witnessed just months before.

When Delacroix first exhibited *Liberty* at the Paris Salon (back then, the greatest annual art event in the Western world) in 1831, it drew huge crowds.

Its portrayal of rebellion in all levels of society helped the French bond and empathize with each other regardless of their social status. It reminded them of what united their country—not politicians, not an isolated group of privileged people, but the people as a whole.

Even with his superb skills, it would have been nearly impossible for Delacroix to make a painting of this significance, one that has moved and inspired so many generations, had it not been because of his empathetic and inclusive point of view. *Liberty Leading the People* became, and continues to be, the symbol of France. It inspired Victor Hugo's most celebrated novel, *Les Misérables* (1862), the musical (1980), and all the films that followed it. It also inspired the French sculptor Frédéric Auguste Bartholdi, who conceived and designed the Statue of Liberty, a gift to the people of the United States paid for by the French people.

EMPATHY, INTEGRITY, AND TRUST

One of the most empathetic artists I ever met was the late Puerto Rican Arnaldo Roche Rabell, the first Latino to graduate with both a BFA and an MFA from the prestigious School of the Art Institute of Chicago. He is considered one of the most important representatives of the neo-expressionist movement. Roche Rabell was the embodiment of this movement whose members wanted to rehumanize the subjects in art. It started in the late 1970s with young artists who decided to portray the human body and other recognizable objects, in reaction to the highly intellectualized abstract art production of the 1950s and 1960s. I had heard so much about Roche Rabell before I finally met him in the summer of 2014. While I was on a business trip to Puerto Rico, his gallerist took me to visit him in his studio outside of San Juan. Arnaldo was waiting to show me how he worked. His excitement for life was palpable. From the moment I entered his airy and enormous warehouse studio, I felt his sincere desire to make me feel at home.

His methods were not only creative, but you could also feel the empathy he had for his subjects. Part of that came from his technique, known as "frottage." He placed a naked person directly under a canvas, wet from layers of oil paint, and then carefully rubbed it over the person's body with a spatula, revealing the contours, marks, and particularities of that body. Each of his models had to spend between three and five hours draped under the canvas. He was deeply concerned about how they felt during the process and sought ways to make the experience more comfortable for them.

I realized that one of the ways he built empathy with his subjects was by asking many questions about their lives. He was genuinely interested in getting to know people and wanted to connect with them. That is a simple but often overlooked cornerstone of empathy: getting to understand who your customers or audience are.

In an interview that Roche Rabell gave to *Visión Doble*, a literary magazine published by the University of Puerto Rico, he said, "I was interested in seeing how close I could get to people, their possessions, and their fears, but this also required their consent. That is why empathy became a tool for closeness. Not necessarily on a level that only shows the occurrence of empathy, but empathy defined as a direct connection with another person. In other words, it becomes a performance in which I persuade you to have faith in me and where I'm going to treat you in the most respectful way, and that I will never mock you or what is important to you. Those are the defining boundaries of Arnaldo Roche's painterly experience."

After explaining how he made his paintings, he told me, "For me, being empathetic is as important or more than all the tools I have in my studio; I couldn't do what I do without empathy." His was a unique type of empathy, something like intimacy with work ethic and integrity. Part of Arnaldo's success came from intently looking for and connecting with other people's physical and psychological worlds, until he could make them visible in his art.

To help me understand how he did it, he gently invited me to sit in a chair. He dragged a small table and another chair over, and sat directly across from me. He placed my hands under a piece of paper and rubbed over them using blue oil sticks. He then took a delicate piece of lace, and rubbed it over with the paper on top of it. The result was the most beautiful composition around my hands. We were so close to each other, but he was so respectful that I never felt weird or uncomfortable while he worked on my hands. Arnaldo's gallerist framed the piece, and I have it in my bedroom close to me. When I look at it, I remember Arnaldo's wise words: "I couldn't do what I do without empathy."

OPENING OTHER WORLDS

As a Latina, I have always had empathy for minorities. Since I opened my company in 2009, I have made it a goal to support Black artists, recommending them to my clients, acquiring them for myself, writing about them, incorporating them in my media projects, and including their works in exhibitions that I have curated. I'm always lured by their wonderful use of saturated palettes, the portrayal of beautiful dark-skinned figures, their trials, tribulations, and triumphs, the narratives of challenge and hope, the stories in their work appealing to my emotions. This was long before most blue-chip galleries realized Black artists' importance, and a decade later, they would go crazy courting them, hoping to add them to their stable of representation.

When I visited the studio of Mickalene Thomas for the first time, a Brooklyn-based megacelebrated multimedia Black artist, I cried. One side of her expansive studio represented all her success. She had studio managers, production managers, assistants, and many other people working with her. Lined up against some of the walls were extremely organized shelves with tubes, cans, and gallons of paint, brushes of all sizes and types of hair, and containers that held, by color and shades, the millions of Swarovski rhinestones she typically uses in her paintings. On the other side, she had re-created part of her incredible living room installations, the ones that she is so well known for and have been exhibited in museums all over the world, from the Art Gallery of Ontario to the Museum of Contemporary Art in Tokyo. These installations were inspired by Mickalene's own childhood home in Hillside and East Orange, New Jersey, the armchairs upholstered with kaleidoscopic patchworks of vintage and African textiles, the walls covered in faux-wood panels adorned with the photographs she took of her late mother, the vinyl records in one corner. Everything was evocative of the 1970s post–Civil Rights Act era, when Black men and women owned and embraced their style and composed and performed some of the best hits of disco music, and the Bronx gave birth to hip-hop. I felt such an intense energy when I sat in one of those armchairs; it was as if I had gone back in time to Mickalene's childhood living room. In a flash of a moment, I felt her throes, courage, perseverance, and ultimately her victory, and I couldn't hold the tears that streamed down my face.

Black artists and Black art are profound invitations to develop empathy. They give us a view that shows us the struggles of Black Americans. There is so much to gain in perspective if you are empathetic, curious, and receptive and if you allow the worlds of people different from you to inform yours.

SEEING INTO THE HEARTS OF OTHERS

Some of the most creative and successful businesses in the world were built on empathy. In 1928, Walter Elias Disney, a folk artist, cartoonist, and animator, had just ended his contract with Universal Pictures. His goal was to create characters and films that his studio would own.

Since childhood, he had enormous empathy for animals, so he drew a mouse. *Aesop's Fables*, which frequently featured mice, and cartoons he had created for Universal inspired him. He called his mouse Mortimer. He showed it to his wife, who promptly told him *Mortimer* was a pompous name and *Mickey* sounded better.

After two failed attempts to find distribution for Mickey's films, in November of 1928, *Steamboat Willie*, an animated short starring Mickey Mouse, came to life in New York. It was the first cartoon in which sound and image were synchronized—a feature that impressed audiences and made Mickey a star. This marked not only the beginning of the Walt Disney Company, but also a pivotal moment in popular culture in the United States.

From the animation of his films to the design of his theme parks, Disney's number one concern was always how people would feel when experiencing his creations. He cared about others; he believed in families and what keeping them together meant for society. His goal was to enrich and elevate entertainment for children and their parents. Disney's historian, Chris Ihrig, attributes an important part of Disney's great success to his empathy: "The core value that drove Walt was his compassion for people . . . it started with his most important relationships and it radiated out to people he never met." Disney tapped into deep-seated human values and emotions. Using them as a starting point, he built an empire that today is worth hundreds of billions of dollars. His original preoccupations and his principles continue to govern the Walt Disney Company today.

You don't have to cry at work or draw animals to feel empathy, but if you are looking to create and innovate in any business, I encourage you to look outside of yourself to develop an empathetic outlook. There are no businesses without relationships. We all need partners, customers, vendors, and collaborators. Empathy in business allows us to understand other people and helps us anticipate their needs and reactions. Empathy is the opposite of self-absorption. It is a vital part of creativity and innovation. After all, how can we serve others' needs if we don't have a grasp on how they think, feel, and behave?

We live in a complex world. Technology separates us socially. People tend to connect less in person than they did prior to the digital age. We spend our days looking at our smartphones. The incessant flow of both empty and valuable information we are bombarded with tends to numb us. This tech-numbness hurts how we develop empathy, since empathy comes mostly from real-life human observation and interaction. Empathy precedes understanding, which is necessary to build a business culture. One of the many reasons we cultivate empathy is so we can do a deep dive into someone else's life and discover new ways to serve them.

ALCHEMY LAB

1. *Leave your biases at the door.* When having a conversation, assume you don't really know what the other person thinks and feels, and focus on listening and understanding.

2. *Position yourself from a different angle.* When you start researching a subject, product, concept, or process, change your perspective. Start fresh. Begin from a position of discovery and remain flexible.

3. *Step outside your comfort zone.* Read magazines, books, or newspapers, or watch movies or shows different from those you would normally go for. Find the other side's perspective. Go further; read or watch stories that usually wouldn't interest you. Whatever is distinctive or even in opposition to what you would normally do, that's where you'll start to find your new sweet empathy spot.

8

Curiosity: Reclaiming the Child's Mind

CLOSE YOUR EYES and open your mind to remember how you saw the world when you were a child. You had a sense of wonder. You were full of questions about everything and filled with exciting new images and sensations. Children have a very playful approach to life, and their lives in early stages center around play. This child's mind is the original mind we were born with. It is not the one conditioned by the lessons we learn from parents, teachers, friends, and others. It has no preconceived notions, and there are no "incontrovertible" laws.

When you visit a foreign country or a city where you have never been, your child's mind returns as you start to see everything new. You allow yourself to get lost, discover new places, and mingle with different people. As we grow older, we are conditioned by formal education, and our minds tighten and narrow. The conventional mind is formed. It begins to conform with society's standards, understand abstract concepts, and relate to others, but it isn't a creative mind. It is a confined mind.

I've never met a successful artist who isn't curious. Not curious as in nosy, but as in inquisitive. Their minds are always on the lookout for joy, inexhaustible exploration, and continuous learning. They ask questions. They are genuinely intrigued and puzzled by materials, shapes, history, emotions, societal issues, and other people. Artists don't settle on one answer; they always want to expand.

The artist's curiosity is akin to a child's. We lose it as we grow older and learn that things function a certain way. Curiosity is a habit that anyone who wants to increase their creativity and innovate in business needs to nurture. Even if you weren't a curious child, you can become an inquisitive adult. Our curiosity bubbles up when exposed to novel information. By asking questions, we elasticize our brains with new knowledge.

LEO, THE INQUISITIVE

The term *Renaissance man* couldn't be better suited to anyone more than it suits Leonardo da Vinci. This polymath, whose interests included architecture, music, mathematics, science and invention, drawing, painting, sculpture, geology, astronomy, botany, paleontology, engineering, literature, anatomy, and cartography, was immensely inquisitive. He spent his life researching, writing, sketching, painting, building, and testing his ideas.

He was so dedicated to finding the truth behind everything that in an era in which the church was one of the most important patrons of the arts, Leonardo couldn't care less about ruffling their feathers. He pushed ahead and came up with conclusions and inventions that threatened the rigid stance that knowledge was fixed by God and therefore immutable. Da Vinci often said that "the desire to know is natural to good men," and his life perfectly mirrored that belief. He was an insatiably curious person who examined and questioned everything. As historian Kenneth Clark said, Leonardo was the kind of guy who wouldn't take yes for an answer; he was never satisfied that he had gotten all the information and always went for more.

Skill without imagination is worthless. Curiosity fuels imagination and creativity. Leonardo was the consummate expert when it came to using his curiosity to open up his imagination, which he then combined with his skill to execute his many remarkable projects.

As an artist, he created the greatest psychological portrait, the one that renders hidden emotions. Da Vinci did this by utilizing a combination of mathematical ratios, the three-quarter position of the subject, the sitter's ambiguous facial expression, and the haunting gaze that follows the viewer across the room. This pièce de résistance is, of course, the *Mona Lisa*. It took Leonardo the last sixteen years of his life to complete, as he jumped from one project to the next and moved from Florence to Milan, to Rome, and then Paris, carrying it with him.

The *Mona Lisa* is the culmination of all the questions and all the answers of his insatiable and inquisitive mind. It embodies the many decisions he took. Everything from the multiple layers of paint, to the shape of her smile, the overall composition, the perspective of the landscape, the choice of colors, and the blurring of his line (a technique that he pioneered called *sfumato*) were the result of decades of living a curious life. He dissected cadavers; conducted extensive experiments in optics, light, and shade; developed equations, which he applied to the proportions of his works; closely observed people and nature; and never took anything at face value. Random luck did not make the *Mona Lisa* the world's most famous painting; rather it is because viewers developed an emotional engagement with her. She had something they couldn't find in any other painting. She seems alive and aware of us and of herself.

Someone with Leonardo's level of curiosity couldn't have confined himself to be just one thing. His creativity extended to many areas. In 1448, he designed a flying machine while working for the Milanese court as a researcher of military technology. Once engaged with the notion of an apparatus that could fly, he filled many notebooks with countless sketches. It became an obsession. He created a blueprint for a helicopter and designed a parachute whose proportions were the same as ones used when the first parachute was invented and tested three hundred years later.

His modern-day biographer Walter Isaacson called Leonardo's notebooks "the greatest records of curiosity ever created." In one of his to-do lists for an ordinary day, Leonardo wrote, "Find the measurements of Milan and its suburbs"; other items read, "get the master of arithmetic to show you how to square a triangle" or "ask Giannino de Bombardier about how the tower of Ferrara is walled . . ." and on and on. His questions and pursuit of knowledge had no end. Leonardo constantly asked hundreds of questions, posing them from many different angles. Studies of this genius from every possible realm abound, from Sigmund Freud's failed 1910 attempt to psychoanalyze Leonardo in his essay "Leonardo da Vinci and a Memory of his Childhood" to Dan Brown's 2003 megasuccessful mystery thriller novel, *The Da Vinci Code*.

BECOMING A PROBLEM FINDER

The most creative artists don't have mental boundaries imposed by experience. By being curious and asking hundreds of questions, the artist's mind can go to many different places. This flexibility allows for a more open exploration of the world than what the conventional mind allows.

Mihaly Csikszentmihalyi, a creativity researcher at the University of Chicago, conducted a one-year-long study at the School of the Art Institute of Chicago. Csikszentmihalyi recruited thirty-one art students and presented them with the task of creating a still life drawing that then would be evaluated by an independent panel on the merits of creativity and originality, among other criteria. Each student also received private evaluations. They were told to choose from a series of twenty-seven objects laid out on a table. Once they made their selection, they were to set them up on a separate table in any composition they desired, and then work on a drawing. There was no time limit to finish. Csikszentmihalyi observed them closely.

Some of the students, we'll call them "type A," chose the objects quickly and with great determination, knowing from the get-go the type of work they wanted to produce. Their decisions were based on preconceived ideas drawn from their art studies. For example, one of them said, "I knew I wanted to create a startling vanishing point." On the other hand, "type B" students had a more emotional approach when selecting the objects and setting a goal. One of them said, "I chose to draw grapes because I spent summers in Michigan with my uncle in his vineyard." This student's decisions did not emanate from some preconception drawn from art history or formal theories of art.

For type B artists, the compositions, and the process of creating each drawing, flowed from a place of discovery and curiosity. They spent a good amount of time evaluating each object and its individual properties. Their quest was to formulate the problem. Neither the method nor the solution was known to them when they started the exercise. Type B students changed the arrangement of the objects they selected and substituted and manipulated them several times before completing their still life. These students' drawings, when evaluated by an independent panel that had no previous information about their identities or process, were considered the most creative and original.

Type A students were presented with a problem (the objects), early on decided on the process (drawing the still life in a way that would create a startling vanishing point), and arrived at what they considered a correct solution (the still life with a startling vanishing point). They were labeled as "problem solvers."

But the study concluded that the most creative artists were the type B students, the "problem finders," those who knew how to focus on the right questions.

Six years after the students graduated, Csikszentmihalyi tracked them down to check on what they were doing. Half of the students were no longer artists, working at other occupations. About 20 percent were somewhat successful artists. The remaining 30 percent were very successful, represented by leading New York galleries and had their work in the collections of several important museums. This 30 percent were type B students, the ones who looked for the right questions.

Most people, when presented with a problem in their areas of expertise, figure out ways to solve it. However, a crucial dimension of creativity rests in people's ability to find problems. If your curiosity leads you to ask the right questions and that takes you to find problems that need solutions in the marketplace, you have struck gold, creatively and probably financially. Curiosity is critical in challenging times. One of its benefits is expanding a person's perspective and reach—wondering and questioning—not just having the right answer. Those who can answer questions but don't know how to ask them won't be as successful as a creative and innovative entrepreneur. A curious leader always seeks fresh ideas and approaches, and keeps asking, "Why?"

CREATIVITY OUTSIDE OF THIS PLANET

Being curious and continually searching is what prompted Elon Musk in 2002 to found Space Exploration Technologies Corp., better known as SpaceX. A serial entrepreneur, founder, and investor in many successful ventures including Zip2, X.com, PayPal, and Tesla, Musk asked himself, *Does human life have to be circumscribed to planet Earth? Can we make it to Mars and establish life there? Can we become a multiplanetary species?* After selling PayPal for $180 million (post taxes) in exchange for his stock representing 11 percent of the company, Musk didn't sit back and relax.

He began investigating space missions and looking for the reason they had stalled. While searching, asking experts, and studying everything he could get his hands on, he realized that the problem was in space transportation. If fabricating skyrockets was so expensive that the United States asked Russia, its favorite frenemy, for a seat on theirs (at a cost of $90 million per astronaut, per mission), then there had to be another way to make space transportation reliable and cost-efficient.

Musk had no experience building rockets or airplanes, but he was an extremely curious entrepreneur willing to learn. SpaceX set out to manufacture rockets that didn't bankrupt the country; that is, by keeping the fees they charge lower than other spacecraft fabricators. On May 30, 2020, after eighteen years, SpaceX's *Falcon 9* rocket was safely and successfully launched into outer space, carrying a capsule with two NASA astronauts. It marked the beginning of a new era for American space flight.

Since elementary school, Musk questioned his teachers, his parents, and whatever information was given to him that wasn't satisfactorily explained. Good thing that Musk never outgrew his original child's mind! Musk's mind is anything but rigid, uncreative, and conventional. His mother, Maye Musk, wrote in her memoir that "when Elon was young, he read everything . . . he was always absorbing information . . . we called him the encyclopedia."

When Musk was fourteen, he read Douglas Adams's science-fiction novel *The Hitchhiker's Guide to the Galaxy* and developed a problem-finder mentality, as he told *Time* magazine's editor-at-large, Jeffrey Kluger, in an interview that aired on *CBS Sunday Morning* in the summer of 2019: "What

[Douglas] was essentially saying is the universe is the answer; what are the questions?" Later he expounded, "If we expand the scope and scale of consciousness, then we are better able to understand what questions to ask. We'll learn more, we'll become more enlightened. And so we should try to do the things that expand the scope and scale of consciousness."

In a video interview Musk gave to the Henry Ford Museum of American Innovation in Dearborn, Michigan, he said that he always questioned whatever set of circumstances, or facts, were deemed to be true. If he saw a slight chance they weren't, he pondered if there could be a better conclusion, adding, "Generally, people are too bound to convention or analogy of prior experiences; it's rare that people think of something on a first-principle basis . . . they'll say, *we'll do that because it's always been done that way*, or, they won't do it because nobody has ever done that, so it must not be good. But that is a ridiculous way to think."

Like da Vinci, Musk's curiosity led him to keep asking questions, in unrelated areas, in realms literally outside of this world, and with each question, new paths were open for innovation.

BUT SERIOUSLY, WHY?

Being inquisitive and asking questions was part of what prompted me to open my business. After observing the behaviors of people in galleries, art fairs, and other events, I started asking myself: Why is the art market so mysterious? Why is there so much hermeticism around it? Why does nobody blog about it? Why are some people intimidated by galleries? How can we serve these collectors better? As the years went by and I kept growing and evolving, I kept asking questions and continue to do so today:

- Why was nobody tackling the super important issues of art and social justice on TV?
- Why should I be circumscribed to just one area of my industry?
- Why do people believe that creativity cannot be taught?
- Why aren't there more dynamic ways to teach how to innovate to a broad group of people?

As I opened my curiosity and connected with more people, I met pop artist and urban legend Kenny Scharf in the summer of 2012. I wanted to photograph him for my first monograph. His gallerist introduced me to him and took me to his studio. Since that day, we have been good friends. Besides Kenny's charismatic and warm personality, there were the many enthralling stories he told me of his times in the fun and crazy New York days (and nights) of the 1980s. He was Keith Haring's close friend and roommate and also hung out with Jean-Michel Basquiat and Andy Warhol. He is one of the very few high-profile artists of that era who didn't succumb to AIDS, drugs, or other diseases.

In addition to the man himself, the other, quite impressive part of our first meeting was the *Cosmic Cavern* that he built in the basement of an old industrial building in Bushwick, Brooklyn. As we walked down the steps, I could barely believe the place. I felt like Alice when she fell down the rabbit hole into Wonderland. It was around two thousand square feet, inside of which Kenny created an immersive world. He covered the walls with thousands of plastic toys, painted in Day-Glo neon colors that came to life under fluorescent black lighting. The vibe was like being inside a 1980s nightclub. "Welcome to my *Cavern A-Go-Go*," he said. "This is a time capsule of generations of objects, and sometimes I throw parties here too."

Kenny, who never lost his childlike curiosity, was experimenting with different materials and testing glow-in-the-dark paint on recycled objects when he created the first version of this installation in 1981. It was in the closet of the small New York apartment close to Times Square that he shared with Keith Haring. The closet then became a cavern, and migrated to the Whitney Museum, which exhibited it in 1985.

Since then, driven by curiosity, he has collected hundreds of thousands of plastic toys, trinkets, and objects picked up from landfills, junkyards, or simply trash left outside people's homes. Since the 1980s, he has re-created versions in places as varied as the Museum of Modern Art in New York and San Francisco's historic Dogpatch district.

There's more than meets the eye to this psychedelic, multisensory experience. Kenny, as curious and playful as he is, is a staunch advocate in the fight against global warming, the effects of pollution, and the impact that the production of plastic has on the environment and oceans. As he gets older, he feels even more urgency about the message and having the *Cosmic Cavern* do double duty. Its mission, first, is to offer a glimpse of the glory of New York's disco years and, second, to bring awareness to those environmental issues with which we grapple every day. Throughout his forty-year career, Kenny has retained his originality. He has no desire to ever stop being curious and experimental.

Being curious also helps develop sharp observational skills. When you are passionately and voraciously asking questions, having conversations, reading, researching, and testing new ideas, it is impossible to "unsee" that which you have seen. In this era of two-minute Google searches and reliance on Wikipedia for everything, those who go the extra mile in the treasure hunt for the missing piece will eventually find the Holy Grail.

Of course, it's a lot easier to scratch the surface and stay content with the basic answers, but nothing creative will come of it. Asking question after question is a lot harder. It requires time and dedication, but it is a very enriching way of expanding your vision. The more curious you are, the more questions you ask, the more tools you will have at your disposal. Curiosity fuels the intellect; if you go digging, you will spark your imagination in ways that are crucial for getting new ideas.

As we learn how to turn our original minds back on, we start looking at things the way they are and not the way we were taught they are. When you observe details, ask yourself why they are there. Why do they exist? Those detailed observation skills promote the association of seemingly disparate, previously explored ideas, the ones that gave birth to disruption and innovation.

In one of his notebooks, da Vinci described a method for acute observation: "Watch the details of a scene or an object, separately, as if examining the page of a book, word by word, then affix those details in your memory, and don't move on to the next detail until you have memorized the first." If you become curious and vested in a new project, especially in an area that is new to you, you can't help but notice all the details that someone else missed, thinking they were mundane.

Having and accepting a preconceived notion of the world leaves people with a passive mind that is good only for consuming (and sometimes regurgitating) information. The artist's mind, the curious mind that retains the childlike perspective, is continually active, processing information and transforming it into something else.

ALCHEMY LAB

- *Ditch the standardized-test mentality. Become a problem finder. Don't focus on just one answer.* No question should be too silly for you to ask or research. Often the most basic questions are ripe with overlooked answers. Don't accept things at face value; expand your reach and, before you start any project, write down the answers to these questions:

  What is the problem you are solving?

  Why is this a problem you are interested in solving?

  For whom are you solving it?

  How can you solve it differently?

  What results are you aiming for?

  Who are the right people to work with you?

- *Conduct discovery interviews* without leading the questions or the answers. Asking "do you think this is a good idea?" is a leading question that will result in false positive, or, worse, false negative answers.

- *Get your interviewees talking about their own lives.* Ask about specific instances where they may have faced similar problems. Let them do the talking while you listen. This is useful if you are looking to introduce a product or a service that solves a problem.

- *Be open to other opinions and balance them out fairly.* Being curious doesn't exclude being wrong.

- *Try something new.* Take a different route to work, engage in a new hobby, try one of your kids' video games, go to a restaurant that serves a type of food you've never tried. Ask the waiter, and maybe even the chef, as many questions as you can about it.

- *Sharpen your observation skills.* Sit comfortably and choose an object in front of you, study it carefully, and then close your eyes and recall the image. Describe it to yourself including colors, textures, shapes, dimensions, and special characteristics. Try to recall every detail. Open your eyes and see what you spotted correctly, what you added, and what you missed. Do this exercise two more times with different objects throughout the day.

9

Silence and Solitude:

A Room of One's Own

SILENCE AND SOLITUDE are prerequisites for intuitive flashes and great ideas. We live in a world that inundates our senses with images, information, sounds, and all kinds of stimuli that distract us, no matter how many high-tech, noise-canceling headphones and other devices people employ to help them focus. Human beings cannot absorb or handle this level of stimulation daily.

The dramatic changes we have had to make, and will continue to make, to adapt to the technological advances of the past twenty years work against generating creative and revolutionary ideas. Artists know that silence is necessary for the creative process to flourish. It anchors them in their work and allows them to face their fears and recognize their feelings. The more artists are in a quiet place, the more they know themselves, and the better they can tangibly express their individuality and their unique ideas.

Creativity and innovation are all about unique and original ideas and their execution. In addition, silence, attention, intention, and focus force artists to fully engage their brains, in both making art and idea-generating activities. I have visited around 450 artists' studios in New York and around the world. Some of them are small rooms partitioned inside bigger, shared industrial spaces. In them, both emerging and sometimes more mature artists work alone or in the company of a couple of assistants. Some are state-of-the-art architectural gems, where the artist works with twenty or more employees in different capacities. All these studios have one thing in common: they are noticeably quiet places. Occasionally, there may be music playing at a low volume in the background, but other than that, silence reigns.

The bombardment on our senses is the norm today. In big cities, millions of people, listening to a podcast or reading an email or text on their phones, cross paths with cars, shops, and billboards simultaneously competing for their attention. Some people glory in their ability to multitask. But at what price?

People are becoming more dependent on technology and less independent in their thinking. They are developing a herd mentality and losing their creative power. A brain that is oversaturated has no room for innovation. Consuming excessive amounts of visual, auditory, and tactile stimuli, as we have been, is like taking a bath in a big tub filled with lavish aromatic salts and bubbles. Once we drain the tub, we are left with a small residue. The rest is down the drain. That's why we feel that even though we are exposed to so much information, our brains receive no benefit. It's almost as if just the scum is left.

SILENCE: CREATIVITY'S INCUBATOR

Spending time in silence and alone doesn't mean you should be isolated or disconnected from the world. It means carving out daily moments to just "be," or, as the writer Virginia Woolf put it, "having a room of one's own." That "room" should be mental, but when possible, also physical. We need pockets of calm and silence daily. Coworking spaces, trading floors, "friendly" open-floor-plan offices, along with our incessant addictions to electronics, social media, and news, are slowly but surely strangling our best ideas.

We live in a world that refuses to appreciate the benefits of solitude and introspection. In 2014, a group of psychologists from Harvard University and the University of Virginia evaluated 431 undergraduate students in eleven separate studies. They found that participants typically did not enjoy spending six to fifteen minutes in a room by themselves with nothing to do but think. Given the option, many preferred to self-administer electric shocks to being alone with their thoughts. Most people seem to prefer to be doing something rather than nothing, even if that something is negative.

Solitude makes artists, inventors, and entrepreneurs observers of their own thoughts and feelings. How can we create or birth ideas of value without a calm mind? Silence and solitude support what Graham Wallas, an English psychologist, in 1926 called the "incubation" effect. When we incubate, we voluntarily take a break from a problem and resume it later (one hour, one day, one week) with a fresh mind and approach, ready to welcome a creative breakthrough. Often, when you don't dwell on a problem and spend some time in silence, the answer comes to you. Have you had that experience? The combination of letting go and clearing your brain through moments of silence often works.

LISTEN TO THE SILENCE FOR ANSWERS

Stillness was central to the life and artistic practice of Georgia O'Keeffe, one of the most influential American artists of the twentieth century. Many consider O'Keeffe the mother of American modernism. Born in Sun Prairie, Wisconsin, in 1887 to dairy farmer parents, she pioneered American abstraction and helped redefine modern art. She is known for her bold, sensual paintings of flowers and plants and dramatic images inspired by the landscape of the Southwest she created during the last forty years of her life. O'Keeffe's husband, Alfred Stieglitz, a New York photographer and art dealer, described her as "grave, silent, meditative, robust, and intense."

O'Keeffe loved to work alone and fiercely protected her solitude. One of her greatest creative breakthroughs came in 1915, when she was in South Carolina teaching art at a local college. She began painting abstract forms, which at that time was completely unusual. She spent most of her time alone, outside the classroom, making art. In a letter to her close friend Anita Politzer, she recounted a particularly exciting experience. She decided to explore the absence of color, working only in black and white. O'Keeffe wrote that, for the first time, she had created images that were hers alone, not influenced by anyone or even her previous work. She started experimenting with shapes she saw in her mind. "The thing is that our own is so close to you, often you never realize it's there . . . I'd never thought of doing [these shapes] because I'd never seen anything like that." She added, "I was alone and singularly free, working into my own, unknown—no one to satisfy but myself." This moment led her to a radical break with her previous work. With that breakthrough, she became one of the first American artists to practice pure abstraction.

In 1918, she moved to New York with Stieglitz, and due to the novelty of her work and uniqueness of her paintings, she received unprecedented acceptance from collectors, critics, and institutions. Within the first few years after moving to Manhattan, she was the highest-paid American woman artist. She spent the next decades of her life working and traveling, especially to New Mexico, a place that gave her all the solitude and silence she craved. In 1946, O'Keeffe became the first woman artist to have a retrospective at the Museum of Modern Art in New York City.

O'Keeffe found that the expansive land and cliffs of the Southwest, the desert, the muted colors, the dryness, and the cool starry nights contained more of what she craved—a sense of transcendence and freedom—reinforced by solitude. She hiked for miles every day, bathed in irrigation ditches, and drove into inaccessible canyons looking for places to paint. After dinner, by herself, she went up to a high mesa to watch the blazing sunset.

In 1949, three years after the death of her husband, she made New Mexico her permanent home. She occasionally socialized with some friends at her ranch, yet, no matter how happy she was to be with other people, solitude was her faithful companion, and society only an aberration. She lived there until her death in 1986 at the age of ninety-eight. O'Keeffe's prolific and triumphant career spanned eighty years. She left more than two thousand artworks that changed the course of art history.

She attributed all her big breakthroughs to her dedication to her work, in silence and solitude. According to a 1987 *New York Times* article, O'Keeffe's estate was valued at $65 million (other sources say north of $76 million), which is $175 million today if we adjust that number for inflation. And if you're thinking to yourself, *$175 million, that's not that much*, well, as of the day of this writing, it's more than the personal fortunes of Barack Obama,

Britney Spears, or Venus Williams. Think how famous all of them are—how many medals and awards they have won and the number of books, albums, and products they've sold. Georgia O'Keeffe was richer than all of them.

In May 2014, one of her paintings, *Jimson Weed/White Flower No. 1* (1932), was auctioned at Sotheby's for $44.4 million, setting a new record for a work by a female artist.

CALM IN THE CHAOS

Silence and solitude were part of the lives and routines of two of the most innovative people of our era: the founders of Apple, Steve Wozniak and Steve Jobs. "Woz," as everyone calls Wozniak, designed, developed, and programmed the Apple I and Apple II, the first successful mass-produced microcomputers. Woz recounts in his memoir that ever since he was in high school, he loved assembling and disassembling computers in his bedroom, quietly on his own. He also likened inventors and engineers to artists, and encouraged them to work alone, outside of big corporate structures.

Jobs got deep into meditation, after discovering at the age of nineteen books like *Zen Mind, Beginner's Mind* by Shunryu Suzuki and the *Autobiography of a Yogi* by Paramahansa Yogananda. He became a student of Eastern spirituality and emphasized the need for quieting the mind. In 1973, he traveled to India for the first time. It was the beginning of his lifelong dedication and discipline to exploring a variety of meditation techniques and participation on silent retreats. Zen Buddhism became Jobs's meditation style, which he practiced daily. He told his biographer Walter Isaacson, "If you just sit and observe, you will see how restless your mind is . . . but over time [with meditation] it does calm, and when it does, there's room to hear more subtle things—that's where your intuition starts to blossom and you start to see things more clearly."

Similarly, Bill Gates, the founder of Microsoft, practices "Think Weeks." It began in the 1980s, when he retreated to his grandmother's house to spend quiet time thinking. Today, twice a year, Gates spends one week in a cabin by a lake in Washington State. Alone, with no technology, he thinks and reads books and innovation pitches written by Microsoft employees.

During those Think Weeks, among several other breakthroughs, Gates came up with the momentous ideas of Internet Explorer (in 1995) and the Microsoft Tabletop PC (in 2001).

YOU NEED ONLY TEN MINUTES

The mindfulness and meditation industry is a $2 billion annual business. While nobody really needs to go into a meditation grotto with special infra-red lights and incense burning, I find that some apps do help keep people on track of their goal to spend a certain number of minutes in silence every day. I'm a fairly social person, but I also spend a lot of time alone, and I enjoy it. My kids call my office "the thinking cave." I often turn off the TV in my bedroom and hand earphones to my husband when he is watching news on his phone. Silence, to me, is as vital as oxygen. I meditate every day, sometimes repeating mantras, sometimes not, and I dedicate time to just thinking, without any distractions. I put my phone on do-not-disturb or airplane mode, and just sit with my thoughts and feelings for as long as I can—ten minutes, thirty minutes, however much I can get.

I compare my daily meditation to taking a shower for the brain. It cleans and keeps it fresh. Spending time in silence will improve your focus and creativity. It surfaces ideas that don't normally come to you when all your senses are engaged in other things.

When you are in silence, your brain is actively internalizing and evaluating the information it has gathered at other times, such as researching, reading, observing, conversing, or brainstorming. If you are a person who doesn't have time to be alone in silence, you need this more than anyone.

ALCHEMY LAB

- *Set a goal of taking one hour every day just to think.* Start with ten minutes for one week, increase it to fifteen the next, and continue in increments of five minutes until you comfortably reach one hour.

If you take walks daily, use that time to think. Turn off your phone and walk in silence.

- *As an alternative, meditate.* Use an app or schedule time to close your eyes and quiet your mind. Focus on the rhythm of your breathing. Start with five minutes and add five minutes each week. When you reach twenty minutes a day, it will do wonders for your creativity and ability to generate new associative ideas.

- *Reduce the amount of you time you spend checking social media, email, and texts, reading the news, and watching TV.* Build up the amount of time until you achieve a complete detox of one day a week: no TV, no podcasts, no social media, no news.

- *Practice setting aside one day where you use your phone only for reading books* and perhaps receiving texts—but only if you need to. Otherwise, keep it on airplane mode or "do not disturb" from 8:00 a.m. to 8:00 p.m. (Nowadays, our phones are our portable offices, organizers, libraries, and daily planners, and I'm not sure we can live entirely without screens anymore.)

10

Intuition: Your Gut Knows

What Your Mind Doesn't

Successful artists and entrepreneurs are very attuned to their intuition. It is an important part of their repertoire when it comes to creativity and problem solving.

- How many times in your life were you guided by something you couldn't explain?
- Have you ever googled something weird that suddenly popped into your mind and it led you to your future business partner?
- What about coming up with a profitable idea seemingly out of the blue?
- Did you ever decide to walk a different route for once, only to run into someone you were thinking about who became helpful in your career or life?

That was your intuition.

That "sixth sense" is innate and part of our hardwiring. Children are very intuitive. That's because they haven't been exposed to false information, theories, or teachings that insist on empirically proving everything. Intuition doesn't depend on logic or evidence. As we rely on education and more and more technology to move us forward, we become rusty in the intuition department.

What is intuition? It's an accurate piece of information that doesn't come up from using our five senses, or from our minds, or our experiences. It comes from a much higher place than our physical perceptions. Intuition manifests as a flash of insight, or a repeated series of insights. When you get hit more than once with the same message, don't ignore it. Intuition is always right. What's sometimes wrong is our interpretation of the intuitive message.

You can consciously direct your intuition, usually by asking questions and being open to receiving the answers. These creative and innovative insights spring from within. Our intuition is always working for us, but we often decide to ignore it. Having good intuition and trusting your gut allows you to make the right decisions most of the time. An added benefit is that once you become a good intuitive, it also allows you to make decisions faster. Artists are excellent at making intuitive decisions as they create their work.

One reason artists are so intuitive is that the physical aspect of creating art requires concentration and mindfulness. Take painting as an example. No matter how intense and slow or how gestural and fast the artist, it requires they be in the moment and pay attention to what they are doing. Part of being intuitive requires being attentive. We think millions of thoughts every day, bounce from one activity to the next, and multitask constantly; artists don't. When they work, they work. They are centered and grounded in what they are doing.

CREATIVITY AND DEEP SELF-APPRAISAL

Henri Matisse was one of the most inventive artists of the twentieth century. He made significant contributions in the areas of painting, sculpture, and printmaking. He dared to give color a much greater expressive power than what other artists had done before him. As if on an acid trip, Matisse looked for fully immersive sensations by embarking on an adventure with colors that lasted his lifetime. After many bold experiments, Matisse parted ways with using color to portray reality. Instead, he heightened his hues to a saturation level not seen before. When he exhibited these first experimental paintings at a salon in Paris in 1905, along with the works of other painter friends, they caused an immediate sensation.

When a critic came to see the show, he called the group *les fauves* (the wild beasts). Matisse started something that propelled him to fame and led him to a successful and lucrative career for five decades. Even today, almost seventy years after his death, his work looks fresh. It serves as a continuous source of inspiration, as well as imitation, for artists, designers, and brands.

Interestingly, Matisse wrote a lot about his own process. He stressed that in order to come up with fresh and creative ideas, he relied on his intuition. What he called a "deep self-appraisal" worked better for him when he had time to commune with nature. Nature and solitude stimulated his intuition. Had he not trusted his gut feelings, he wouldn't have made the bold decisions he did in 1905. Matisse defined intuition as "the expansion of our consciousness . . . which brings about . . . endlessly continued creation."

He called his flashes "the truth" because they were self-generated and unique to him. In 1906, he followed the same process, this time listening to his intuitive hunches. It was as if he injected his colors with steroids. That's how he painted *Le Bonheur de Vivre* (The Joy of Life). *Bonheur* is a seven-feet-wide-by-six-feet-tall canvas, onto which Matisse turned a landscape into a stage, flanking the composition to look like the curtains of a theatre. He painted the trees with green trunks and the foliage ochre, orange, and magenta. For the ground, he chose a deep lemon yellow and, on the line of the horizon, a wide stripe of indigo blue resembles a lake or the sea. At least a dozen bodies in sensual positions engaged in conversation, kissing, dancing, or playing musical instruments complete the scene.

Bonheur was a radical departure from the past. When it was exhibited, American writer and art collector Gertrude Stein bought it on the spot. She immediately hung it in her dining room at 27 Rue de Fleurus in Paris, where she held weekly salons attended by poets, writers, and artists. When Picasso, who until that time had had only modest success, saw *Bonheur*, he was shocked. He made it his mission to outdo Matisse. A year later he did, when he painted *Les Demoiselles d'Avignon,* one of the most important artworks in history.

In a 1907 interview with Guillaume Apollinaire, a French poet and critic, Matisse said that his artistic personality came from following his intuition and returning to the fundamentals—colors, canvases, and reviewing his early works. He expressed his intuition "with purity . . . in the briefest manner by putting down, for instance, four or five spots of color, or by drawing four or five lines." Matisse attributed his choice of balancing colors and shapes in a way that hadn't been seen before to his intuition. It continued to be a trademark of his work for years to come.

"Instinct" is where Matisse's creative power lived, in feeling the sensations of the moment and allowing intuition to be the guide. "Feeling the sensations of the moment" is a combination of what modern intuition experts call "the body check" and "mindfulness." The body check is a quick way of taking a mental inventory of the impressions and feelings in and around you. You start with the weight of your body on a surface, and continue with the sounds you hear, the fragrances you smell, the things you see, and the taste in your mouth. Mindfulness is the practice of staying in the present moment by avoiding thoughts about the past or worrying about the future.

AN EMPIRE BUILT ON HUNCHES

Every successful entrepreneur uses their intuition to their advantage, whether consciously or unconsciously. One of the most striking cases of building a business on instinct and gut feelings is that of Josephine Esther Mentzer. Josephine was born in 1906 to Hungarian-Jewish immigrants, who settled in Corona, a low-income neighborhood in the borough of Queens, New York. Right after her birth, her mother gave her a nickname, "Esty," and she grew up with her six siblings and parents in an apartment located on top of the hardware store her father owned. One of her uncles, John Schotz, had come to New York with a strong knowledge of chemistry. Schotz and Esty, who was six at the time, became quite close.

In 1924, Schotz opened a small lab to manufacture homemade creams, lotions, and potions. Esty, who was eighteen and had just graduated from high school, joined Schotz and quickly realized that her uncle wasn't good at sales. She took over that task and had great success. With neither previous business experience nor a technical background in cosmetics, Esty intuitively devised a marketing strategy for Schotz's products. She named one of his concoctions "Super Rich All-Purpose Cream" and sold it to her friends, using her own skin as proof of the cream's miraculous powers. When that worked—all of her friends obsessed over the cream—she started giving attractive names to Schotz's many formulations and began selling them door-to-door to beauty salons, hotels, and clubs.

Esty later changed the spelling of her name to *Estée*, adding an accent over the first *e* to make it look and sound French (France, at the time, was where the most aspirational beauty products were created). As an entrepreneur, her creative ideas were completely guided by intuition. Decades before the most skilled marketers and advertising agencies figured it out, Estée, then a teenager, knew that "to sell a cream, you first sell a dream."

In 1930, Estée married another child of European immigrants, Joseph Lauter, an accountant who tried his luck selling silk and buttons to minimal success. She continued selling potions under a new business name, Lauter Chemists. Shortly after, they changed their name to Lauder to correct a misspelling that occurred when Joseph's parents emigrated from Austria to the United States. Selling the idea that beauty was attainable using her products, Estée Lauder worked for many years, mostly by herself, demonstrating her products on other women's faces.

It wasn't until 1946 when Estée Lauder, Inc., was formally incorporated. The only two shareholders were Estée and Joseph. Lawyers and accountants warned her not to sell through department stores, claiming her profit margins would become too slim and other brands with more capital and trajectory would have prevented her from succeeding on the cosmetics floor. But she followed her intuition and convinced Saks Fifth Avenue to place a large order. Her creams sold out in two days, and Saks gave her a tiny counter on the cosmetics floor.

Estée had another intuitive insight: if she wanted to play with the big brands, she couldn't stay long at that small counter. She ordered thousands of printed invitations and mailed them to her clients, announcing the grand opening of her new Saks point-of-sale location. The day of the opening, all the women who received the invitation mobbed the store. They had no option but to relocate Estée to a bigger counter close to the main entrance.

In 1950, Estée visited an advertising agency hoping to engage them in her marketing efforts. They told her that the $50,000 she had earmarked as her annual marketing budget wouldn't take her anywhere. Undeterred, Estée followed her intuition and shifted the $50,000 to a different strategy that resulted in one of the greatest marketing innovations in the cosmetics business. First, she originated the idea of "free gift with a purchase" and giving "free samples" to anyone who wanted to try her creams. Second, she asked Saks if they could insert invitations to her demonstrations and announce the "free gift with purchase" in their monthly credit card statements to customers. Both innovations proved extremely successful. The giveaways brought women back for more. Over the years, the samples and their gift packaging became Estée Lauder's signature, annoying her competitors and building loyal customers everywhere.

Later, every cosmetics company followed her innovation, transforming the cosmetics floor of department stores in the United States and elsewhere. Dismissing those who attributed her success to pure luck, Estée repeatedly told employees and the press, "People do make their own luck by following their instincts and taking risks." It was one of the maxims that governed her business decisions throughout her life. Today, Estée Lauder is a leading cosmetics manufacturer. Its products sell in 150 countries, and it is valued at $115 billion. Not bad for a business initially built on its founder's hunches.

SHOWERS AS IDEA INCUBATORS

When you are in harmony with your intuition, you follow cues that aren't evident through your senses or your logical mind. You are open, willing to receive them, and act on them. Intuition is so intertwined with one's own identity that only each one of us can ask the right questions and receive the right answers. The trick is to invite—and follow—your hunches. Not in a crazy way; trusting your intuition doesn't mean going with the first image that crosses your mind or making hasty decisions. To learn how to trust your intuition, you first must nurture it, interpret its symbols correctly, and respect it when it speaks to you.

The idea to open my own business came to me intuitively when I asked myself in deep silence, *What do I do next? I can't stay in this law firm; I loathe being a lawyer. What are my true gifts?* All those images of my childhood visiting museums and galleries with my parents and painting landscapes with my grandfather hit me consecutively. My husband told me that what I was attempting to do, with no clients and no experience in the art world, seemed quite difficult. Although he was full of doubts, he nevertheless offered me his support.

I knew of a handful of art advisors and emailed them requesting an exploratory call. Only two answered, one of them because she was friends with a friend who made the introduction via email; the other one answered out of kindness. The first told me, "You'll never make it in this business; it is too small, and you don't have the qualifications." The second said, "I spent all this money getting a master's in art and business, and I've yet to see the return." I heard them; I didn't counter, just listened. In both cases, as soon as I hung up, my intuition calmly said, *But they aren't me. I know I will make this happen.*

My intuition guides most of my moves in more concrete ways. I have far too many examples, but a striking one occurred a couple of years ago. I was taking a shower (yes, there is truth in the many anecdotes about people getting their best ideas in the shower, because there's silence and you take your mind off, albeit temporarily, the many things that are distracting you) when I suddenly remembered the face of a client I hadn't seen in a few years. That day, I sent her a text message to say hello. She answered right away, telling me she'd been thinking about me, and mentioned that she had a very large painting she acquired decades ago that she wanted to sell. When she sent me a picture, I knew it wouldn't be an easy sale. She wanted close to $1 million for it, and only a very small group of collectors would be interested in the piece.

I was up for the challenge and gladly offered to work with the painting for one month to see if I could find a buyer. I emailed and called a bunch of collectors and other art advisors who could have been interested; none of them were. I also tapped a couple of museum curators. Nothing. After three weeks, almost ready to give up, I closed my eyes, took three deep breaths, mentally scanned my body sensations from head to toe, and asked, *Who is the person who buys this painting now?* Hoping to see someone's face, all I saw was an image of the Eiffel Tower, again and again for about thirty seconds. *What does this mean?* I asked without getting any particular feeling or symbol. *I welcome any answers.*

I went on with my day, and almost twelve hours later, I remembered an old conversation I had with the owner of a gallery in Paris, who collected the work of that artist. I knew this person was very daring and his collection was quite bold. I barely knew him, but I emailed him anyway and within minutes he wrote back asking if he could send someone he trusted to see the painting in person, which I arranged. Five days later, he made an offer, which my client happily accepted. My intuition was right. I didn't get the exact answer right away, but I was open to getting any information, which happened when I made the connection between the Eiffel Tower and the French art dealer.

ESTABLISHING THE LINK BETWEEN CREATIVITY AND INTUITION

A team of psychologists from the Queen Mary University of London and Goldsmiths University of London sought out to establish the link between creativity and intuition. To do so, they performed an extensive search of relevant databases like the Web of Science, PubMed, PsycINFO, Google Scholar, and Scopus. They combed through hundreds of studies that gathered data and interviews from Nobel laureates from the fields of physics, chemistry, and medicine as well as remarkable filmmakers and inventive chefs.

They identified the role of a "big leap" and how intuition contributes to scientific discoveries as well as business and artistic breakthroughs.

Big leaps in knowledge occur if someone creates a new paradigm to solve a problem in the absence of any clear, reasoned path. This new piece or pieces of information cannot be explained by analysis or by following rational steps.

Someone who relies on a gut feeling to generate creative answers combines separate chunks of gradually acquired information about what could be working and boils them down to form a new coherent construct via associations.

The team of psychologists concluded that the role of intuition in creativity should never be neglected as it is often reported to be a core component of the idea generation process, which, in conjunction with idea evaluation, is a crucial phase of the creative process.

Depending on the complexity and importance of the question, your intuition can guide you to an answer that can be immediate, clear, and visceral. Or it may be very subtle, delivered as pieces of a puzzle, and take a week or even longer to surface. The key always is asking the right question, letting your mind interpret the symbols, and inviting your intuition to give you the right answer.

ALCHEMY LAB

- *Acknowledge that you are already highly intuitive.* Commit to developing your insights in a way that benefits and guides you, your business, and the market you serve.

- *Take inventory of your senses.* Every day, early in the morning, in silence, quickly scan your body sensations head to toe and mentally repeat them to yourself, including how your body feels, what you hear, what you see, what you taste, what you smell. Then, take a couple of deep breaths, and ask, "What are my goals for today?" Whatever the answer, symbol, or sensation, write it down in a journal or notebook and follow up with another question: "What's the best way of accomplishing these goals today?" Write down those answers. Stay open and receptive to any other piece of information that may come up during the day. Keep writing and checking those answers periodically.

- *Don't let your mind get stuck.* If you hear your mind protesting, *I'm not getting anything, I'm totally blocked*, that is valuable information too. Keep asking: "What is the block? Does the block have a shape? A name?" The first impressions, feelings, or thoughts that come to mind could be the answer. When you are afraid that you're going to be wrong, you won't hear your intuition. It is important you trust yourself and leave fear on the side. Second-guessing inhibits the flow of intuition, creativity, and business ideas.

- *Frame the question correctly.* To access your intuition with more specific concerns, this is very important. It may take several attempts. To get to the right question, your state of mind has to be calm. You won't get an accurate answer if you are highly emotional, when you're extremely tired, or when you have had a very difficult day.

- *Be specific, but don't put your intuition into a chokehold.* Don't ask leading questions, and avoid those with a *yes* or *no* answer. For example: "Is Joe a good investor for my company?" is a leading question whose answer is yes or no. A better question would be, "Who are the investors best aligned with my company's values?"

- *Stay in silence waiting for hits of intuition; be open to receiving whatever you get.* Intuition gives you the power. It gives the answers to your questions. They are generally neutral and come immediately as very short words, symbols, images, or feelings. Sometimes it also presents a question to which you must find the answer.

- *Put the pieces together.* Write the words, symbols, feelings, or images down and wait for another hit. Record them daily. You will get the right answer, and the written record serves as a fact-checker should you need it. This is where most people tumble, but the more you practice, the more accurate your answers will be.

- *Practice the art of monotasking.* Give your undivided attention to doing one single activity for thirty minutes: reading, doing chores, answering email (no music, no talking to anybody at the same time, no checking social media). Increase the amount of time you spend monotasking by five minutes every week.

- *When it feels like butterflies in your stomach, pay attention.* Having an "instinct" is essential to coming up with creative business ideas of value.

11

Daydreaming: The Earthly Delights

of Dreaming with Open Eyes

ARTISTS ARE DELIBERATE daydreamers. Their work is to bring their imagination and fantasy outside of them and materialize it in a piece of art. For artists, the act of daydreaming is neither just a wandering mind nor being absentminded or distracted. Instead, daydreaming is a crucial habit they cultivate to stimulate their ideas.

Artists enrich their fantasies with more art. They direct their minds to daydream of beauty, colors, shapes, new concepts, fables, stories, experiments with new mediums, and infinite possibilities. Many times, they look at other artists' work. Where most people hide their fantasies, artists manifest almost all of them, at least those that can be painted, sculpted, filmed, digitized, performed, or written.

THE FANTASTICAL VISION: FIVE HUNDRED YEARS BEFORE SURREALISM

Having studied art history as a formal subject when I was a teenager, and even during that first trip to Europe when I was fifteen years old and visited all those museums, I now realize that I was too young to have the knowledge to be impressed with certain things.

When, as an adult, I stood in front of the astonishing oak triptych that is *The Garden of Earthly Delights* by Dutch painter Hieronymus Bosch at the Museo del Prado in Madrid, I nearly lost it. The combination of its elements, narrative, vivid colors, and great size (almost seven feet high by thirteen feet wide) blew me away. When I saw the caption, I had to look twice to make sure I read it correctly. It said Bosch painted the panels sometime between 1490 and 1500. How was that possible? Bosch was translating his fantasies, dreams, and imagination into his work in a way that no artist until the surrealists, four and a half centuries later, did.

The painstakingly detailed panels depict three scenes from left to right. The first panel evokes the creation in the book of Genesis, but with a twist. Adam and Eve appear with Jesus between them in a landscape filled with beautiful animals. In the center of a pond, Bosch painted a rosy fountain made of crab legs and shells. The wide middle panel is an extravagant, bright, dreamlike scene of an expansive green field on which several hundred nude figures perform pleasure-seeking activities. Mermaids cavort and pink and blue structures that look like sci-fi capsules float on a turquoise lake. Intermingled are life-size fruit, fantastical animals like unicorns, and enormous colorful birds, some of which are ridden by humans.

The third panel is a dark depiction of hell with hybrid beasts. One creature wearing a blue suit and a cauldron hat eats human beings; crustacean parts engulf humans; and a "tree man" looks back at his cavernous torso formed from a broken eggshell. Five hundred years before James Cameron and Guillermo del Toro turned themselves into wealthy filmmakers creating ogres and enchanted lands, Hieronymus Bosch had designed the set and the characters.

Little is known of Bosch's life and practice, but throughout the centuries, scholars and historians pieced several details together and made some assumptions. It is possible that he attended religious pageants and theatrical plays, where he probably got many ideas from. He also spent a good deal of of time reading and gave in to the impulses of his imagination. Bosch took whatever information was available to him and magnified it in his works through the power of daydream and fantasy.

Due to the novelty of his paintings, Bosch became a well-paid and sought-after painter in his own country as well as in Italy and Spain. His patrons and collectors had never seen anything like his characters and fantastical narratives. He was the embodiment of innovation and inspired a multitude of copyists and imitators for years after his death. It took many centuries until we again saw this type of fantasy and dreamlike imagery.

GIVING UP CONSCIOUS CONTROL

The realm of the unconscious and dreams were some of Sigmund Freud's chief preoccupations. Daydreaming also became a subject of his interest. While some of his theories have been challenged and his methods and conclusions disputed, he garnered enormous attention, and respect, for elaborating arguments that were completely novel. In 1908, when he wrote a short essay titled "Creative Writers and Day-Dreaming," the concept of creativity wasn't as widely accepted as it is today, so he circumscribed his analysis to novels written by successful authors with mass appeal. Freud concluded that these writers had a common denominator. They indulged in daydreaming in order to create a world of fantasy, evoking their childhood at a time when all they did was play. From childhood play to fantasies, dreams, and novels, Freud found a thread: people attempt to change the unsatisfactory world of reality by inventing one in which wishes are fulfilled. That is exactly the domain of the artist. They can alter every bit of reality through their minds and with their hands.

The modern heirs of Bosch were the surrealists, a movement that started when the French poet and critic André Breton, strongly influenced by Freud's studies of dreams and what they revealed about the unconscious mind, published the first Surrealist Manifesto in 1924. Breton aimed to free a group of artists' imaginations from conscious control by encouraging automatic, uncensored, free imagery that merged fantasy with reality.

Two of the most popular surrealist styles were (1) paintings that originated from the artist's dreams, which required conscious interpretation, and (2) free-associative paintings, where the artist automatically and without much conscious control quickly expressed whatever came to mind. In both cases, the goal was to let the artist's imagination go anywhere, without shame.

Around the same time, Salvador Domingo Felipe Jacinto Dalí i Domènech, a twenty-one-year-old Spanish art student living in Madrid, also became seriously interested in Freud's work. He decided to try his luck and moved to Paris where he later became a member of the surrealist movement that included Max Ernst, René Magritte, Giorgio de Chirico, Francis Picabia, and Yves Tanguy.

The closest I ever came to the brilliant mind of the great Dalí was when I visited his house and studio on the Costa Brava, a couple of miles away from the town of Cadaqués, Catalonia. That day I fully realized that he embraced the surreal as a way of life; his genius did not just come from his talent for painting or random luck. He invited the absurd and his boundless imagination to rule his life. Reality played only a small part in it. Dalí's house, which is in a small bay in Portlligat overlooking the Mediterranean Sea, was constructed by joining several white fisherman's huts, creating a labyrinth of rooms and passageways on different levels. From a distance, it looks like a bunch of sugar cubes resting on a small beach.

As soon as I crossed the door into the foyer, I was greeted by a seven-foot-tall taxidermied standing polar bear holding a functioning lamp in his right paw and adorned with a dozen ethnic necklaces around his neck. A giant open Chinese parasol hung from the ceiling above the curved staircase, forcing the visitors to bend down as they climbed up. Pink, yellow, and blue silk covered the walls of one of Dalí's studios and his "Model's Room." Red and yellow fabric stripes resembling a circus tent draped the ceiling. Jute or zebra rugs covered some of the floors; others had black-and-white checkerboard tiles.

Dalí's artwork and sculptures were everywhere. All the rooms had windows of different shapes and frames. The narrow patio flanked a long pool built in the shape of a penis and culminated in a lounge area with colorful poufs and pillows. Stuffed, fake snakes sewn from zigzag-patterned fabrics hung from the ceiling and came down the walls. The rooftop terrace, planted with olive trees, donned giant plaster eggs, some holding their perfect oval shapes, others sculpted to look as if they had cracked. Certainly, this is the most magical studio I have ever visited. It's a shame that Dalí had been dead for two decades before I made it to his house.

The Persistence of Memory is probably the most famous surrealist painting ever made. Dalí painted it in 1931. It was bought by Julien Levy, an

American art dealer who visited Dalí in August of that year, a few days after he finished it. Levy told Dalí that he considered his work both "extraordinary" and "unsalable." Nevertheless, Levy resold the painting and, in 1934, an anonymous donor gave it to the Museum of Modern Art in New York, where it still hangs. The small oil on canvas measures only nine and a half by thirteen inches. The background shows a melancholic seascape with rocks and cliffs, like Dalí's view from his house in Cadaqués. To him they represented the softness and hardness of life. In the foreground, he painted a barren olive tree; a melting pocket watch hangs from one of the cut branches. Farther down is a sleeping sea creature with long lashes, which Dali probably borrowed from Bosch's *The Garden of Earthly Delights*. Three other watches complete the composition. Two of them are melting, and the third, a closed-case gold one, is covered in ants, which to Dalí symbolized decay. A critic who wanted to sound smart in front of Dalí asked him if the watches referenced Einstein's theory of relativity, to which Dalí replied that they were his vision of Camembert cheese melting in the sun. Dalí called *The Persistence of Memory* a "hand-painted dream photograph."

Besides painting, drawing, creating sculptures, making movies, and taking photographs, Dalí spent his time inventing and designing objects, experiences, and products. He never shied away from going where his most absurd thoughts led. He knew they were fertile territory for innovation. Dalí questioned why most people dismissed their own outlandish ideas and daydreams and labeled them "impossible" or "irrational." The people he pitched his inventions to considered them pretty absurd, but years later other inventors would make similar things viable. Dalí wrote in his 1942 autobiography that he had invented "artificial fingernails made of little reducing mirrors in which one could see oneself." This happened twelve years before Fred Slack, an American dentist, invented and patented the first commercial acrylic artificial nail in 1954. That invention led to a market that, aided by fashion and female hip-hop performers, is projected to reach $1.2 billion in 2024.

Dalí, who was obsessed with filmmaking, also wrote about another of his inventions. The "tactile cinema" would "enable the spectators, by an extremely simple mechanism, to touch everything in synchronism with what they saw: silk, fabrics, fur, oysters, flesh, sand, dogs, etc." Everyone thought he was crazy. It took four more decades for the first commercial 4D film, *The Sensorium*, to be screened in a Six Flags theme park in Baltimore in 1984.

Dali's "tactile cinema" was also the precursor of virtual reality and augmented reality, as well as interactive and immersive surrealist theatre experiences, like the smash hit *Sleep No More* by British theatre company Punchdrunk. This experiential play, inspired by Shakespeare's *Macbeth* and Alfred Hitchcock's film noir, has been performed daily in New York City since 2011 (with a break for the pandemic). It started as just an immersive and interactive experience, where the audience follows actors and explores, freely, multiple darkened floors, labyrinthine realistic interiors, and fantastical spaces. After two hours, the audience finishes the experience in a 1920s-style cabaret setting that offers drinks for sale. The experience takes place in a one-hundred-thousand-square-foot building in Chelsea, which Punchdrunk and an investor company baptized "The McKittrick Hotel." Through a combination of smart and creative business moves, these two companies capitalized on the success of the play, and the building now houses a couple of bars, a rooftop restaurant, more cabarets and speakeasies. They also host a variety of lavish theme parties every month. The estimate is that altogether the experiences that happen inside McKittrick bring close to $60 million in sales annually.

INDULGING YOUR CREATIVE ECCENTRICITIES

Daydreaming is a powerful and eccentric mental instrument. Many entrepreneurs use it to feed their fantasies until they build empires that reach millions of people and generate billions of dollars. They set out to create work rich in imagination and fantasy. One of those entrepreneurs is Guy Laliberté, a Canadian from Quebec who developed a passion for the circus when his parents took him to one when he was a little boy. This childhood experience nurtured his interest in performance, and instead of going to college, Laliberté left for a year of "busking" on the streets of Europe, where he played music and juggled to entertain people in squares. Eventually, a troupe of sword-swallowers, fire-breathers, stilt walkers, and acrobats found him. He joined the group and learned how to perform other acts.

Back in Canada in the early 1980s, Laliberté and two partners organized a summer performing fair that enjoyed moderate success. The government of Quebec gave them a $1.5 million grant, which they used to launch *Le Grand Tour du Cirque du Soleil* in 1983. The brainchild of Laliberté and his partners was a creative quantum leap. They reinvented the circus by marrying a solid business sense with a passion for the surreal.

Cirque became a cutting-edge show, without animals, that focused on spectacular acrobatics, exceptional music, and acts that defied logic. The *Cirque* artists perform feats of athleticism and contortionism that come from the realm of dreams. Their bodies sculpt stories, touching the hearts of the audience. For Laliberté, nothing is off-limits when dreaming up a new show. Fantasy and reality constantly overlap, and the boundaries between one and the other are completely blurred. Dreaming is fundamental for *Cirque* and lies at the core of its values. The company prides itself on offering their artists and creators the resources to make anything they imagine a reality on the stage. Between 2015 and 2017, Laliberté sold 100 percent of his *Cirque du Soleil* stock for approximately $1.7 billion.

Take daydreaming seriously, even if in the beginning all you get out of it are a bunch of bizarre ideas. Don't let your conscious mind take you away from what could be a revolutionary innovation. In the end, the unconscious mind rules most of our human functions. Daydreaming helps tap our subconscious, is the engine of information processing in our brains, and it is filled with valuable fantasies, memories, and dreams.

ALCHEMY LAB

- *Approach a current product or service you or someone else offers with an alternative mindset.* Add elements that make it surprising, confusing, absurd, or unpredictable. Do not censor yourself; keep exploring. If somebody would have told us twenty years ago that our phones would play music, contain an entire library of books, and allow us to open up a live screen with an interlocutor on the other side of the world just by pressing a button, we would have laughed at the whole thing.

- *Design this product or service* by sketching it out or cutting and pasting pictures of the parts or digitally Photoshopping them.

- *Take a creative challenge.* It is another way of seeing things differently. See it as if you were part of the audience in an experiential theatre, where you get to choose your own path and your own ending. Welcome all your ideas freely, in all forms, shapes, and combinations, no matter how outlandish they may seem. What is required for them to happen? What prevents you from developing the ideas you generate through this process?

- *Draw music.* Listen to your favorite song and what comes to mind when listening to it. On just one blank page, doodle, create a variety of shapes, use different colors or just a pencil.

- *Ask "What if?"* Use it as a positive preface in your business projects and in your day-to-day activities. Push your boundaries to the max and write down the ideas that come to mind every time you ask yourself or others, "What if?"

- *Engage in automatic writing as soon as you wake up.* Keep a pen and notebook by the side of your bed and grab them as soon as you open your eyes. Write down your dreams or whatever crosses your mind without stopping. Try to do it as rapidly as possible without consciously editing your thoughts.

- *Keep a journal* for at least two weeks and then go back to read your ideas. You'll be surprised at your hidden unconscious treasures.

- *Study art.* Look at art in museums, galleries, or even online. Inhabit it. Insert yourself in it. What if you were a color? What if you were a part of the narrative? Create your own story around it. Amuse and indulge yourself.

- *Play.* I mean it. As people grow up, they cease to play, and they forget the pleasure they had playing when they were children. Spend time playing video games (in moderation) or assemble a team for a board game night. Do you have kids? Play with them and give them your undivided attention while playing.

- *Go to the circus or to an immersive or interactive theatre experience.* When it's over, write down your impressions and feelings. What called your attention? What was unique? Is there anything you can borrow and adapt in your business?

12

Risk-Taking: Creativity Abhors Complacency

THRIVING ARTISTS AND entrepreneurs are always willing to take risks. Strict formulas for coming up with new ideas, whether in an artist's studio or a start-up, is a surefire way to kill creativity. Anyone trapped in producing work to fill a specific demand, who operates with tunnel vision, or lacks the time to devise a new offering, product, or way of solving a problem won't ever be able to innovate.

People get complacent when they experience some success. It's easy for them to repeat an effective modus operandi until it doesn't work anymore. Then panic sets in. That loop is a legacy of how things once were. As things are now, we have to keep moving. Instead of being reactive, we must proactively innovate.

Good artists and visionaries despise comfortable loops. Evolution comes from blazing a trail and taking chances. That's how artists and great businesses keep delighting and surprising their audiences. Fear of failure or criticism are two of the main reasons people stall. If anyone is going to talk about you, it will be done whether you take a chance or not. You might as well venture into unexplored territories, even if you don't know the outcome.

Parisian neoclassical artist Jacques-Louis David knew how to take big chances. He blurred the boundaries between life, politics, and art in a way nobody before dared. Like many of his contemporaries, David started his career painting scenes from the classics, Greek mythology and Roman history. He used the style he learned in school—bright colors with rococo influences. It was fashionable and pleased the monarchy.

In the late 1780s, social unrest in France swelled, food was scarce, taxes were high, and there was a huge budget deficit exacerbated by France's involvement in the American Revolution. As a result, the French resented King Louis XVI and his wife, Marie Antoinette, and held them in contempt. David had aligned himself with Maximilien Robespierre, one of the most influential anti-monarchists of the time. He played a key role in the French Revolution.

Other artists stayed away from political movements. Others left France to find new opportunities in other countries. David, on the other hand, joined the Jacobin Club, a political organization that supported a centralized republican state, free of any royals. In this serious moment, he changed his style, finding his earlier work frivolous. He began to paint canvases that sought to educate people about the benefits of a republican government. The vibrant colors and adornments of his first paintings gave way to sober compositions and muted tones that displayed maturity and reflected his political beliefs.

In 1793, following the overthrow of the monarchy, David painted his masterpiece, *The Death of Marat*. It is thought to be the first political painting in history: Jean-Paul Marat was a staunch anti-monarchist journalist, publisher, and politician. His incendiary newspaper and extreme views made him many enemies among those who supported the nobility, clergy, and aristocracy.

David was Marat's friend. He actually visited him the day before his murder, and had last seen him in his bathtub, where Marat, who suffered from dermatitis, often took medicinal baths to relieve his condition, and worked. On July 13, 1793, Charlotte Corday visited him under the pretext that she had information about a group of Girondins (a loosely affiliated moderate political faction) who had fled to Normandy. Marat was in his bathtub when she arrived. As she spoke, he took notes of the names she recited. Suddenly Corday, also a Girondin, rose from her chair, pulled a five-inch knife from her corset, and fatally stabbed Marat. He died almost instantaneously. In an unprecedented political move, David painted Marat's death portrait, idealizing and beautifying him. He removed all traces of his skin condition, and portrayed him calm-faced, lying in his bathtub. The dark background and sparse composition were a glaring contrast to the opulent interiors that surrounded the portraits of the nobility.

David added elements that were not in Marat's crime scene. He painted the victim holding a pen in one hand and a bloodstained piece of paper in the other that reads, "July 13, 1793. Marie Anne Charlotte Corday to Citizen Marat. Given that I am unhappy, I have the right to your help." That took the spotlight off the murderer and placed it on Marat. He added a bill on top of a crate and next to it a note that said, "Give this banknote to the mother of five whose husband died defending the fatherland." In this way, he portrayed Marat as an everyday man who became a martyr and a hero.

As the radicals' official painter, David used reproductions of this paint-ing as propaganda to fire up the people and fuel the revolution. The origi-nal painting was hung in the assembly hall of the National Convention of Deputies.

Years later, when Marat was no longer in favor, the painting was returned to David. After Napoleon's fall and the restoration of the mon-archy, David self-exiled in Belgium, where he died in 1825. Today, many have forgotten Marat, but not this painting. It also served as inspiration to many generations of artists who, centuries later, made political state-ments through their art.

THE CHOICE: TO RISK OR TO SETTLE

In the spring of 2017, I received an email from the owner of a big gallery, inviting me to the opening party and a private visit to British artist Damien Hirst's extravagant show *Treasures from the Wreck of the Unbelievable*. The exhibition took over the two locations of the contemporary art museum Punta della Dogana and Palazzo Grassi in Venice, Italy.

I accepted immediately, since I was going to be in Venice for the Bien-nale, and everything Hirst did was truly worth seeing in person. I avoided searching for early images on Instagram or anywhere. I really wanted to experience it for the first time in person. The press had already maligned much of it, saying that it was a cross between *The Pirates of the Caribbean* and the Atlantis Casino in the Bahamas. I didn't care. I was excited to enjoy the experience and form my own conclusions.

When I arrived at Punta della Dogana, I was escorted inside the museum by the gallery owner and one of his directors. I was impressed. Hirst had fashioned an entire fable around a shipwreck found off the coast of East Africa. The wreck contained thousands of treasures dating from the first century AD amassed by a wealthy collector of eclectic taste. Hirst was the underwater explorer who two thousand years later found the remains of the ship. He baptized it the *Unbelievable*. This fantasy world of sculptures, videos, lightboxes, vitrines, and drawings was a huge departure from his dot paintings, medicine cabinets, and sharks floating in formaldehyde. He took an enormous gamble.

He produced more than three hundred different sculptures and objects for this work. Some were as little as a piece of jewelry in the shape of a scorpion, cast in gold with precious stones. Others were collections of jugs and vessels placed inside vitrines; each vitrine comprised a single piece of art. One was twenty-two feet high with meticulously detailed carvings in the shiniest black bronze, depicting a beautiful woman with six arms fighting a dragon with several heads. There was also a three-dimensional version of the head of Caravaggio's Medusa, molded in malachite.

It was kitsch, spectacle, Hollywood, good and bad taste rolled into one. The monumental scale of the restored 1682 building, which once had been a customs house, is in a triangular area of Venice where the Grand Canal meets the Giudecca Canal. Every window looks out over the green waters of Venice, which helped create an even more extraordinary setting for the show.

In the internal courtyard of the museum's second location, Palazzo Grassi, Hirst had placed his pièce de résistance, a colossal sixty-foot-tall, black resin, perfectly sculpted beheaded male body covered in corals and seashells. He called it *Demon with Bowl*. Nearby, a giant head, presumably the one the demon lost, made of bronze to simulate the greenish and bluish tones of oxidized metal, lay on the floor. The other three stories exhibited more sphinxes, busts, objects, lightboxes, and drawings of the wreckage.

That night, at the Rialto Fish Market, we congregated in a lavish party to celebrate the exhibition. As I chatted with Hirst, I told him I was awestruck not only by the quality of the sculptures but also by the jokes he inserted throughout. One, for example, was the body of a decayed Mickey Mouse; another a pharaoh's bust modeled after musician Pharrell Williams's face. He winked and told me, "Everything is as real or as unreal as you'd like it to be."

Hirst, whose career is riddled with peaks and valleys, never cared much about curators or critics. It took ten years from the moment he had the idea until the day the exhibition opened to see it to fruition. He had reportedly invested $50 million to fund the production of all the pieces—in itself, a huge risk. Deep-pocketed collectors funded the project with an additional $15 million. More than one thousand different vendors and fabricators from all over the world were involved in making the show. Making it an even greater gamble, thirteen years had passed since Hirst's last major retrospective in Naples, Italy. All the sculptures in the exhibition, as is customary in contemporary art, were editions. Hirst chose to produce three of each in different versions plus two artist's proofs.

We saw one iteration, but for each piece, there were four more for sale. Prices ranged from $100,000 for the small objects to north of $5 million for the gigantic ones. In November of the same year, when Hirst was preparing to de-install the six-month-long show, he told a journalist from *New York* magazine that the show had already generated $330 million.

Betting on this body of work paid off. Hirst didn't disappoint his patrons and collectors, who always admired his readiness to expose himself to danger and his wild inclination to take the greatest risks. Hirst's name became synonymous with provocation, shock, and rule-breaking. Some people don't like the work, some people call him commercial, others call him tacky, but he is definitely someone with a guaranteed spot in art history books and a fortune to boot. Mostly because he took chances.

JUST DO IT

Every great innovator is willing to gamble. In 1962, Phil Knight, an MBA student at the Stanford Graduate School of Business, had a crazy idea. He wrote a paper explaining that if Japanese brands took over the greatest market share and disrupted the German camera market with their superior quality, low prices, and edgier models, they could do the same to traditional German running shoes.

Knight was an avid runner and felt that the options available in the US market for running shoes were limited. They didn't allow for speed and agility, which is what every runner wants. Upon graduation, he decided to take a year to travel the world and asked his dad to lend him $1,000 to start a business. He planned to go to Japan, meet with a shoe manufacturer, and ask to become their distributor in the United States. Knight's dad thought his child was losing it, but he acquiesced.

Many months later, on his ambitious world trip, Knight made it to Kobe, a large city in southern Japan. He was there to visit Onitsuka, a manufacturer of sports shoes. He told them that he thought the Japanese shoes could sell in the billions of dollars in the United States. He offered to be their exclusive distributor. The Japanese men heard him with curiosity, while taking notes. They inspected and observed him in silence. Knight had barely any work experience, let alone experience selling shoes. By the end of the meeting, Knight had placed an order for several samples with the $1,000 his dad had lent him. That day, Knight christened his business as Blue Ribbon. It was the only name that came to mind during the meeting.

Back home in Portland, Oregon, Knight waited for more than a year to receive his shoe samples. When he did, his track coach, Bill Bowerman, went crazy for them. He asked Knight if they could partner. Knight agreed. They went on to form a 51–49 percent partnership, giving Knight control. He sold his shoes in sports arenas, in training tracks, and from the back of his car. The business grew and expanded to many other states. The shoes were lighter than what was available and cheaper than anything on the market.

As the business grew, so did the problems. The shoe stores didn't pay on time, and the factory in Japan wasn't delivering what Knight envisioned. It was taking too long and no bank wanted to lend Blue Ribbon any money. Onitsuka was also pressing for greater sales numbers and looking for another distributor. If they succeeded, it would cut Knight and his company out of the only brand they represented.

In 1971, when he was close to losing the business, Knight had an epiphany. He asked himself, "What if I manufacture my own shoes and don't have to be under the heel of these factories? What if I open my own retail stores and don't have to be at the mercy of late payments from the sports stores?"

He took a huge gamble. After many attempts and testing factories in Mexico and Japan, he found the perfect one. He knew he needed a cool name for his new shoes. *Blue Ribbon* didn't cut it. He considered *Dimension Six*. A member of his team wanted to name them *Falcon*; nobody was 100 percent convinced.

Finally, the deadline to file the paperwork with the US Patent Office arrived and they had no name for the new shoes. Jeff Johnson, a team member, called the office in the morning. He awakened in the middle of a dream and saw a name—*Nike*. Phil then remembered his solo trip around the world, and his visit to the Acropolis in Athens where he learned about Nike, the Greek goddess of victory. He didn't love the name, but he liked its connotations. There was no more time; he had to choose. That summer of 1971, one of the most recognizable brands was born. Today, Nike is the biggest athletic footwear company in the world and is valued at $236 billion.

NOTHING VENTURED, NOTHING GAINED: OPEN-ENDED OUTCOMES

In business, any problem that has an open outcome promotes risk-taking. White-knuckled control freaks have a hard time creating and innovating. They can't stand to leave anything to chance.

Opening my company and leaving behind the certainty of a big corporate job to start something from scratch, with no clients and no proven track record, was certainly a big bet. I take calculated risks every day in my company. I know that I have to take those chances if I want to stay relevant and forge my own path.

I fell in love with Greece the first time I visited it in the summer of 1991. The evocative beauty of the mainland and the islands got me dreaming of epic stories. Gods and humans, like Zeus and Athena, Hercules and Achilles, hung out together, sailed the waters, engaged in battles, and defeated their enemies. I went back a couple of times, including once with my husband a few days after I discovered I was pregnant with my first child. We didn't return for seven years, until the summer of 2015, when I couldn't control the Greek itch and my two boys were old enough to have fun in the Aegean.

I never read in-flight magazines. I typically have enough writing and reading to catch up on. That day I intuitively picked up one of the magazines on the flight from Rome to Mykonos. While mindlessly flipping through the pages, I found an article about a "contemporary art center" opening their doors for the first time that summer. I was intrigued. In 2007, the last time I visited, Mykonos was an underdeveloped rocky island. Its stark contrast of blues against the arid landscape made it one of the most beautiful places I'd ever been to. I took a picture of the article, and, when we arrived at our hotel, I emailed the new art center asking for directions and requesting a visit. Much to my surprise, I heard back within an hour. Marina, the owner, answered my email. In typical Greek fashion, she told me to come at night. She would be open at 5:00 p.m. every day and close at 2:00 a.m., following the nocturnal rhythm of Chora, the island's main town.

That night, after my husband and I got lost a few times in the maze of narrow cobblestone streets, we found the place. Marina was there, a cute pregnant woman who had stayed late, battling her exhaustion as she waited for me to come. What awaited us blew me away. Dio Horia, a three-story vernacular Mykonian white house with indigo blue doors and windows, was unlike any gallery I had ever visited before. On the lower level, there was a small intimate patio, with plants, chairs, tables, art books, and magazines. Huge double doors opened to a large exhibition space. A beautiful staircase led us to second-floor exhibition rooms and balconies. A third floor followed, with more art and a rooftop bar overlooking the town. I was speechless.

The gallery exhibited some of the most interesting young European artists. I couldn't believe this place existed in a hard-to-find alley in the middle of the town. We spent about fifteen more minutes chatting. Marina told me she had worked for DESTE, one of the most respected private art foundations in Europe, one that I was quite familiar with. We exchanged phone numbers and I told her I'd be in touch.

Back in New York, I emailed her. We had met for exactly thirty minutes in Greece, yet, in my email I proposed that I curate a show in the entire Dio Horia space. Incredibly, she readily accepted. Once we agreed on the financial terms, I was free to do anything I wanted. I immediately thought about bringing the work of New York artists and juxtaposing their styles and ideas against sixteen cultural inventions of ancient Greece such as democracy, stoicism, and satire. I see New York as a cultural center that resembles Athens 2,500 years ago.

Marina loved the concept and gave me carte blanche. I knew I was taking many levels of risk. Dio Horia had been open for only a few months. It was Marina's first gallery. Greece was going through the worst financial crisis in history. Last, I had to convince many artists to produce new works, consign them to us, and ship them thousands of miles away in the hope they would sell to a different collector base.

I named the show *Greek Gotham* and was so excited about it that barely any artist said no to participating in my project. Soon after, Marina said, "I feel this is going to be epic! We should try to print a catalogue, which you can write and design." Music to my ears! I contacted a friend, who had a connection to Absolut Vodka. Elyx, their high-end brand, liked my idea so much they decided to underwrite the printing of the catalogue and the opening party. Jeffrey Deitch, legendary art dealer and former director of the Museum of Contemporary Art in Los Angeles, agreed to write the introduction.

I recruited sixteen phenomenal artists, some of whom were on the verge of big breakthroughs and huge market shifts, for this group show. It seemed like a dream. Nina Chanel Abney, KAWS, Austin Lee, and Erik Parker were among the artists who were part of that show. It took a lot of negotiation. Organizing the shipping was borderline nightmarish. In the end, we made it. By opening night in the summer of 2016, 75 percent of the fifty works exhibited were sold and we had already grossed a cool mid-six figures. We were all thrilled and grateful.

More than twenty press outlets, ranging from the *New York Times* to the *Economist*, covered the exhibition. The artists who traveled to Mykonos had a blast. Marina and I became really close friends and still continue working on projects together. *Greek Gotham* was the very first art exhibition in Greece showing exclusively New York artists. It also built Marina's program for years to come because the artists loved Greece so much they kept coming back and bringing others along. Had I not taken a chance on the whole thing, none of this would have happened.

Part of being creative and innovative entails taking risks. That comes with rewards and penalties. You may gain fans and followers and you may have detractors and critics. It's impossible to please everyone. People become risk averse in business because they fear coming up short. Our society's expectations in the quest for perfection, which is unattainable, are so high. The most brilliant creative work is always the result of huge risk. It is inevitable that some people won't like your ideas, or that you will be judged harshly, but others will embrace your risks. It's much better than staying stuck. Neither Damien Hirst's art nor Phil Knight's shoes are everyone's cup of tea. That never stopped them from betting on their wildest ideas.

ALCHEMY LAB

- *Take one risk today.* What is it that you usually steer clear of? Are you good at writing emails but dread talking on the phone? Do you want to contact a prospective client, but are afraid of rejection? What's the worst that could happen? If you name the worst outcome aloud, overcoming the fear is much easier.

- *Accept a project or responsibility that lies outside your comfort zone.* Stretch your boundaries beyond your current abilities. Say yes to something even if you don't exactly know how to do it.

- *Do things differently; add a new element or make a complete shift.*

- *Get out of your comfort zone.* The longer you have been doing the same thing, the more you need to take a chance and find something new.

- *Take calculated risks on a creative level.* You don't have to bet all your money or sell your soul. If you do not feel fully ready, take risks where the stakes are lower. In business, any problem that has an open outcome promotes risk-taking. If you have a structure that is solid, you can take risks; if you fail, you still have the structure to fall back on. *If you don't take those risks, someone else will.* Risk-taking is what defines you as a creative and unique voice. If you want to be creative, increase your leadership, and stay relevant, you must take risks.

13

Improvise: Jazz Things Up

THE ABSTRACT EXPRESSIONIST artists of the late 1940s, most based in New York, emphasized spontaneous, improvised expression. Reacting against the subject matter, techniques, and structured compositions of their European predecessors, the impressionists and cubists, they leveraged the physical characteristics of their processes and the paint: violence, dynamism, sensuousness, lyricism, and speed.

In the summer of 1947, Jackson Pollock, the pioneer of abstract expressionism, produced his first action painting. Ditching the easel and stretcher bars, spilling paint onto the unstretched canvas he tacked to the floor, he applied paint in a loose, vigorous, rapid, and improvised manner. Using sticks, trowels, knives, and hardened brushes, he walked around the canvas tossing paint everywhere.

Continuing his improvisation, he even poured the paint directly from the can. Depending on the way he tilted it, the dribbling line became thicker, thinner, or puddled. No type of paint was off-limits to Pollock. He used oil, enamel, plumber's aluminum, and, most frequently, house paint, which was cheap and fluid. Pollock knew that to get to this point of improvisation took many years of experience.

In an interview with the Sag Harbor radio station on Long Island in 1950, Pollock said, "With experience, it seems to be possible to control the flow of paint, to a great extent, and I don't use the accident." Later he added, "I don't work from drawings . . . the more immediate, the more direct—the greater the possibilities of making a statement." Improvisation turned Pollock into a radical innovator. His paintings shocked many viewers, but, ultimately, they changed the course of modern art.

FIRST KNOW THE BASICS, THEN BREAK AWAY

Jazz musicians are always improvising, riffing, and jamming. That is the beauty of the genre. Jazz builds on a foundation, a combination of learned and rehearsed notes and compositions, which are then improvised on. Whether in music or painting, while spontaneous and intuitive, the artist must know the deep structures that ensure the new note, brushstroke, or gesture remain coherent, even if surprising. The balance between novelty and tradition, structure, and freedom constitutes the essential tension that shapes improvisational work.

It was no coincidence that Pollock listened to jazz records on repeat, day and night in his studio and at home, as his wife, Lee Krasner, recounted. The most improvisational of all the music genres, up to then, was part of what inspired one of the most improvisational artists in history. The unpremeditated approach in Pollock's creative process was as spontaneous and surprising as Billie Holiday's notes and riffs. A critic from the *San Francisco Chronicle* rightly compared Pollock's "flare and spatter and fury in his paintings" to "the best jazz that is the result of inspired improvisation."

Drawing from experience and impromptu moments, there is both harmonic structure and an element of chance in Pollock's drip paintings, now considered landmarks of modern art that, decades later, sell at auction or in private sales from one collector to another for more than $200 million each.

Artists interpret emotions and sensory data into physical representations. Many improvise as they deal with the reality that confronts them when bringing their work into being. A sculptor, working with stone or wood, confronts the imperfections in the medium. Painters often must manipulate the paint, its thickness and color, and the surface upon which they create. Ceramicists constantly encounter myriad unexpected challenges with clay. If it is too wet or too dry, after the shape has been molded, it can collapse or crumble. If it's not bone-dry when it's fired, the piece may crack or explode in the kiln. Firing is a science all its own, which, if done incorrectly, leads to cracks and explosions.

Artists react, improvise, and make hundreds of moment-to-moment decisions about the best way to bring the project to a successful conclusion. Improvisation in art refers broadly to the practice of suddenly composing or inventing something new through a responsive departure from preformed plans or expectations. Improvisation in business is about reacting creatively to possibilities not previously envisioned.

LEAVE A PERCENTAGE TO CHANCE

When I saw Israel-born, New York–based artist Nir Hod working in his studio on his newly developed "chrome paintings," I realized how much he thrived on improvisation. He developed this technique while pondering how seductive people found their reflection in a mirror, how fascinated they are to see themselves on shiny surfaces. To replicate that effect on the canvas, he explored different mediums, looking to create an abstract painting that added an element of reflection.

He didn't know how to get there. After much trial and error, he found his formula. First, he added a layer of oil paint onto the canvas. When the paint was dry, he applied a layer of chrome, using a machine like those used in car factories and garages. His process is physical and energetic. When the chrome is sprayed onto the canvas, it looks like black paint and slowly turns into a mirror effect. It's like magic, even for Hod. He uses three or four different methods to expose the colors of the oil paint underneath the chrome. One of them is extreme air pressure, which gives the surface an old patina. It's very accidental. He controls about 60 percent of the outcome; the rest is chance. Another way to remove the chrome is to throw ammonia, which heats the chrome but doesn't affect the canvas or the oil paint. A third way is to scratch the chrome by dragging the canvas up and down the road next to his studio. He can use any or all of these methods in one painting. He never knows with much certainty the result.

While not every artist works like this, Hod is the perfect example of how improvisation can lead to innovative results. The key is that, for thirty years, he was an accomplished painter. He had already mastered the more traditional techniques. He had the structure, the deep foundation, and knowledge of materials. Now, after all these years, he could leave a percentage of the process to spontaneity.

A BALANCING ACT: THE TRADITIONAL AND THE IMPROVISATIONAL

You have to be able to balance your tried-and-true methods and structures, the steps that you mapped out to get to your end goal, and the knowledge you already have about your business to embrace the contingencies that will arise. You must take care of them quickly, sometimes in ways you hadn't considered. This is improvisation in action. Improvisation isn't a substitute for planning, but rather an instrument to be used in situations that catch us off-guard or when our strategies haven't prepared us for an unforeseen circumstance.

The paradox of improvisation is that the more prepared and competent you are, the more creative and unpredictable you can be. The greater your preparation, the easier it is to relinquish control. If you trust that you know enough about your craft or your business to come up with a new gesture, as Pollock did, you can experiment wildly with a method you have used before to see what happens.

Leave a percentage of your project to chance, but be mindful that improvisation is not for every project. Know how to balance the stakes. An impromptu move can add that unexpected quality of surprise that keeps your clients wanting more, or it can save you at a moment's notice.

Using these elements of improvisation regularly will help you achieve mindfulness—the state of being present, focused, and aware. Mindfulness will increase your emotional intelligence, which will also lead to intuitive insights and creative breakthroughs.

IMPROV: THE "YES, AND" TECHNIQUE

Bob Kulhan is an assistant professor at Duke University's Fuqua School of Business. He teaches improvisation to students and executives. He asserts that in business, improvisation is "about reacting, being focused and present in the moment at a very high level."

We live in a time of constant change and uncertainty. The ability to react is necessary to finding solutions that fulfill the demands of the marketplace. One of the improvisational techniques taught by Kulhan, borrowed from American actor and coach Del Close, and adapted to business, is the "yes, and" improv method. It starts with one person presenting an idea, or "offer"; the second responds "yes, and," adding something. This can go back and forth multiple times and helps move your creativity forward.

Let's say you're having a conversation with a client who asks you to do something impossible by tomorrow; rather than automatically saying "no, that's impossible," start your response with a "yes, and." Move on with something like "let's please review the scope of that request to make sure we can get it done by tomorrow." Your client is happy, because people love hearing "yes." Also, the information added after "and" offers an opportunity for you and your client to review the project. In the process, it clarifies the request. If you immediately jump to saying, "That's not something we can do," it shuts down the conversation. "Yes, and" keeps building on it. Cultivate this method and use it every time you are caught by surprise with a request or a question you aren't sure how to answer.

Shonda Rhimes, the brilliant showrunner, TV and film creator, writer and producer, and CEO of Shondaland, the company that creates all the magic, wrote a memoir titled *Year of Yes* published in 2015. In it she confessed how, after years of hiding behind noes and avoiding the limelight, one day in November 2013, her older sister confronted her and told her, "You never say yes to anything."

This statement shocked Rhimes. Her company was already generating several million dollars and she was reaping the fruits of her successful shows. Deep inside, she knew that something was off, in her life and her business. She made a commitment to saying yes to everything, or almost everything. From there, things went pretty much from "great" to "astonishing."

Engaging in public appearances, being a part of the Hollywood milieu, and doing press is necessary for anyone who, like Rhimes, is in the thick of writing, creating, and producing smash-hit TV series. But she just didn't want to do it. She was content being behind the scenes. That attitude, however, was hurting her image and diminishing her opportunities.

Any other entrepreneur in the entertainment industry would have killed to have Rhimes's contracts and talent. They would have done anything to be on the cover of magazines, receive awards, or be interviewed on high-rated late-night shows. Not Shonda Rhimes. She was shy, busy, and saying no to every invite that came her way, until the day her sister uttered those stinging words. That was the turning point. Rhimes went from being hyper-planned and predictable to being spontaneous in her business and press engagements.

Those first twelve months saying yes (which she continues to do) launched *How to Get Away with Murder* in 2014. That was when, together with *Grey's Anatomy* and *Scandal*, Rhimes got her own prime-time block (8:00 to 11:00 p.m.) on the prime day (Thursday) on one of the biggest television networks in America (ABC).

Starting that "year of yes" and continuing until 2017, Rhimes's shows accounted for 14 percent of all of ABC's prime-time advertising revenue (new episodes and reruns). That same year, she also said yes to delivering the commencement speech at Dartmouth College; appearing on *Jimmy Kimmel Live!*, *Good Morning America*, and *The View*; hosting charity events; being on the cover of *Entertainment Weekly*; accepting awards; and all sorts of things she would have normally turned down.

Finally, the world had a chance to know Rhimes, and the world liked her even more. In 2017, Rhimes and Shondaland entered into a $100 million, four-year agreement with Netflix. Shondaland only grew from the moment Rhimes decided to say yes. Today, her company is one of the most innovative in the United States. Besides writing and producing film and TV, Shondaland is now a full multimedia business that produces videos, podcasts, and other content, hosts a website in partnership with Hearst, and collaborates with many companies in different capacities.

A LEADER IN CHARGE IS MORE CREATIVE THAN A LEADER IN CONTROL

When you accept the idea that there is improvisation in business, you become a leader in charge, not a leader in control. Too often, people think the leader should know everything and tell everyone what to do. A great leader, who is innovative and always looking toward the future, knows that sometimes their job is to ask the right questions and not have all the answers. It leaves room for improvisation. When you improvise, if you have the underlying knowledge, you give yourself permission to innovate and to move the needle quickly.

In 2011, two years after I had opened my business, improvisation served me well. An important client who lived in London called and said, "I want to buy a piece by Banksy . . . and I want to buy it directly from his studio . . . it is a gift for my husband's birthday." I got chills all over. I wanted to please the client, but her request seemed impossible. Banksy, a British street artist, prankster, and provocateur, always operated anonymously. I had no connection to him. Still, I answered, "Yes, sure, I'll arrange something for you." A million thoughts raced through my mind: *How could I find his studio manager? Did he have one? Does Banksy even exist?*

I had a deadline to meet, which was fast approaching: the husband's birthday. There was an email address listed on Banksy's website, but I had a hunch that wasn't my route. I closed my eyes for ten seconds. In my mind, I saw the face of a Brooklyn-based street artist I had done business with. I had no idea if he knew Banksy, but I immediately texted him to explain the situation. He called me back right away wanting to know who the client was and what I needed.

An hour later, I had an email from that street artist introducing me to Banksy's studio manager, a woman in East London who replied cheerfully. We hopped on the phone and she told me that Banksy had created a series of large paintings on wooden panels, some of which were sold, and the others were going to a museum show. "But I have one left that is a beauty," she said.

When I told my client, she asked, "Can I go and see the work at the studio myself?" Her request made me sweat profusely. The situation was quickly becoming more complicated. However, I said, "Of course you can!

Let me figure out the best way to do it." I asked the studio manager if she'd be amenable to my client's visit and, thankfully, she agreed. A couple of days later, following cryptic instructions as if it were an FBI operation, my client went to Banksy's studio. She loved the painting and, later that day, I helped her close the sale.

ALCHEMY LAB

- *Use these four elements when improvising in business:*

  Be present and focused in the moment so that you know exactly
      when to improvise.

  React quickly to what's being given to you.

  Be aware and adapt to how people around you react to your
      improvisation. That's how you know if you are moving in the
      right direction or if what you are saying is not well taken.

  Practice being a good communicator across the board. Choose
      the right words so that everyone understands what your
      improvisation is about.

- *Practice the "yes, and" technique.*

14

Embrace Failure:

When Disappointment Breeds Innovation

Doing something new and creating something of value requires experimentation. If you want to do something unique, you must be at peace with the idea that you don't know the outcome and you may fail. There is no wisdom and no success without a letdown. Handling failure well is something that good artists and entrepreneurs know how to do. To succeed in new and creative fields, you must become comfortable with being uncomfortable.

THOSE WHO CREATE ALSO FAIL

Artists approach failures not as dramatic occurrences, misfortunes, or tragedies, but more like inevitable events. They often see their mistakes ironically or humorously. Failure, paradoxically, is sometimes a hallmark of artistic success.

The French artist Marcel Duchamp, considered the father of conceptual art, was always experimenting in search of something radical and new. In 1912, he painted a half-futurist, half-cubist naked figure walking down a staircase. Duchamp used lines and planes in a geometric composition and painted it to look like wood. He wanted to create a way to depict movement, so he repeated the figure many times to give the illusion of motion.

The result was completely novel. He called his painting *Nude Descending a Staircase, No. 2*, and submitted it to the Salon des Indépendants. The art shown at this annual exhibition in Paris was widely discussed. The committee reluctantly accepted *Nude 2*. The cubists labeled it too futuristic and found the title disturbing. It had "too much of a literary title," they said; also, *one doesn't paint a nude descending a staircase; that's ridiculous, a nude reclines* . . .

STICK WITH YOUR UNPOPULAR IDEAS IF YOU BELIEVE IN THEM

Duchamp wouldn't change the title and withdrew the painting from the Salon. He had sufficient confidence to know that he had done something completely different. If viewers struggled to relate to the piece and its radical idea of the human figure, so be it. Later that year, Galerie de la Boétie in Paris, owned by Duchamp's brothers, exhibited it. The controversy and criticism didn't subside.

Duchamp, although somewhat hurt and disappointed by *Nude 2*'s rejection, didn't give up on it. An American art dealer called Walter Patch saw *Nude 2* and was so impressed that he had the canvas shipped to New York to exhibit it at the Armory Show. That show was then the most important exhibition of contemporary art in America. In February of 1913, *Nude 2* made its debut in New York. The more open-minded Americans didn't show much love to it either.

The *New York Times* labeled it "an explosion in a shingle factory." It became the punch line of a cartoon published in the *Evening Sun*. The satire contained hundreds of people on top of one another. The caption at the top read, "Seeing New York with a Cubist"; the caption below, "The Rude Descending the Staircase (Rush Hour at the Subway)." *American Art News* offered a $10 prize to anyone who could find the nude.

The painting garnered so much attention and was mocked so many times that even former president Teddy Roosevelt, who had attended the Armory Show that year, wrote a piece for *The Outlook* (a weekly New York magazine that ran until 1935). In his satirical review of the exhibition, he wrote, "Take the picture which for some reason is called *A Naked Man Going Down Stairs*. There is in my bathroom a really good Navajo rug which, on any proper interpretation of the Cubist theory, is a far more satisfactory and decorative picture." However, at the end of the Armory Show, the piece sold to a San Francisco lawyer and art dealer for its asking price of $324 (around $10,000 today).

Nude 2, and the criticism it generated in America, became a symbol of the new. Other artists started thinking about what it would be like to create art in the modern era. Duchamp, far from defeated by the critics, delighted in all the attention his work received. He moved to New York City in 1915, where he quickly realized how important *Nude 2* was in paving the way for his arrival. After it was sold a couple of times, the piece found its way into the permanent collection of the Philadelphia Museum of Art. It was bequeathed by collectors Louise and Walter Arensberg. *Nude 2* is widely regarded as a modernist classic. It is one of the most famous paintings of its time.

Duchamp, who also invented the "readymade," a term he applied to works of art he created from manufactured objects (like a bicycle wheel mounted on a wooden stool, or a men's urinal, which he called *Fountain*), never stopped experimenting and changing his style. He went on to become one of art history's most famous—and most admired—artists and provocateurs.

THE IMPORTANCE OF GOING FAR ENOUGH

Good artists don't fear failure—they embrace it because it means that they have gone far enough. They are fully aware that with much experimentation and willingness to take risks, it is likely some innovative things will happen, and others will go wrong.

Jeff Koons, one of the most important living American contemporary artists, had to go through many perceived "failures" and setbacks at different stages in his career. Koons, whose work is rooted in many different movements, including pop, conceptual, and minimalist art, experimented with readymades. Influenced by Duchamp at the beginning of his career in the late 1970s, he moved to New York in 1977. His first gallerist, Mary Boone, was able to sell only two or three of his works. He then worked with Annina Nosei, who got equally disappointing results. Nobody understood Koons's work. Frustrated, he moved to Florida with his parents in order to save money until he was able to come back to New York. He did and worked as a commodities broker at Smith Barney to sustain himself and to finance the manufacture of his work.

PERSISTENCE IN ADVERSITY

In 1983, while still working in Wall Street, the idea for a new body of work consumed Koons. The inspiration was a basketball, which, because it is inflatable, is connected to the experience of life. Every human needs air to live. Koons wanted to submerge the ball under water, suspended in the middle of a tank, without it floating up to the surface. That defied the laws of physics and seemed an impossibility. He tried everything. In his obsessive quest, he even called the 1965 Nobel Prize winner in physics, Richard P. Feynman.

Luckily, Feynman had an answer and explained how Koons could do it. He had to mix a highly reagent-grade sodium in the water. That made the water in the bottom part of the tank heavier, and, by adding fresh water at the top, the ball would be suspended in the middle of the tank. It works but has to be reset every six months as the water homogenizes and the basketball loses its equilibrium.

After much experimentation, Koons displayed his water tanks with Spalding basketballs suspended inside at an East Village gallery in New York called International with Monument in 1985. He called the show *Equilibrium*. Besides his metaphor comparing basketballs to humans, Koons went further. He said they symbolized an embryo in utero and also had a relationship to social mobility. In his view, the sport of basketball is associated with aspiration, particularly by those who admired or dreamt of becoming an NBA player. Philosophically, Koons was asking the viewer to look at the suspended basketball and associate it with how people could reach a yearned-for state of perfect equilibrium. The work is profound, but at face value, it was hard to understand.

This was Koons's first solo show, and after working so hard to find the perfect suspension formula, he had great expectations. The art critics, who were very important, tore the show and Koons apart. Some called it "commodity sculptures that substitute kitsch for art" and "a nightmare." Some found Koons "repulsive." The show was a flop from a critical standpoint.

Nevertheless, collectors bought the tanks, finding them inventive and innovative. One of those collectors was the wealthy Greek-Cypriot Dakis Joannou, who became acquainted with Koons through this exhibition and paid $2,700 for one of the sculptures. He became one of Koons's most important patrons and supporters.

With the passage of time, the water tanks in *Equilibrium* became some of the most influential works in the history of contemporary art. They were exhibited in Koons's retrospectives in major museums around the world. The last time one of them sold at auction, it went for $15 million. Where would Koons be had he not embraced his early failures? What if he had said, *The critics were right; the hell with these water tanks and readymades, I'm going to make abstract paintings that conform with what people want?*

In business, as in art, the only way to know that you've used your creativity to the max and gone far enough is when you fail. But that is actually a good sign. It is important to stretch all the limits. If you don't fail in the process, you can be sure that you didn't push hard enough, and, therefore, didn't get your best idea. Having your own business is full of minefields. Being innovative in any area will inevitably involve many different failures.

CREATIVITY AND FAILURE:
A CREATIVE SOLUTION TO FUTURE CHALLENGES

Barbara Corcoran founded her first real estate firm in New York in 1973. For almost twenty years, she worked relentlessly building her name and that of her company. In 1992, for the first time in many years, she turned a profit—exactly $71,000 (about $130,000 today).

She decided to reinvest it in her business, and she had a creative idea about what to do with it. She hired a photographer to videotape all seventy-three of the Corcoran Group's listings. She even hired a professional makeup artist so the agents would look flawless. Then, for a refundable deposit of $20, clients could take the tapes home and see the listings in comfort—a perfect solution for the busy New Yorker.

Corcoran announced her brilliant upcoming initiative at a companywide meeting with her two hundred salespeople. She closed her remarks with a bang: She titled the video *Homes on Tape* or *HOT*. The room erupted in applause. Her idea was innovative and way ahead of their competitors' marketing efforts. That was, according to her, one of her best ideas not just in 1993, but in ages.

The result was quite different from her expectations. After spending her $71,000 profit throughout 1993 on those videos, not a single person took one. Brokers from other real estate agencies didn't want to show their clients another salesperson's face and contact information. Internally, the Corcoran Group's agents feared the same. To add insult to injury, the photographer had created each video with a slideshow that was so fast, not even the speediest New Yorker could properly watch. Her big idea flopped. She had wasted her hard-earned profit.

A few weeks later, talking with her husband and a friend, Corcoran discovered the internet, which was just coming into general use. A light bulb went off. What if she could put those videos on the internet? They would need to get a website. By January of 1994, she had a domain name, built a website, and the photographer reverted the videos to photographs.

At the first big meeting of the year, she announced phase two of the *Homes on Tape* project: "The Corcoran Group will be one of the first companies in America to take our listings into cyberspace!" Within a month, four clients found new homes browsing the Corcoran Group's properties listed online. A failure turned into a victory launched the company into the future. Her innovative marketing strategies paid off. In 2001, Corcoran sold her business to NRT LLC for $66 million.

As you move ahead creatively, testing new concepts, innovating, offering unique services or products or upgrading them in imaginative ways, you will have a stream of ideas that may seem like failures. Keep a record of them and periodically go through that list. Those ideas may hold surprising solutions or show you a way to begin again in a more intelligent way.

MAYBE NOT NOW, BUT THERE'S ALWAYS THE FUTURE

If you are in for the long haul, no matter how many different products, projects, services, upgrades, and pivots you have made, your failures can become solutions to unknown future challenges. Don't forget these flops. Instead, look back at them. Analyze the process that led to them, and reexamine them, reframe them, and use what you learn to your advantage.

Culturally speaking, success and failure are different perspectives on performance based on society's different values, a variety of points of view, and diverse interests at any given time. Assessing a perceived failure from different angles helps us see other perspectives. The critics thought that Duchamp's futuristic painting and Koons's water tanks were failures, but the marketplace thought otherwise. In any creative business, failure must be, if not welcomed, accepted. It is necessary for growth. Entrepreneurship is personal, but business is not. Every failure hurts. I know. The trick is to learn from each one of them, so they don't happen again.

When I started my company, a close, trusted friend referred me to a client, an allegedly "big art collector" from Brazil who wanted to work with me. He asked for several works from specific artists. I had been able to get him an excellent piece by one of those artists. The dealer who sold it to me had a direct relationship with the artist, trusted me, and paid me a big commission. I was elated. I told the "big art collector" that he had to follow the art world's ethical protocols. In this case, out of respect for the artist and the dealer, he couldn't sell the work at auction for five years. He readily agreed: "Of course. I am a pro; I respect the artists and you."

Four months later, with a new client at an art fair, I ran into the dealer. I was so happy to see her again, but her expression told me she didn't feel the same way. "That work showed up at auction in Brazil last month. I will never sell you anything again," she said. I was taken aback. My heart sank. I took a deep breath. I did not want to make a scene. My new client had heard the whole thing!

I was just nine months into my incipient business. I didn't know what happened. Had I contributed to this epic fail? I calmly told the dealer that I was sorry to hear that and knew nothing about it. If it was true, the collector had acted on his own. I said I would investigate it and, if true, confront him if need be.

Back home, I immediately did my own research and confirmed that the "big art collector" had dumped the work at a São Paulo auction house. I emailed and told him I would never work with him again. I said I didn't need him, that I valued my reputation more than his patronage. Then, I did what I should have done first; I asked several gallery owners and directors if they knew him. They told me they no longer sold to him because he did the same to them.

I couldn't save my relationship with the dealer, but it's now twelve years and counting and such a thing never happened to me again. I failed by not doing sufficient due diligence on the "big art collector," who was nothing more than a charlatan. He was addicted to profiting from and gambling with art. He used and took advantage of my inexperience.

That episode was crucial. Since then, I have developed a natural radar for spotting speculators, cheaters, and con artists. I never work with a client without researching their past art dealings and how they conduct their lives and businesses. I have made many other mistakes, but I believe having an adaptable mind and spirit, as artists have, helps me understand that when things don't turn out as expected, it is not a failure. It simply is something that didn't work out.

ALCHEMY LAB

Evaluate the events you deem failures by asking yourself these questions:

- *Who told you this was a failure?* Who evaluated the merits of this project and called it a failure? Is it a client? The marketplace? A teammate? You? *Look for comparisons and similar precedents* that prove or disprove your "failure." Sometimes all it takes are a few tweaks to turn something from a flop to a hit.

- *Were you able to connect emotionally* with your target audience or your customers, explaining in depth the merits of your product or service?

- *Do you feel a sense of ownership of your own idea?* Or has it been altered so many times that it isn't your original idea anymore?

- *What in the past did you do to push an idea that was met with resistance?* How did you refine it so that it became a success?

Use the answers as an anchor to hold you strong when you feel like you want to give up. Let them propel and push you forward to continue toward your goal.

PART III

TOOLS OF THE TRADE

■

Artists and entrepreneurs think differently and throughout history have used diverse techniques, media, and ideas to come up with novel ways of making art, creating products, and getting their creativity flowing. Here is a selection of my favorite ones. I have witnessed them in action in the artists' studios, in works in progress, and in final works. I have learned about them in museums and through curators and historians, and I have thought about ways they can be adjusted and applied by anyone in any business. Each one can be used separately or combined with others. You just have to be open to try them.

15

Deconstruct: Break It Down

FRENCH ARTIST GEORGES Seurat was invested in the idea of creating something new in painting. He obsessively studied books on color theory. He wanted to prove that it was possible to scientifically apply color to canvas and invent a new visual language. What he developed was a technique he called divisionism (later called pointillism). It consisted of painting small dots of color, which, when seen together, formed an image. The result was the beginning of the neo-impressionist movement.

Seurat thought that deconstructing a figure into its smallest part, a dot of paint, brought the greatest amount of luminosity to the painting and enhanced its optical properties. It took him two years to finish his masterpiece, *A Sunday Afternoon on the Island of La Grande Jatte*, which he completed in 1886. Meticulously painting dot by dot, Seurat's stunning work shows Parisians of different backgrounds mingling in a park on the banks of the Seine between Neuilly and Levallois-Perret. The painting measures almost ten and a half feet wide and almost seven feet high. Seurat was thrilled with the result of his innovative technique. He even painted a faux frame around the composition—made of dots—onto the canvas. With pointillism, Seurat invented a painted precursor of the pixel in art. Neo-impressionism succeeded in departing from the impressionists and, ultimately, influenced the cubists, who studied his work as they considered breaking up shapes and forms.

Picasso and Braque, the two pioneers of cubism, were quite interested in Seurat's idea of fracturing the image into many distinct parts. In 1906, albeit in a very different way, they began doing just that. On their canvasses they broke down parts of an object, or a space, and later people. They overlapped the faceted parts to create something completely different—a piece of an object here, another there. The cubists deconstructed reality into geometric pieces and recombined its fragmented parts in a novel, radically innovative way. Cubism became the most influential art movement of the twentieth century.

The most graphic example of this deconstruction is Picasso's *Guernica*. In 1937, the anti-Franco Spanish Republican government commissioned him to paint a large mural for the Spanish Pavilion at the Paris World's Fair. Almost at the same time, Picasso, who supported the Republican side in the Spanish Civil War, heard about the aerial bombing of Guernica, a Basque city in northern Spain. Thousands of innocent people died. Horrified by the news, Picasso painted, in light shades of gray over a dark background, deconstructed figures—a wounded horse, floating heads, heads on the ground, arms, legs, feet. These disembodied shapes conveyed the horrors of the war more powerfully than if they were connected to each other.

Nina Chanel Abney, an African American contemporary artist based in New York, is another deconstructionist. She forms angular bodies, sometimes disembodied heads; at other times she includes detached forms—flames or birds—mixed with graphic and geometric elements—the dollar sign, the letter X.

After having worked with Nina and attended many of her shows, I see how cubism's deconstructed forms have inspired and influenced her cartoonish figures and symmetrical compositions. At the same time, her work is distinctively hers. Using vibrant colors, she tackles hot topics including race, sexuality, celebrity culture, the media, and police brutality. Her incredibly strong paintings, prints, and murals made her one of today's most sought-after young American artists.

Seurat, Picasso, and Abney lived in quite different times. Yet each used deconstruction to advance their views on art and to assert and develop their own styles. They didn't invent the dot or how to paint angular faces or geometric backgrounds, but they took elements of an object and positioned them differently. Each devised a completely different visual language that excites people and makes museums and collectors want to buy their art and build markets around them.

FINDING THE CORE

One way to apply the idea of deconstruction to a product or service is to start by looking for unique isolated elements and then extract and combine them with something else. That's how the remote control for TVs was born.

Although several attempts to create a remote control for other objects began in the 1890s, it wasn't until 1950 when Zenith and its engineers thought about creating one for the TV. They considered attaching a wire to a "remote" that they had deconstructed from a TV's control panel. Later, in 1956, they figured out how to use directional light to facilitate channel changing. Since then the remote control has mutated millions of times and expanded into other areas, ranging from car keys to air conditioners to apps on our phones that adjust just about everything.

Every year, the computer company Dell engages some of its designers in the exercise where they take apart old and broken computers. They work on those that are beyond repair. The point of this deconstruction is to have new insights into the life cycle of these devices. Often overlooked by most manufacturers, the end of the product itself provides valuable insights. Why did one part last longer and another didn't? By deconstructing several old machines, can we find patterns that will lead to new solutions? These and many other questions help Dell create better products.

Twitter is another example of how deconstruction can lead to enormously profitable and creative business ideas. Blogging started in 1994, with students publishing their writing on rudimentary websites they created. These online personal diaries became quite popular. In time, blogs became more sophisticated. They contained longer posts, pictures, and videos. The platforms got fancier and catered to every blogger's need.

Enter Jack Dorsey and his partners, who, in 2006, decided to launch a social network, on which users expressed themselves in microblogs.

Originally, posts on this platform were limited to only 140 characters; in 2017, they doubled to 280. While blog posts became longer and their content more robust, Twitter stuck to its original intent of deconstructing its users' long thoughts. By 2012, more than 100 million users posted 340 million tweets a day. In 2013, Twitter went public. Today, the company is worth $54 billion.

Another way to deconstruct is to shut down pieces of your business that take up too many hours of your day and don't produce the revenues you expect or where the headaches are bigger than the return, even if profitable.

Deconstruction can be used as a technique for opening up concepts and subjecting them to separate questions. In order to turn a problem into a fruitful creative challenge, you need to deconstruct it so that you can identify its causes and consequences and, potentially, find the solution.

In my case, I loved creating products for limited-edition collaborations with artists. I designed more than forty objects in eighteen months working closely with twelve different artists. We were profitable. More than thirty press articles, including in the *Wall Street Journal* and *Vogue*, featured them. I placed them in some of the best concept stores and boutiques in the United States, Europe, and Asia.

But the headaches of dealing with factories, stores that didn't pay on time, and all the moving pieces that handling manufacturing and distribution entailed were too much of a pain. I'm very proud of the collaborations, and people ask me to bring them back. But this is a piece of my business I decided to cut even though the products were successful and the profits good. If you are not 100 percent, or at least 50 percent, dedicated to the retail business, it's not for you.

To deconstruct successfully, think of your core products or services:

- What are you known for?
- What are you exceptionally good at?
- Would you reduce it to its most simple form?
- What about using that core differently, in other markets or with other customers?

The human brain loves to cluster ideas and make associations. That is good, except when the ideas are so ingrained in the same loop that our associations prevent creative thinking. When that happens, deconstructing them leads to creative solutions.

ALCHEMY LAB

Our mind is preconditioned with ideas that are attached to each other, which sometimes limits our creativity. The result is that we repeatedly get the same answers to our questions. Write down all the words that come to your mind that are associated with the word *summer*. Do it for fifteen seconds. What did you write? *Sun, sea, heat, beach, sand, bikini, sandals, ice cream,* and so on. Now assume you are a New Yorker and spend your summer in Patagonia, Argentina, where it's actually their winter. What might you answer?

The brain likes to embrace that moment when it understands that the whole can be broken into parts. But you have to prompt it. You can apply the following method to anything, from coming up with a new product to solving a customer-service issue. It is a variation on the "Five Whys," a technique used to get to the root cause of an issue, invented by Sakichi Toyoda, a Japanese entrepreneur and inventor who established the Toyoda Automatic Loom Works, and later, Toyota.

For example: Assume you are a salesperson in a business and not meeting your goals. You might think the solution is to ask yourself, "What do I need to do to sell more products?" Because the challenge is so general, asking that question might generate a lot of ideas, but they won't really address the underlying problem. Instead, start by formulating a series of concise questions, each addressing only one issue. They can't be so broad as to invite irrelevant solutions or so narrow that they won't generate potential solutions. Follow these steps:

1. *Ask yourself five times, "Why is this a problem?"* (In this example, "Why is it a problem that I am not selling enough?")

This might be a possible answer:

a. Because I am not generating sufficient income to justify my salary or because I am not generating sufficient income to keep this part of the business healthy and afloat.

That's definitely a problem, but you need to ask this question five times. "Why else":
Subsequent answers may be:

b. We cannot finance the growth of the business.
c. We are losing market share to the competition.
d. I am becoming demotivated, making it even harder for me to sell.
e. We are in danger of losing our existing customers to the competition.

Now we have a clear view of the consequences of insufficient sales.

2. *Ask five times, "Why has this occurred?"*

You now need to understand what happened. You must dig deeper to get to the root cause so you can find a creative solution.
Initial answers may be the following:

a. Outside competition is killing us; there are way too many options out there.
b. What I sell is too expensive.
c. I am not generating enough good leads because I am not targeting the right clients.

    d. There are many salespeople in my company and I'm facing internal competition since they have a bigger part of the customer base than I do.

    e. Clients are cutting their budgets.

Now you have a series of deconstructed answers you didn't have before.

3. *Ask questions based on your prior findings* and formulate a variety of answers to come up with a solution:

For example: "How can I generate more leads?"
These might be potential answers:

    a. Find better prospects.

    b. Get serious about networking.

    c. Take risks.

    d. Send emails every day to my contacts, inviting target clients to an event, and so on.

    e. Consider how to make it financially easier for my customers to buy my products: lowering prices, offering bundles, extending financing, installment plans, incentives, and so on.

If you use this method of deconstruction when you face a complex issue, you will become a creative problem solver and an innovator. You will see the pieces of the puzzle in isolation rather than as an overwhelming whole. Prompt your brain to deconstruct instead of immediately forming associations.

16

Aggregate: See the Big Picture

I SEE AGGREGATION as the practice of combining different elements into one integrated whole. I know it is the opposite of deconstruction, but each has its place. Many different artistic inventions result from joining disparate three-dimensional objects. For example, Picasso used scraps of wood and pieces of tablecloths when he invented the assemblage in 1912. And what, if not aggregation, did the Gutai group do, when they came up with installation art in 1955?

The idea of spectacle rooted in the "experiential," such as in the Museum of Ice Cream and the Color Factory, can trace its origins back to installation art. These extravaganzas generate millions of dollars annually, drawing lines mainly of millennials, hoping to get a selfie in one of their multicolored settings.

BUILDING A WORLD OUT OF EXPERIENCES

The Gutai group, based in Osaka, was one of the most important artist collectives in postwar Japan. It lasted from 1954 to 1972, enrolling fifty-nine artists throughout its lifetime. These artists experimented with direct engagement with materials and, in 1955, staged their first festival-like event. It was a complete novelty. Previously everything related to art appeared in the confines of galleries or museums. The Gutai artists were the first to combine and integrate performance, painting, the environment, everyday life, their own bodies, nature, time, space, and technology into one event.

As the Gutai continued experimenting, they added light, sound, sculptures, immersive installation, and video. They influenced generations of Western artists, including Allan Kaprow, an American known as the pioneer of "Happenings." Happenings were events that started in 1959. Kaprow aggregated installation, performance, games, and activities and engaged both artists and participants for the sake of play. Later, he created Happenings in stores, gyms, lofts, and parking lots. No place or material was off-limits. Thanks to him, installation and performance art became popular in the West.

BEYOND AGGREGATION, IMMERSIVE SPECTACLE

One of my favorite modern-day master aggregators is Philadelphia-based multimedia artist Alex Da Corte. He works with a variety of objects that he strips from their original function and combines into something new. His large-scale immersive installations usually include floor pieces, sculptures, neon, deeply colored walls and carpets, videos, sound, and sometimes scents. He has an ability to combine familiar objects and images in unusual ways, mixing high and low, pop culture, TV, and cartoons, using references that range from Mister Rogers to Prince. He creates and performs in the videos in his installations, wearing costumes, prosthetics, and layers of makeup.

Da Corte creates worlds that are ravishing and cool. When I am inside one of them, I always gasp and dream. For his first museum survey at the Massachusetts Museum of Contemporary Art, Da Corte took over the second floor of the museum. My eyes could barely believe what he did in the main gallery. Yellow, pink, and green rugs divided the sprawling one-hundred-foot-long room. Giant neon rectangular sculptures hung from its thirty-foot-tall ceiling. A shallow pond with motorized ducks, the façade of a suburban house, a giant bull's-eye reminiscent of Target's logo, and many more incredible objects filled the space. I felt as if I were on the set of a contemporary *Willy Wonka and the Chocolate Factory*.

WHEN MORE IS MORE

When we think about innovative aggregation, the guiding principle should be that the whole offers so much more than the sum of its parts. Even if the parts are available individually and can live independently, they won't represent or convey the same feeling or meaning when brought together.

Aggregating is what "concept stores" have been doing since their inception in the 1990s. They were first conceived by European retailers, who developed the idea of tailoring a shop with a lifestyle focus, carrying a curated selection of handpicked products across categories like fashion, art, books, and jewelry. The beautifully designed spaces felt more intimate and distinct, unlike any department store, and became cultural destinations in their own right.

In 1991, 10 Corso Como opened in Milan, pioneering the concept store and changing the business of retail forever. Its owner, Carla Sozzani, wanted customers to hang out and have an unrushed experience that happily married art and commerce. She believed they'd be enticed to come back again. Her motto was "slow shopping." People visited her store and the many others that popped up all over Europe not only to buy things but also to discover a group of cool items in a unique setting.

Ever since Sozzani's store opened, the idea has been copied and adapted all over the world. Independent retailers as well as brands like Nike, Urban Outfitters, and Nespresso opened specialty shops, trying diverse approaches to the idea with different segments in select cities. These days, the bar is quite high. Buyers are well traveled, live on Instagram and TikTok, and apparently have seen it all. Today's concept store blurs the line between retail and hospitality. Some offer cocktail bars, others restaurants, a few even offer spa services. That's aggregation at its best.

Facebook started in 2004 as an American college-wide phenomenon spearheaded by Mark Zuckerberg, a Harvard student. As a child he learned coding and enjoyed building websites and inventing easy-to-use features not yet available anywhere. He also saw an opportunity to leverage user-generated content that was initially limited only to college students and extended it to a broader audience who could benefit from the platform's features as well. Besides personalizing each page, users could share pictures and updates about themselves with their network of friends.

As the private equity money poured in, Zuckerberg decided to drop out of Harvard and dedicate himself full-time to his growing venture. He realized that to thrive, Facebook needed to aggregate many more attributes. Facebook pages for business became the rage among early adopters. Its first ads rolled out in 2007.

He added the "like" button, now ubiquitous on every social media platform, in 2009. Two years later, instant messaging made communication within the platform easier. In 2012, Facebook launched its own App Center to help users find games and other applications. Every year, new features like news articles, 3D posts, and "Stories" are added.

Despite some flaws and its fair share of scandals, Facebook became the preferred social media platform worldwide. As of 2021, it had 2.9 billion users and was valued at $995 billion. The aggregation of features kept users spending more time on the platform, which allows Facebook to run more ads and make even more money.

GREATER THAN THE SUM OF ITS PARTS

There has not been a more revolutionary product in the past fifty years than the smartphone. It, too, is so successful because it aggregates many things. It's a phone, camera, text messenger, internet browser, music player, video screen, email provider, and source of entertainment and distractions, all in one.

Smartphones changed the way we communicate, allowed people to have a portable office with them at all times, and enabled social media to achieve stratospheric numbers. Without their suite of hundreds of different functions combined in a single instrument, smartphones would not have succeeded the way they did.

When I developed my online creativity class, I had to combine a few elements to make it a fully aggregated offer. Videos are broken down into modules and seen on a specific learning platform. PDFs with written summaries and exercises accompany each lesson. Once a week, on Zoom, the entire class meets with me to discuss what they learned on the other platform's videos. I also created a private Facebook group for participants so they could interact with each other. To put together this product, I aggregated three different technology platforms and delivered content in three different ways.

Adding parts that may or may not relate to one another in an interesting and unique way can be one of the most creative sources of new ideas in business and in art. To elude the pitfalls of producing something that lacks innovation, avoid playing it safe. Neither the Gutai nor Da Corte, much less Zuckerberg, were afraid to mix things to create a better experience and make a bigger impact than if they were offered in isolation. If there is a technique that calls for daring experiments, it is aggregation.

ALCHEMY LAB

To get your creative juices flowing to put together an experience, product, or business that aggregates various parts, follow these steps:

1. *List each element that you'd like to see together.* Collect digital images of them. Create online mood boards with apps that make photo collages and add all the parts you want to include. This gives you a visual clue of what you want to accomplish and how the elements look next to one another. That type of visual imagery is immensely powerful and helps you see new connections or edit out those that are not right.

2. *What is the product, service, or business intent?* What are you aiming to accomplish?

3. *Can the concept be brought to reality?*

4. *Add elements of storytelling.* Think carefully about the parts of an aggregated project and what they say to the costumer. Ask the following questions:

What story do you want to tell? Put yourself in the place of your customers. Think about what they will do when they have the experience, visit the website, or receive the service. How are they going to interact with the space? Or with the website? Or with you?

What would you want your customers to say after visiting your business or website or using your product? Write down each thing you think they would enjoy.

What will strengthen the experience? This is the question with the cherry on top. This is where you go the extra mile. There is always one more thing you could do to enhance and strengthen the experience. That is when you know you are striving for creative excellence.

17

Repeat: The More You Do It,

the More Original It Gets

IF I SAID the words *creative repetition*, you'd probably say that was an oxy-moron. But repetition can be a source of creativity if we see it through the eyes of an artist.

Repetition in the visual arts may give birth to a particular style or series. In business, a recurring message, image, logo, or slogan is the mother of branding.

Claude Monet, a leading French impressionist painter, was the first modern artist to repeatedly paint the same scene. In 1883, he moved from Paris to Giverny, a village in Normandy, in the north of France, where he rented and eventually purchased a house and two acres of land. For the next forty years, until his death, almost everything in his life revolved around Giverny or two miles around it. In a letter to his second wife, Alice Hoschedé, in 1884, he said that he was enticed by repetition because "it always seems to me that in the beginning again, I will do better."

TAKE IT FROM MONET: YOU CAN DO IT BETTER

The first series he created at Giverny were the stacks of hay he saw outside his door. He fixated on how to capture the transience of light, depending on the time of day. Between 1890 and 1891, Monet created twenty-five canvases, endless variations of those stacks. Each rendition captured them at a different day or time. The motif was constant, but the colors and his impressions at the moment were not. The time or the day varied, but not his perspective or his tools. Collectors loved them. Monet gave Paul Durand-Ruel, a Parisian dealer, fifteen of the *Haystack* paintings to exhibit in his gallery. They all sold within days. In 2019, one of the *Haystack* paintings sold at auction for $110.7 million.

Between 1892 and 1893, Monet made more than thirty paintings of the Rouen Cathedral in Normandy. He rented various spaces across the street, which allowed him to produce the most nuanced renditions of the cathedral's Gothic façade. Each had its own tonal gradations of pinks, blues, yellows, violets, oranges, and ochers. He worked at least on fourteen of them at the same time. When exhibited, the series enjoyed critical and commercial success. Monet's friend Camille Pissarro wrote to his son urging him to see the exhibition in Paris before each canvas was sold. "They ought to be viewed as a whole," he wrote.

In 1893, Monet applied for permission to divert a nearby river to his Giverny property. He wanted a pond on his expansive grounds. Once granted, he dedicated himself to designing his garden. He bought water lilies from Egypt and South America and built a bridge over the pond inspired by the Japanese gardens he loved. In 1899, he started painting a series that included that bridge and parts of the lush shoreline.

Later he tightened his focus on the water lilies alone and their reflection on the water. Obsessed with seizing the moment, the way the light affixes on surfaces, the shadows, the seasons, the things of the moment, Monet lined up five or six easels in his garden and spent only a few minutes at each one of them every day at different times. The series grew like organic documentary photographs into more than 250 *Nymphéas*, or *Water Lily* paintings. He gifted the last eight to the Musée de l'Orangerie in Paris. He had spent the last thirty years of his life repeating the same motif.

There are not many words with which to express my astonishment on entering for the first time the all-white oval rooms at l'Orangerie. The monumental *Water Lilies* are still exhibited there. Each of the paintings is almost seven feet in height and between twenty-one and fifty-five feet long. They adapt to the curvature of the walls, as Monet intended. The colors range from purple and indigo to musk and aquamarine. The visual and emotional impact of this series seen together is something I never experienced before and haven't since in relation to art. They expressed beauty, hope, nostalgia, faith, peace, abundance, reverence for life, the ethereal and sublime all at once. Working on repetitive themes served Monet well. There isn't an artist, museum curator, or serious art collector who hasn't seen and appreciated his many extraordinary series of paintings.

WARHOL: MASTER OF THE VALUE OF REPETITION

Repetition turned Andy Warhol into the ubiquitous and revered international pop artist sensation he is known to be. He forever changed the course of art history by turning day-to-day objects, celebrities, and logos into a form of high art.

In the process, Warhol became the greatest artist-businessman that ever existed. It started after he moved to New York from Pittsburgh in 1949. He worked as an illustrator for magazines like *Glamour, Harper's Bazaar,* and *Vogue.*

At the same time, he started experimenting with repetition, using a technique called blotted-line, a rudimentary form of printmaking. He created a master illustration and drew over the lines with ink or watercolor, pressing a clean sheet on top of the wet lines to make a print. He did this several times, generating many variations of the same master drawing. He hoped that, when a demanding magazine asked for an illustration, he didn't have to create many handmade originals in different color combinations. His thinking was dead-on. These early tryouts made him realize that through subtle variations of the same thing, he could please the most discerning eye and even a greater group of people.

The idea of a series and multiple images stuck in Warhol's mind, and in 1962, far gone from the world of commercial illustration, he had a solo exhibition at Ferus Gallery on North La Cienega Boulevard in Los Angeles. There he showed thirty-two hand-painted twenty-by-sixteen-inch canvases portraying a Campbell soup can in one of its thirty-two varieties. Warhol carefully mimicked the red-and-white can, over and over again. The only change was the variety on the label. By the end of 1962, after much experimentation with series and repeated visuals, Warhol found his golden goose. He blew up photos he sourced from tabloids, magazines, or newspapers and reproduced them on materials like plexiglass, paper, or board using the mechanical process of silk screen. Until then, silk-screening was used only for printing commercial posters and ads. In Warhol's words, "It was all so simple, quick, and chancy."

When questioned about his unorthodox methods, Warhol answered: "I don't think art should be for the select few . . . it should be for the mass of the American people." The process allowed him to work faster than creating each image by hand. The innovative use of commodified symbols, ordinary items, and portraits of celebrities he idolized like Liz Taylor, Marilyn Monroe, and Mick Jagger, among hundreds of others, made his work stand out.

Throughout his career, Warhol created unique paintings and silk screens on canvas in different color combinations and thousands upon thousands of screen-printed editions on paper. Animals, flowers, reproductions from old master landscapes, mythological figures like Botticelli's Venus, still lifes, dollar signs, Mickey Mouse, portraits of politicians, actors and athletes, sunsets . . . nothing was off-limits.

In addition to publishing editions in quantities ranging from twenty to one thousand, he offered many of them as portfolios. People wouldn't buy just one but the entire series. It was not a coincidence that Warhol named his celebrated studio the "Factory" and often said "repetition adds to reputation." At the time of his premature death in 1987, Warhol was worth $220 million. That's about half a billion in 2021.

THE MOTHER OF CREATIVE BRANDING

One of the most crucial aspects for any entrepreneur, whether at the start-up phase or in the middle of a successful venture, is branding. Branding springs out of consistency and repetition. What is an ad campaign but repetition that leads to cultural imprinting in the minds of consumers?

No ad money? No problem. Today, small brands become relevant and stay in the minds of people through social media. The ones that take branding seriously and understand who they are, what they sell, and to whom repeat variations of their story, messaging, color, logos, and ethos. The point of effective branding is not repetition for its own sake, but to do it creatively.

Whatever form of communication you use, whether it is social media posts, ad campaigns, or email newsletters, you can use it as frequently as every day if it provides value with surprising and innovative content. When it does, you'll get your target audience's eyes and their hearts and minds engaged.

Some of the most successful and creative ad campaigns came from the Italian fashion company Benetton. In 1982, before everyone else rushed like crazy to portray racial and cultural diversity in their marketing efforts, Benetton was doing so. When Luciano Benetton, the chairman of the company, hired artist and photographer Oliviero Toscani as creative director, the brand took off.

When I was around ten, my mother kept stacks of glossy fashion magazines. I was always mesmerized by Benetton's double-page spreads in which young models—Black, Asian, Native American, Latino, and white—were photographed happy and hugging, wearing knits in every imaginable color. I always looked forward to the next magazine so I could see more of those ads. I also begged my parents to purchase one of those knits for me. After I got my first, I asked a few more times. The Benetton ads worked on me and many of my schoolmates. There was nothing like those repeated images of a bunch of racially diverse teenagers wearing fun clothes.

Years later, Benetton continued pushing the envelope. The intercultural theme was always present, but the ads became more conceptual—a Black woman breastfeeding a white baby, a black hand and a white hand cuffed together. The only constant was the green logo in one of the corners that read, "United Colors of Benetton."

By then, I was traveling abroad and saw the ads on street billboards and airport lightboxes. They looked like Benetton, the messages were the same, yet each was more interesting and intriguing than the last. In the '90s and early aughts, Benetton's ads turned political—oil spills, refugees, AIDS victims.

Luciano Benetton told the *Washington Post* in a 1993 interview that the ads had two purposes: the brand and the values equaled Benetton's worldview. He added, "It was difficult to choose what product to show, so we decided to concentrate on social issues, since these are common problems that are recognized around the world." How revolutionary, disruptive, and creative is that for a fashion brand that made knits at a low price point? Much has changed since Benetton's heyday, but what has not is the impact those ads had worldwide. Benetton was unequivocally recognized as the pioneer of the fashion ad campaign that felt anything but boring.

HOW MANY TIMES IS TOO MANY?

In the 1930s, Hollywood movie studios conducted a study that revealed that a prospect needs to hear a message at least seven times before they'll buy the product or service. Today, in the digital age, seven times won't even scratch the surface. There is so much clutter in front of people's eyes and ears. Being repetitious can be intimidating, but bear in mind that not everyone will see your Instagram post, read your newsletter, see your ad, watch your video, or answer your survey at the same time.

I use Instagram almost daily, and 95 percent of the time I use images with saturated and brilliant colors, which resonate strongly with my brand (I even wear similar colors year-round). I try to surprise my audience with original content that I create and pictures I take of art and beautiful places. It is quite unusual for me to post a black-and-white photo. I do it only if the image is high-quality and the caption clearly expresses my message. That sure can be surprising and engaging.

Sometimes my captions are short and witty, puzzling or intriguing. Sometimes they are long and heartfelt. Using a combination of blogging, licensing my content to third parties, and repurposing the content for IGTV, I developed a thought-provoking series of videos inside artists' studios. I released them to my audience once a month. Those posts later led to my TV show when someone who worked at PBS noticed them. Consistent repetition of my message in different ways didn't alienate my audience. It helped me expand my reach because people were definitely watching.

How can repetition feel fresh? What can we borrow from Monet, Warhol, and Benetton? A couple of things, including their sense of artistry and aesthetics. Today, it doesn't matter what you are selling, there are no excuses for presenting low-aesthetic social media posts or ads. It is one thing to show a natural image, and an entirely different thing to post a poor-quality one. Photo apps and tools are available for free or at a minimal cost. Inspiring examples abound to encourage our own creation of interesting, compelling visuals.

Equally important is to strive for originality. Monet's *Water Lilies* bordered on abstraction at a time when that was a style barely known in France. Warhol used machines that were intended for other purposes, and no subject matter was ever off-limits. Benetton sold clothes without even advertising them. Consider what is rare and unique even if it has no relationship to what you sell. Could you be daring with words if you can't do it with images?

ALCHEMY LAB

No matter how long you've been in business, write down the answers to the following questions:

- *What are the core attributes, values, and strengths* of your services and products?

- *What colors, feelings, and words* are associated with your services or products?

- *Whom do you sell to?* Who is your ideal customer?

- *What is your brand story?* People remember through stories; do not neglect telling yours.

Use your answers to distill or strengthen your branding. It is the repetitive message that you must use time and again to teach your audience about who you are and whom you sell to. Think about different ways to repeat the same messages with visuals and words. Create themes and variations around your message or take what you have done a notch further.

18

Creative Tension:

When Opposites Attract

Dᴜᴀʟɪᴛʏ ᴄᴏᴍᴇs ᴏᴜᴛ of contrast that results from combining opposites. Like electricity, the tension between two opposite poles generates energy. The greater the tension, the greater the power. Feminine and masculine, strong and soft, abstract and figurative, traditional and modern, familiar and novel, past and future.

Contrast in art is a distinctive quality that emerges when opposite elements, such as light and dark, are arranged in the same composition.

THE STRIKING POWER OF CONTRAST

One of the most remarkable uses of contrast in painting goes back to da Vinci's chiaroscuro technique. He intensified the darkness of a color by adding black pigments instead of saturating or layering the tones. *Madonna and Child with Flowers* (also known as the *Benois Madonna*) was da Vinci's first independent painting, although he was still an apprentice to Andrea del Verrocchio. Finished in 1478, the painting is full of strong contrasts: the dark background, the lighter skin tones of Mary and her baby, the use of color and shadow in the blue drapery of her clothes and the folds of fat on chubby Jesus. With the *Benois Madonna*, da Vinci was the first painter to achieve a full, three-dimensional illusion on a flat surface. He did it by innovatively and methodically developing contrasting moments of light and shadows.

A century later, a twenty-four-year-old Milanese painter known as Caravaggio took da Vinci's contrasting techniques to new levels. Caravaggio's first use of this dramatic illumination technique was his 1595 painting *Saint Francis of Assisi in Ecstasy*. The two subjects, Saint Francis and the angel who is holding his unconscious body, are bathed in light that comes from the top of the canvas. Everything around the figures is extremely dark. The two bodies' ethereal look came from Caravaggio's radical use of light and dark.

Chiaroscuro wasn't cutting it as a name for this dramatic juxtaposition. Instead, the term *tenebrism* (from the Latin *tenebrae*, meaning "darkness") was born. This way of painting was so innovative that it influenced artists all over Italy and signaled the dawn of baroque painting. Later, it was widely imitated in the rest of Europe throughout the seventeenth century.

Caravaggio's spotlight effect also inspired the cinematic choices of many filmmakers, including Orson Welles's 1941 masterpiece, *Citizen Kane*, Francis Ford Coppola's *The Godfather* trilogy (1972–1990), and Martin Scorsese's 1973 *Mean Streets*. Referencing Caravaggio's paintings, Scorsese told BBC's *The Culture Show* in 2005, "I was taken by the power of his pictures . . . because of the moment he chooses to illuminate the story . . . you come upon the scene midway and you are immersed in it. The use of light and shadows, that's one of the things with Caravaggio . . . very stark, very powerful, very determined light, and this is the kind of thing we were looking to do in the '70s."

DRAMATIC BORROWING: DUALITY WITH A TWIST

Another creative way in which artists play with duality is by looking at the past and re-creating it with a twist. Many artists incorporate fragments of art history in new work and even reinterpret masterpieces to give them their own spin.

The French artist Édouard Manet revered the art of the past. When he painted *Le Déjeuner sur l'Herbe* in 1863, one of the most famous and recognizable artworks, he took fragments and inspiration from two historical works: one, by the celebrated Venetian painter Titian, a 1509 oil-on-canvas titled *Pastoral Concert*, in which two naked women and two dressed men hang out together on a lawn; the other, a collaboration between the great Italian artist Raphael and engraver Marcantonio Raimondi's 1510 print, *The Judgment of Paris* (not the city, but the Greek mythological character, whose elopement with Helen, queen of Sparta, triggered the Trojan War).

More than 350 years later, using elements of Titian's and Raphael and Raimondi's works, Manet combined two bourgeois, well-dressed Parisian men next to one woman *sans* clothes in what could have been a picnic in a Parisian park. A second woman in the background, wearing a sheer undergarment, is bathing in a stream. The result was scandalous. Manet himself called it the "Foursome."

Almost sixty years later, in 1932, Picasso, inspired by *Déjeuner*, came up with his own versions: six paintings, one hundred forty drawings, and six engravings. He gave his cubist variations the same title his French predecessor did.

RECOMBINATION: THE MASH-UP OPPOSITES

I've admired Allison Zuckerman's work since I first met the artist in 2016 when she was twenty-six. She had already embraced many dualities in her strong paintings, which showcased explosive combinations in a creative and frenetic way.

Mixing opposites, like technology and analog techniques, the old and new, the familiar and the novel, Zuckerman pulls digital images from among the thousands she keeps in her computer folders and uses Photoshop as her drawing pad to recombine them.

She creates her own art history–reloaded mash-up, remixing, for example, a foot from a Picasso painting, a fruit bowl from American pop artist Roy Lichtenstein, a body that resembles Michelangelo's Adam from the Sistine Chapel ceiling, a bird from Disney's *Snow White,* and enlarged pictures of her own lips or eyes. She prints her creations on large canvases and adds brushstrokes using traditional painting methods. Of course, she has made several contemporary re-creations of Manet's *Déjeuner,* complete with a classically American white-and-red checkered picnic blanket.

The tensions and polarities in her work have caught the eye of some of the most influential art collectors in the United States and beyond. In December 2018, three years after her MFA graduation, she had a solo show at the Rubell Museum in Miami, owned by a family of art collectors who are in part responsible for the development of that city's cultural scene.

The show opened with great fanfare during Art Basel Miami Beach when the attention of the art world is concentrated in Florida for a few days. Several sold-out gallery shows and solo exhibitions in international museums followed. Her use of dualities keeps her work fresh, her ideas flowing, and her supporters wanting more.

HARMONY IN CONTRADICTIONS

The complex play of these dualities is fertile terrain for innovations in business too. Gabrielle "Coco" Chanel was very adept at combining opposites. She was the first fashion designer to create the androgynous look. In 1906, she befriended Étienne Balsan, a young man who had inherited a fortune. He took Chanel to live with him in his château in northern France, where they became lovers.

Bored with this life, Chanel started to wear Balsan's clothes: his tweed coats and open-collared shirts mixed with her own. To complete the look, she added his straw boater hat. That was her big "aha" moment. Freed from tight Victorian corsets and ridiculous headpieces worn by women at the beginning of the twentieth century, she felt at ease.

Balsan was thrilled with Chanel's look and introduced her to his tailor so she could have masculine pieces made for her size. Since that moment, she created her signature look mixing male and female garments. Her style quickly caused a sensation among the women who would become her loyal clients. Her famous open jersey cardigan, those that sell today for thousands of dollars, came from cutting one of Balsan's sweaters and sewing golden buttons to it. This newfound style was so well received it allowed Chanel to open a boutique in Deauville, Normandy, in 1913. In 1918, due to her earlier success with androgynous clothes, Chanel purchased the building at 31 Rue Cambon in Paris.

In 1920, another mix of opposites came to life: Chanel No. 5, the iconic perfume that put her name everywhere around the world. When Chanel met French-Russian perfumer Ernest Beaux, she gave him a wish list of polarities. First, to make a fragrance that was "artificial, something that has been made like a dress . . . a woman should smell like a woman and not like a flower." Second, a perfume that blurred the line between a respectable girl and a seductress. Mixing synthetic aldehydes, Beaux found the elixir that Chanel approved—a blend of opposing ideas and scents.

Even the design of the bottle was a paradox for a women's perfume. It wasn't ornate and curvy like the competitors'. It was masculine, rectangular, strong, and inspired by a whisky decanter that belonged to one of Chanel's lovers. Chanel No. 5 was a sensation almost instantly, and, today, a century after its creation, the French government prides itself in saying that every thirty seconds, a bottle is purchased somewhere in the world. In 2020, an estimated 2.25 million women bought a bottle of Chanel No. 5 in the United Kingdom alone. Annual sales are estimated to be north of $3 billion, but that's a number that the brand, being a private company, doesn't disclose.

FINDING THE NEW IN THE OLD

In business, consumers like the old and the familiar when they are rein-vented and re-created in interesting and useful ways. The camera is not a new thing. The first one was made in 1816 by French inventor Nicéphore Niépce. In 1885, George Eastman pioneered the photographic film for his first camera, which he called Kodak. He released his invention in 1888.

I don't think either Niépce or Eastman could have imagined that, in 2006, Frank Wang, a Chinese student, would design and build a flying device carrying a light camera that could take pictures and videos from miles high. In 2014, after testing many variations and launching several drones, Wang's company, DJI, released a fully integrated camera drone. It could fly for almost half an hour, with a range of seven hundred meters, and be manipulated by a remote that allows the user to control the navigation and return the camera drone to its user. The latest models can fly three miles and for up to four hours without a recharge. This innovative duality, an old camera and new invention, led DJI to control about 70 percent of the camera-drone market, which is currently a $27 billion industry.

Today, Frank Wang is doing the work that needs to be done now, managing the day-to-day operations at DJI. He is also constantly reframing and evolving. He is grounded in the present, but pays close attention to technology and consumer trends. Wang looks to the future in order to keep innovating and improving on the products he has launched.

REIMAGINING TIME AND CULTURES

In March 2019, when I was invited to curate a group exhibition for the inauguration of a large commercial gallery in Beirut, Lebanon, I wanted to play with the creativity that comes out of marrying old and new with East and West. Beirut is a five-thousand-year-old city. Since childhood, I have been inspired by *One Thousand and One Nights* (or *Arabian Nights*), one of the most famous pieces of literature from the Middle East.

Dating back to the early ninth century, *Arabian Nights* follows the brilliant Scheherazade, who volunteers to marry King Shahryār, knowing he killed a wife a night in retaliation for his first wife's unfaithfulness. Scheherazade tells the king what becomes a series of linked stories, ending each night with a cliffhanger, so that he will want to hear the rest and not kill her. She does this for 1,001 nights until Shahryār has a change of heart. Isn't Scheherazade the OG queen of creativity?

Throughout history, *Arabian Nights* has inspired artists. Among them are Eugène Delacroix, René Magritte, Marc Chagall, Salvador Dalí, and Henri Matisse. *Why not reinterpret these tales now?* I thought. I invited seven contemporary American artists to participate. I showed them pictures, told them passages, and really excited them about bridging the many dualities with their own ideas and styles.

Some of them were unfamiliar with the tales but were curious to research it. The results couldn't have been more beautiful. For example, Allison Zuckerman used her engaging mix-ups of art history to make a large, twelve-foot-wide painting showing Scheherazade luring the king with nightly tales so she could escape on a horse.

New York–based Jonathan Chapline made paintings and sculptures in intense neon colors. They showed the actual book next to "Aladdin's Wonderful Lamp" and Moorish interiors and architecture adorned with palm and date trees.

Georgia-based Holly Coulis painted still lifes with figs, oranges, and pomegranates next to Arabian tea sets in spectacular contrasting colors. LA-based Canyon Castator re-created "Ali Baba and the Forty Thieves," adding portraits of politicians, a masked hacker in front of a laptop stealing data, and other famous fictional crooks like the Grinch and the Pink Panther.

These artists were unknown in Lebanon, but all fourteen artworks sold out rather quickly. I baptized the exhibit *The Thousand and One Nights*. The Beirutis were moved by the concept and the inventiveness in the way the artists embraced the familiarity and the novelty, the Middle Eastern traditions and the American ways. Hundreds of people, from politicians to bohemian writers, came to the opening and *The Thousand and One Nights* got its Western contemporary revival out of the sweet marriage of polarities.

ALCHEMY LAB

Think about the following dualities and examine how you could integrate them in your project, product, or business:

- Charity and profit

- Popular and elite

- Average and exceptional

- Conscious and unconscious

- Past and future

- Light and darkness

- Masculine and feminine

When tinkering with dualities, the creative part comes from knowing how to balance them. Like Janus the Roman god who had two faces—one that looked to the past, the other to the future—the ability to handle and juggle dualities is what keeps leaders relevant and their creativity flowing.

19

Cross-Pollination:

Fertile Ground for Creativity

For the first ten years of his career as an artist, Gustav Klimt painted portraits and landscapes in a conservative traditional European style. He also decorated museums and theatres in his natal Vienna. While he had a great talent, nothing was out of the ordinary or innovative in his work.

THE ALCHEMY OF SCIENCE AND ART: GOLD

That changed in 1900, when one of Klimt's supporters and patrons, an Austrian woman named Bertha Szeps, who collected art and led an important salon that Klimt attended frequently, introduced him to her new husband, Hungarian anatomist Emil Zuckerkandl.

Zuckerkandl tutored Klimt in biology and gave lectures and seminars arranged by Klimt. Zuckerkandl projected slides of microscopic tissue, cells, and human eggs. He explained how these eggs, when fertilized, became fetuses and eventually humans. This fascinated Klimt and permeated his art for the following decade.

One of the assignments Zuckerkandl gave Klimt was to read Darwin's 1859 book, *On the Origin of Species*. Klimt was impressed with Darwin's theories and the science-based conversations he had with Zuckerkandl. His paintings started to reflect new themes and hidden meanings.

He became obsessed with understanding humans biologically the way Darwin did. In 1903, he traveled to Ravenna, Italy. There the Byzantine architecture of Italian churches, their interiors decorated with luminous golden mosaics, influenced him. The combination of biological symbols and gold leaf in his paintings marked the beginning of Klimt's famous and financially successful "Golden Phase."

In her autobiography, Szeps wrote that Klimt's paintings were not just "decorative" but showed symbology, referencing the very mystery of life. After attending Zuckerkandl's biology classes, "an abundance of shapes . . . reminiscent of epithelium cells with black nuclei in whiteish cytoplasm" appeared in his work. In *Hope I* (1903), Klimt painted a naked redheaded woman in the last stages of her pregnancy. In *Danaë* (1907–08), there are sperm symbols impregnating the ancient Greek princess and early embryonic forms that symbolize conception. Klimt innovated in the arts by using this cross-fertilization of diverse disciplines—art, science, and decorative references—in a way not commonly used back then. As a result, Klimt became the leader of the new modernist movement in Vienna.

In 2006, art collector and Estée Lauder's son Ronald Lauder paid $135 million for Klimt's *Portrait of Adele Bloch-Bauer I* (also called *The Lady in Gold*), which Klimt started painting in 1903 and finished in 1907. The painting for a long time was embroiled in battles and controversies. It was stolen by the Nazis in 1941, then given to Galerie Belvedere in Vienna, and finally reclaimed in 2006 after a seven-year trial by Maria Altmann, the niece and rightful heir to the Bloch-Bauer painting. She sold it to Lauder with the help of Christie's.

What most people don't know is the iconography of Adele Bloch-Bauer's ornate dress. It is composed of complex symbols: rectangles for sperm and ovals for eggs. As art historian Emily Braun puts it, "These biologically inspired symbols are designed to match the sitter's seductive face to her full-blown reproductive capabilities." Lauder called the painting "our *Mona Lisa*" and hung it at the Neue Galerie, Lauder's museum of German and Austrian expressionist art in New York City, for everyone to enjoy.

CREATIVITY: MUCH MORE THAN MEETS THE EYE

These interdisciplinary mergers of sciences and humanities enhance creations and serve people in unique ways. One of my first memories interacting with large art installations comes from the time I traveled with my parents at the age of four. We went to the airport in Caracas, the city where I was born. There, the floors and part of the wall in the check-in areas were covered by hundreds of thousands of mosaic tiles. The Venezuelan kinetic master artist Carlos Cruz-Diez placed them in a precise geometric grid, forming lines in yellow, blue, red, and black, creating an optical illusion. The colors behaved in different ways, forming gradients of greens and fuchsias, even though those hues weren't used. The floors seem to move as you move and the perspective changes depending on the angle whether you walk straight ahead or sideways.

Years later, I met Cruz-Diez in Caracas. He explained that he spent many months studying the scientific properties of materials. He knew when he was assigned this massive project that millions of people would step on these floors. He traveled to many countries in Europe and finally found a compound of feldspar and silica called Sialex. It comes from the banks of the Loire River in France. The material is inherently colored and practically indestructible, ideal to withstand the abrasion of constant footsteps.

He said there was a social element to everything that he did. He wanted the people who came in contact with his work to engage deeply with it. He accomplished that and more. For me and the many Venezuelans who left our country and never returned, these floors are one of the last memories we keep in our minds and hearts.

Considered one of the greatest artist-innovators of the twentieth century, Cruz-Diez developed some of his most interesting inventions in the early 1970s. With the oil crisis, the plastic products like the PVC sticks Cruz-Diez had been using for his intricate artworks disappeared from the market. Instead, he decided to work with aluminum sheets. He would print lines of color and create other effects he hadn't before considered.

He was unable to find the cutting and piercing machines with the millimetric precision he needed, so he designed and manufactured his own machines. They lasted decades and as he adapted them to newer technologies they became more efficient with time.

He had to experiment quite a bit to get the colors to stick to the aluminum without chipping. He bathed the sheets and rods with nitric acid, but that didn't work. It almost caused an explosion. Then he tried degreasing the aluminum with detergent—that didn't work either. Finally, sanding the aluminum first, then washing it with soap, next applying a coat of zinc chromate, then sanding again, finishing it with a coat of white acrylic paint, and, at last, screen printing on them line by line gave him the result he wanted.

Every artwork, intervention, and installation that Cruz-Diez worked on, no matter how little or how huge, always involved rigorous mathematical and geometric precision. One millimeter out of place, and the expected visual effect of an entire composition was ruined. An inexact cut or an opening, and the sheet or rod had to be discarded.

Cruz-Diez lived in Paris most of his adult life and died there at the age of ninety-five in 2019. Scientific, technological, and mathematical concerns—particularly color theory—alongside the aesthetic ones deeply consumed him. This successful cross-pollination from the fields of science, technology, math, and sociology integrated in his art and aided his practice.

He had a lucrative and fulfilling seventy-five-year career. His work was the subject of almost 300 solo exhibitions in more than 20 countries and more than 140 architectural interventions. Among them are the platform of the Saint-Quentin-en-Yvelines railway station near Paris, France; a gigantic undulating sculpture at the Juan Carlos I Park in Madrid, Spain; a suspended wall in the Olympic Park in Seoul, Korea; and the walkways at the Marlins ballpark stadium in Miami.

The impressive 118,403 square feet of colored lines that fill the entire turbine halls and walls of Venezuela's largest hydroelectric plant highlights his humanity. He accepted that project because he said that the workers, who had to spend so much time in such a cavernous place, needed to have some art and color brighten their lives. Cruz-Diez turned an inhospitable space into a welcoming, humane one that created meaning for those who worked there every day.

MULTISENSORY ART: CREATING SOCIAL CAPITAL

The relationship between humanity, science, nature, and technology is the center of everything that Korean American artist Anicka Yi does. She integrates holography, textile design, video, fragrance, biology, and neuroscience, among other disciplines, into her art.

Instead of going to traditional art schools and following an art training path, Yi studied film and worked at the labs of Columbia University, and did residencies in places such as MIT. There she learned from and collaborated with engineers, geologists, physicists, virologists, and scientists.

This unique and innovative spin on an artistic practice allowed Yi, in less than ten years, to earn the representation of a blue-chip gallery and win the prestigious Hugo Boss Prize in 2016. This led her to an exhibition at the Guggenheim Museum in New York, to represent Korea in the 2019 Venice Biennale, and to be selected by the Tate Modern to create a monumental work that was exhibited in the museum's Turbine Hall in 2021.

Yi's conceptual work engages the audience's minds and senses with different elements. She worked with a chemist to develop the fragrance of "prehistoric wetland" for a show in a gallery on the Lower East Side in New York. She evokes sound when she adds music and edits out certain instruments in her videos.

During her show at the Guggenheim Museum, she installed a diorama that held a colony of twenty thousand living ants inside a network of computer parts. The ants were lured by scents distilled from a mix that perfumers helped Yi formulate.

For an exhibition in Brussels, she created round lantern sculptures made of kelp that hung from the ceiling. Each hosted a flying insect inside. The insect's shadow was projected onto the wall through the greenish light of the lantern. She wants to call the attention of the spectators to look at issues related to climate change, the importance of preserving the environment, the reactions we have to smells, and something she describes as the "biopolitics of the senses."

MIXING INTELLECTUAL CAPITAL: A KEY TO INNOVATION

The complexities of the world today require collaborations, teams, projects, services, and products that are born out of interdisciplinary approaches. This is one of the most fertile spaces for creativity and innovation. All the successful internet companies founded in the past thirty years were born out of the cross-pollination of fields. The success of e-commerce, online services, digital platforms, and social media came out of the integration of technology with traditional fields like retail, shipping services, customer services, entertainment, and countless others.

The wearable technology market was valued at $116 billion in 2021. It is one of the most innovative fields that sprang out of cross-fertilization. Starting in the 1960s with rudimentary computers strapped around the waist, wearable tech didn't advance much until Finnish company Polar launched the first wire-free heart monitor in 1982. Invented at the intersection of medical equipment, science, industrial design, and technology, Polar became the go-to brand for anyone who wanted to monitor their heart rate, speed, effort, distance, and other variables while exercising or practicing sports.

Polar dominated the wearable-tech-for-fitness market until 2007, when Fitbit, a company based in San Francisco, started selling clippable trackers that measured the steps, distance, calories burned, and sleep cycles of the people who wore it 24/7. In 2013, Fitbit launched its first wrist-worn tracker. In 2019, Google announced that it would buy the company for $2 billion.

In 2014, Apple upped the ante. It released the Apple Watch, whose newest versions can get messages and notifications, play music, track workouts, warn of abnormal heart rates, take electrocardiograms, among many other things. Sony, Adidas, and Samsung followed Apple, releasing their own sleek smart watches.

Cross-pollination is attainable when artists and entrepreneurs are humble enough and have the presence of mind to know that they can't possibly know everything. Avoiding the mentality that things have to be self-contained and "pure" allows us to invite the perspective of others who can add an expansive dimension to ours.

ALCHEMY LAB

When artists and entrepreneurs take concepts, ideas, and techniques from separate fields and blend them, magical things can happen. This also is the way life is—multiple realms colliding through cross-pollination.

If you want to cross-pollinate, follow these steps:

1. *List your strengths and areas of competence.*

2. *Identify the second and/or third different fields in which you need to develop expertise.* The depth of competence can vary significantly depending on what it is you want to do. Consider the integrative structure of the product, company, or service that will be developed from cross-pollinating. Be flexible, dynamic, and fluid, whether you are working alone or in a team. This is the fundamental characteristic of cross-pollination and is the only way it can lead to fruitful outcomes.

3. *Pay attention to the process.* Accidents and unintended consequences can bring myriad creative discoveries that weren't seen from the outset.

20

The Analog Method:

Use Your Hands to Access Your Brain

Leonardo da Vinci carried a notebook with him at all times. He had a small one hanging from his belt. He was obsessed with writing down his ideas, observations, and whatever around him piqued his curiosity and deserved exploration. He was a genius who intuitively knew the value of putting pen to paper.

WHAT'S ON YOUR MIND: NOTHING'S TOO BIG OR TOO SMALL

Many of his incredible inventions, if not all, originated in those notebooks. Anatomical and machinery sketches, recipes on how to mix and grind pigments, extensive writings on light and shade, and to-do lists were copiously recorded in those notebooks.

Some pages have notes on how to use a mirror to find potential mistakes in his paintings. He was used to looking at them straight from the same perspective and wouldn't see what was wrong until he reversed the image.

There is even a study for his famous 1498 fresco, *The Last Supper.* It includes many notes about what each character is doing in the final scene. For example, da Vinci wrote "one who was drinking and left the glass in its position and turned his head towards the speaker . . . another one twisting the fingers of his hands together . . . another speaks into his neighbor's ear," and so on. He noted the tasks for each of the thirteen people in the scene that he would later paint on the wall of the refectory of the convent of Santa Maria delle Grazie in Milan.

Today, about 7,200 pages of his journals exist. That is thought to be about one-quarter of the total. Da Vinci's notebooks were not just about art. There were jokes, reflections on domestic problems, philosophical musings, ideas about air and water. Art historian Kenneth Clark called these notebooks "the most astonishing testament to the powers of human observation and imagination ever set down on paper."

As Walter Isaacson explained his process for writing da Vinci's biography, the starting point for his extensive research was da Vinci's notebooks, not his paintings. There is no doubt that through the process of constantly writing down his ideas, da Vinci unleashed his vast creative power.

SPARK YOUR CREATIVITY: WRITING AND PLANNING

Throughout history, many artistic geniuses left records of their thoughts in notes and journals. Words, stories, hypotheses, doodles, sketches, preparatory drawings, anything that was worth recording became a part of their process—a way of revving up their creative engines. These early planning stages were a way of emptying out their minds and organizing ideas before going onto the canvas, the marble slab, or any final medium.

From the time he was thirteen years old in 1894 until 1965 when he was eighty-four, Pablo Picasso doodled, wrote, sketched, and drew in many notebooks, filling 175 of them. He dated them carefully and kept them hidden until at least the late 1960s. Then, he would occasionally tear out pages for friends or offer one of the sketches to his dealers. He was protective of these notebooks. They were very intimate to him. It was almost as if all his magic stemmed from them.

They only surfaced after his death. Their discovery made many art historians rethink Picasso's genius and his process. He was an intense and prolific artist, full of energy. He could make a complete painting in hours. His legendary artistic practice always seemed visceral and unplanned. The sketchbooks proved that he was indeed planning. The thoughts, scribbles, and sketches he recorded in them were the genesis of his immense creativity.

The world saw Picasso's notebooks for the first time in 1986 in an exhibition that started at Pace Gallery in New York and traveled to the Royal Academy of Arts in London, the Los Angeles County Museum of Art, and many other museums around the globe. The notebooks were brimming with gorgeous watercolors, pastels, sketches made with pen and crayons, collages, studies for many of his paintings, copies of old masters' works, and ink drawings of his lovers and the interiors of his studio in his villa La Californie in Cannes, with variations upon variations of each.

He also kept records of his ideas, reflections, and thoughts about the people he knew. He considered all of his entries in his diary to be part of his work. Many of them were kept in a security safe at the bank. Among those were the eight notebooks with all the preparatory sketches for his breakthrough 1907 painting, *Les Demoiselles d'Avignon.*

He had such a close relationship with his notebooks that he even wrote on the cover of a 1906 volume, *"Je suis le cahier"* ("I am the notebook"). Picasso's son Claude said it best in the foreword of the catalogue commemorating the notebooks' exhibition, that they were "the stepping stones to trampolines for somersaults."

THE WRITING IS ON THE WALL

With the advent of technology, many people have forgone the magic that comes when using a pen to put thoughts on paper. A series of studies conducted by Indiana University revealed through brain scans of five-year-old children that neural activity was far more enhanced when generating letters on paper. They were accessing forms of creativity that couldn't be activated when typing on a keyboard.

A different study on children from second, fourth, and sixth grades carried out by the University of Washington also demonstrated that the subjects wrote more words and expressed better ideas when writing by hand versus using a computer. The interactions of the use of hand movements and the tactile experience of holding a pen against a piece of paper bring the information that's being expressed close to the forefront and makes the brain pay more attention. But the studies on the creative benefits of writing longhand don't stop with children.

In 2014, researchers from Princeton University and UCLA studied the behavior of Princeton undergraduate students. They were divided in two groups: those who took notes with laptops and those who took notes with pen and paper. The unequivocal conclusion was that using laptops to take notes impairs learning. Their use results in shallower brain processing. The students who took notes on laptops performed worse on conceptual questions on tests and in classroom participation than the students who took notes longhand.

Those who wrote by hand with pen and paper came up with more original content. They processed and reframed information in more interesting ways, and used a lot more brainpower than those who typed on a keyboard.

There is also stimulation caused by a collection of cells at the base of the brain. It is called the reticular activating system (or RAS). RAS helps the brain filter information to focus more attention on what the person is currently writing. This helps in the process of associative ideas and acute observation. And what is creativity without associations and sharp observation skills?

Although it is impossible to go without computers altogether (and we wouldn't want to!), if you'd like to enhance your creative powers in the early stages or planning a creative project, it is an excellent idea to let ideas flow through the process of longhand writing. The sequential finger movements activate multiple regions of the brain associated with processing and remembering information. Creative thinking requires the connection of different types of ideas. Handwriting activates multiple areas of the brain in a way that typing does not.

Sir Richard Branson wrote in an entry on his blog that he had shared the stage with Bill Gates at the Bill and Melinda Gates Foundation Grand Challenges event in London in the fall of 2016. That day, Branson was thrilled to discover that Bill Gates, one of the most tech-oriented minds in the world, had notes for his speech scribbled on a piece of paper, which he reviewed often. Branson added that he also always carries a notebook, and has instilled the notebook culture in all his employees at Virgin. As he put it, "An idea not written down is an idea lost."

I like analog methods myself and go through six or seven Moleskine notebooks every year. I get them in different sizes and colors. I find that when I'm writing following my unconscious impulse for increased creativity or writing letters to people I can't talk to, which will never be mailed, the letter-size notebooks without lines work best. It is almost as if my ideas need all that space to breathe. Taking the time to write things down in a journal gives us the pause we don't ever get while multitasking on the phone or in front of a computer.

Don't get me wrong: I don't live without my iPhone, whose Notes app I use often. I also constantly take thousands of pictures that serve as visual memory. But almost every day, I do take handwritten notes. When I write the jumble of ideas running through my head—my goals, plans, diagrams, ideas for my business, and even the first outline for this book—the smaller notebooks with ruled pages do the job.

I then review those ideas and go through them again at night or at the end of the week to see what gems I can unearth. Often, when I have a specific objective in mind (versus automatic writing), in the process of writing I generate more ideas. I add them to the pile. And I do believe, wholeheartedly, that longhand writing multiplies creative thoughts and unravels ideas in ways that other methods can't.

ALCHEMY LAB

Carry a notebook with you everywhere you go.

Take notes throughout the day. If something pops into your mind, write it down. If you have time to flesh out an idea, go for it. Plan and document your projects in longhand. Try it for sixty-six days—the time it takes for the brain to form new habits and neural pathways.

If carrying a notebook at all times is impractical, make it a daily habit to write down your thoughts with pen and paper in the morning, before your day starts. Jotting down whatever crosses your mind (automatic writing), no matter how absurd, is quite conducive to generating creative breakthroughs later in the day or week. It is unlikely that you will find the solution to all your problems or your best ideas while you are engaged in automatic writing, but expect genius thoughts and aha moments at any time during the hours or days after you start this process.

Some prompts to get you going:

- Daily to-do list

- A list of business concerns and worries

- Specific goals for the day

- Strategies to tackle a project—write as many as you can

- Ideas for the future

- Tasks that you are avoiding

- Things that call for your attention

- Improvements that you'd like to implement in your business

- People you are looking to connect with

- Synchronicities and serendipities

- The biggest accomplishments of the past week

PART IV

THE WAY FORWARD

■

Creativity is like a wheel we have to keep pushing if we want to see our big ideas come to fruition. All the habits, methods, tools, and experiments in the Alchemy Labs are spokes in that wheel, constantly rolling. Their role is to get you to a place of momentum, to the point where you can materialize what you envisioned in your mind, dreamed about, deconstructed, aggregated, cross-pollinated, written on a piece of paper, or talked about with your team.

The following chapters present different ways of integrating, shifting, adjusting, and strategizing what you already learned in parts I, II, and III in order to help materialize creative ideas into real accomplishments.

21

Mixing Intuition and Rationality:

Balancing Premonition and Logic

Witnessing the creative process from start to finish, sometimes in one take, is one of the most interesting things about working with artists. For example, when I curated the exhibition *Greek Gotham* in Mykonos in 2016, Austin Lee and Mira Dancy, two of the artists who were in Greece for the opening, decided to paint the gallery walls. Austin used spray paint to tackle a wall indoors. Mira grabbed brushes and traditional paint for a mural outdoors. Both transformed the space before our eyes. A nondescript white slab of concrete became a work of art in a matter of hours.

It was a clear moment where intuition and rationality were integrated in the final product. They had a strong foundation—the materials and mediums. They knew what to expect from applying paint to a wall. They were intuitive enough to create something meaningful, under a tight deadline, in a place they had seen before only in pictures.

People who don't know artists or haven't ever worked with them may think that they are all spacey and bohemian. Sometimes that's the case. However, the majority of successful artists also use their logical minds. They know how to make good business decisions. They use their intuition to their advantage, and leverage both their logical and intuitive minds in their creative practices. As good entrepreneurs also know, part of being relevant and innovative requires balancing that higher form of intelligence, our intuition, with real-world empirical knowledge.

Rational thinking is developed through traditional education, by having day-to-day experiences, doing the work, understanding culture, and developing practical knowledge. This is sequential thinking. When we observe a phenomenon, we make a deduction. We understand the consequence and react or form a conclusion in our mind. It is the thinking process that follows logical steps and the one that is favored by traditional education and the fields of science, technology, math, and anything that can be proven with data. It helps us manage complex layers of information. It gives us a sense of how the parts interact and come together. Having a good sense of the whole comes from rational thinking. It grows from learning new skills, reading about new things, and anything else that enhances knowledge.

THE WINNING FORMULA: GROUNDED AND INSTINCTUAL

Peter Paul Rubens, one of the most famous painters of the seventeenth century, knew how innovative (and lucrative) the union of his rational mind and his intuition was. Rubens grew up in Antwerp but lived in Italy and Spain for eight years, acquiring a wealth of knowledge and real-life experiences that no amount of intuition on its own could have provided.

He didn't want to leave Rome. He had learned to speak fluent Italian. He had developed a good network of friends and a handful of patrons. But his mother got quite ill, and Rubens returned to a war-ravaged Antwerp in 1608. He intuitively sensed that the city was about to experience a great boom in art, architecture, and reconstruction. Following his intuitive insights as well as the rational knowledge and observations he had accumulated during the past decade, he bet on Antwerp. He married a young woman named Isabella Brant, bought a large house on Wapper Square, built a massive studio, and began to work.

Due to a 1609 truce between the Southern Netherlands (Belgium today) and the Northern Netherlands (Netherlands today), artists, craftsmen, artisans, and architects flourished in the reconstruction of Antwerp. Rubens was spot-on on his predictions. From the moment he sensed that Antwerp's art business would bounce back, he intuitively knew he should hustle his way into different sectors of Flemish society. Public servants, socialites, members of the clergy, wealthy patrons, and of course the highest local nobility, including Albert, archduke of Austria, and his wife, Isabella of Spain, were all in Rubens's circle. The archduke and his wife appointed Rubens court painter in September 1609. They also exempted him from all taxes, guild restrictions, and official duties in Brussels. What a deal!

SUCCESS: INTUITION, RATIONAL THINKING, AND HARD WORK

From then on, Rubens launched a formidable practice combining intuition and rationality that resulted in a phenomenal artistic and business enterprise. He employed several apprentices and produced work at a speed that was unusual at the time. He took control of his creative ideas and assured each of his patrons that no matter how many assistants worked in his studio, the paintings were his.

Between 1609 and 1620, Rubens completed twenty-two enormous altarpieces and sixty-three paintings to be hung in Antwerp's religious buildings. That's not counting the hundreds of private commissions, including portraits and mythical scenes, that he also produced during the same time. In 1616, Rubens, wanting to expand his practice, rationally signed a contract to make the first of many tapestries. This began a new venture that generated an excellent amount of revenue for the years to come.

In 1618, he became the first Flemish artist to launch a printmaking business, multiplying the money earned from the engraving and printing of his designs. These were sold and disseminated all over Europe, increasing his fame and, at the same time, acting as marketing devices for his already well-established name. In 1620, he was commissioned to design thirty-nine ceiling paintings for a Jesuit church. For the rest of his life, these jobs never stopped coming. It is estimated that Rubens produced some 2,500 paintings in the thirty years that he remained in Antwerp, something quite remarkable even by today's standards.

Throughout his career, Rubens remained guided by his sixth sense and grounded by the expertise developed during so many years of day-in and day-out work. He continued accepting a wide range of commissions from kings, queens, churches, and friends and enjoyed great wealth and recognition all over Europe.

It was the ability to balance instinct and logic that led Rubens to become the prolific artist-entrepreneur that he was. Had he not followed his gut and acted on his premonition about Antwerp, the conditions for Rubens in Italy or elsewhere in Europe would have been very different. By staying, he found favor with the royals and benefited from the pent-up demand that he found in his city. Once he gained momentum, he didn't let it go. He continued paying attention to his insights, offsetting them with a robust foundation: his ability to execute artistic commissions big and small.

SIXTH SENSE PLUS COMMON SENSE EQUALS GOOD DECISIONS

As the world becomes more complex, making the right decisions becomes harder. As humans, we use rational thinking all the time, but we have to trust that we can use our intuition as well. Logical thinking on its own doesn't produce creative ideas. Intuition alone borders on the vague and abstract. We must use our higher sense to help us make the right decisions. Our intuition gives us answers that could otherwise not be accessed through rational thinking, and many times it saves us from taking the wrong path.

The Otto Beisheim School of Management in Düsseldorf, Germany, studied managers who made business decisions that were purely intuitive, purely analytical, or combinations of both. Their research, published in 2017, showed that the purely intuitive approaches didn't work well because the managers had no idea how to interpret their intuitive cues. The purely analytical worked a little better but were still subpar, and those who combined the two fared the best.

In 1961, Ray Kroc acquired most of McDonald's Corporation, after having closed a deal with brothers Dick and Maurice McDonald. The company was to pay the founding brothers a percentage of the profits for life. It also was contractually obligated to get their approval for some decisions. Kroc was at the end of his rope with the brothers and their demands, which dragged down any business development that he wanted to implement.

Against the advice of his lawyer, who told Kroc not to make an offer to completely buy the brothers out, Kroc followed his intuition. It told him the gold mine that McDonald's was to become. He asked Dick McDonald to name the brothers' price. McDonald told Kroc they would sell for $2.7 million. Kroc was already overleveraged. He had to pay for the first deal with the McDonalds, and three insurance companies had lent him $1.5 million. Then one of Kroc's associates found John Bristol, a private investor in New York, who said that he would loan the $2.7 million plus interest plus 0.5 percent of the gross sales of McDonald's over three contractual periods. When reviewing the offer with his accountants, Kroc and his team determined that it would take thirty years to pay back the loan based on McDonald's then-current sales.

Furthermore, his lawyer told him, once again, that it was a huge risk and a very long-term financial commitment. This time, Kroc didn't waver. He had the same gut feeling he had when he decided to purchase that San Bernardino burger joint. He went with the private investor's money against the judgment of his advisors. He bought the McDonalds brothers out, and completely repaid the loan in 1972, a full twenty-four years earlier than projected.

CHART YOUR COURSE AND FOLLOW YOUR THOUGHTS AND INTUITION

In 2017, I was invited to preview an exhibition at the Museum of Sex in New York. *Quite an unusual place to have an art show*, I thought. I was curious and intuitively guided, so I went anyway. The show was titled *NSFW: Female Gaze*, and I was pleasantly surprised to discover the work of many female artists in their twenties that I hadn't known of before. Among the artworks was a life-size sculpture of a half-naked curvy woman sitting on a chair. I was impressed by the fact that it was made from papier-mâché. It looked like anything but. I also connected with the vulnerability of the subject and the artist's honest approach to the work. The caption said that the sculpture was by a Philadelphia-based artist, Shona McAndrew. That work intrigued me, and after I left the museum, I posted on social media a picture I took of it. That day, McAndrew started following me on Instagram. About a year later, I invited her to participate in one of my video series, focusing on the topic of today's beauty standards.

I was paying attention to her work and seeing a good evolution in the pictures she posted. She also exhibited in group shows, where I experienced the works in person. I even bought a couple of her paintings and a sculpture for myself. Although she had a lot of room for improvement, I sensed a great future for her and her work.

In early 2019, the owner of CHART Gallery in Tribeca asked me to curate a show. I thought a solo exhibition with McAndrew would be a good idea. The owner of the gallery was very unconvinced. My intuition told me it was the right thing to do. My rational mind had been following the fast advances the young artist was making. She was producing better paintings, refining her sculptures, meeting deadlines left and right, and seemed responsive and organized. The owner of the gallery was still reluctant. She was weighing her risks. She didn't necessarily want to have her gallery full of paintings and sculptures of naked women. She also didn't think she could increase the prices of an emerging artist's work to a point where the show would make sense financially. Last, she didn't think the quality was up to par. I was 99 percent sure about what I was suggesting.

After much push and pull, the owner of the gallery agreed. I told McAndrew the premise of the show. Up until then, she used only herself or her boyfriend as models. Now she was to find other people and also incorporate art history in her work. She said she was interested in exploring what women do in their private time and spaces—Do they do their hair? Wear green facial masks? Eat at midnight out of the fridge? I thought that was a great take and suggested she look at French Romantic artists who painted the ultimate male fantasy of female spaces—harems filled with odalisques such as those created by Eugène Delacroix and Jean-Auguste-Dominique Ingres.

McAndrew did so, asking her friends to send her smartphone pictures of themselves in the same poses of women found in those historical paintings. I wrote the press release explaining the show's premise. I also priced each of the stunning eight paintings and five sculptures she made for the show. I named the exhibition *Muse*.

Not only did every artwork sell out shortly after the opening, but people asked for more commissioned paintings. Jerry Saltz, the senior *New York* magazine art critic, named it one of the top ten shows of 2019. Had I not trusted my intuition, and backed it up with my rational findings, none of this would have happened.

BE CREATIVE BY MEETING IN THE MIDDLE

Mixing intuitive feelings with a rational process leads us to events that click and help spark the greatest ideas. This isn't about making haphazard, visceral, risky decisions or about dragging along, analytically second-guessing everything. That is barren territory leading nowhere creatively. It is about finding a comfortable middle. If anyone has a hunch and does a decent amount of due diligence, or has sufficient experience to forecast parts of the outcome, this is the space where creativity happens and even unproven ideas can blossom.

When rational thinking has taken over, it is a signal that you are stuck and it's time to break the habits that keep you there. Allowing yourself to break free from repetitive habits that kill creativity will also help you understand the aspects of a task or a project. By identifying the points that are flexible and those that are rigid, you can find creative ways to work around those that can be bent.

ALCHEMY LAB

Let your rational thinking and intuition guide you. One way to do this is by decreasing the amount of technology you use each day and letting intuition flourish alongside logical thinking. Technology has helped us tremendously, but it also has made our minds lazy and us slow to acknowledge our gut feelings. If you are stuck in the middle of a project and can't come up with ideas, or if you can't find a solution to a problem, ask yourself the following three questions:

1. Why are you doing what you are doing the way you are doing it?

2. Are there limiting circumstances that make you do what you are doing in a particular way? Let your rational mind answer.

3. List a variety of possibilities that you could implement if you didn't have a limiting element, an obstacle, or rules to adhere to. Let your intuition and your imagination do the talking this time.

If, based on this exercise, you can propose to your industry, your clients, your audience, or your team that they do things differently, go ahead and try. You will be perceived as a leader and an innovator.

22

Collaboration: 2 + 2 = 5

IN 1422, DONATELLO, the greatest sculptor of the fifteenth century, was commissioned to create a large bronze sculpture for Orsanmichele. This important building in the center of Florence combined the functions of a church and a grain market. Donatello was incredibly skilled with marble but didn't have the same dexterity with bronze casting. However, he had the presence of mind to be fully aware of that fact. Enter Michelozzo di Bartolomeo, an exceptionally experienced sculptor in bronze. He was part of Donatello's circle of friends. Donatello enlisted Michelozzo to help him finish the bronze casting of his sculpture faster.

THE WHOLE MAY BE GREATER THAN THE SUM OF ITS PARTS

This was a time where partnerships among painters and their apprentices were fairly common, but not between sculptors. However, Donatello realized how much time, physical space, and skill working with bronze required. In 1424, he formalized a collaborative partnership with Michelozzo. They would receive equal credit and split the profits. Additionally, they were free to take on their own individual projects, which they both continued to do.

The next commission Donatello and Michelozzo worked together was the tomb of Antipope John XXIII at the Baptistery of Florence adjacent to the Duomo. Donatello designed the effigy with the pope's face, the Madonna and Child, the mythological figures of the "virtues," the cherubs, and other ornamental elements. All the casting and polishing was Michelozzo's job, who also was in charge of designing the architectural settings.

When the twenty-four-foot tomb was completed in 1431, it became the tallest monument at the time in Florence. Moreover, there was no precedent for a three-dimensional gilded-bronze effigy. The tomb became an artistic reference of the early Renaissance and a precursor of many more funeral monuments in Florence and beyond. The collaboration between Donatello and Michelozzo lasted around seven years. They produced several important pieces, including the celebrated outdoor pulpit of St. Stephen's Cathedral in Prato, Italy.

Good artists are the ultimate collaborators. They need galleries, curators, and collectors. Depending on what they do, they may also partner with fabricators, printmakers, fashion labels, hospitality companies, toy manufacturers, or with anyone else who has the skills and expertise they may be lacking. What remains constant is how they bring their own influence in the quest for innovation to each project.

ART AND COMMERCE

The first collaboration between a fashion house and an artist dates back to February 1937. Salvador Dalí and his friend Elsa Schiaparelli, an Italian designer who had been making avant-garde dresses since the 1920s, decided to join forces. The result was an off-white silk organza evening gown. The fabric was imprinted with one of Dalí's favorite and recurrent motifs—a red lobster. Dalí saw it as a symbol of female sexuality. The dress was daring and innovative and almost immediately acquired iconic status. It captured a tremendous amount of attention when it was photographed by Cecile Beaton for *Vogue*. Today, the dress belongs to the permanent collection of the Philadelphia Museum of Art. It's constantly on loan to other museums for Dalí or Schiaparelli exhibitions. What the collaborators would have never guessed is that in the eighty years following the "Lobster Dress," thousands of visual artists would partner with fashion brands to create products ranging from one-off garments to entire seasonal collections.

CROWDSOURCING ORIGINALITY

Robert Rauschenberg was one of the greatest crowdsourcers of all time. He partnered with other visual artists, artisans, writers, musicians, engineers, actors, dancers, retailers, technicians, and printmakers from all over the world in his pursuit of innovation. He used to say, "With two people, you always have three ideas."

His work came to life when he started collaborating with choreographer Merce Cunningham and composer John Cage in 1952. They worked together on an event called *Theater Piece No. 1* at Black Mountain College, North Carolina, an experimental school that Rauschenberg had attended and where Cage and Cunningham taught.

But things started to take a more collaborative shape in 1954 when Rauschenberg officially began working with the Merce Cunningham Dance Company. Cunningham favored the idea that no medium should be subordinate to any other. He let Rauschenberg run wild and free with his ideas. During the ten years that followed, Rauschenberg contributed lighting, set, and costume designs to more than twenty of Cunningham's performances. Their incredibly bountiful collaborations were only revealed to all the parties involved at the final rehearsals. Only then did the dance, costumes, music, and sets come together. Rauschenberg recalled, "It was the most excruciating collaboration, but it was the most exciting, and most real, because nobody knew what anybody else was doing until it was too late."

The collaborations between Rauschenberg and Cunningham ended in 1964, and not coincidentally, that was the year when Rauschenberg became the first American and youngest (at the time) to win the prestigious Golden Lion for painting, the top prize at the Venice Biennale. That event opened the door to recognizing the United States' ascendancy over European artistic dominance.

Many historians, artists, and friends attributed Rauschenberg's success to his openness to all the ideas that flowed through his multiple collaborations. However, the one with Cunningham was particularly unique. Early in his career, it influenced Rauschenberg's creative freedom as well as his sense of improvisation, spontaneity, and surprise, attributes that took his work to the next level.

Collaboration was so central to his practice and added so much to him personally and professionally that in February 1977, in a rare interview with *ARTnews*, Rauschenberg said, "That's why I like dance, music, theatre, and that's why I like printmaking, because none of these things can exist as solo endeavors. Also, the best way to know people is to work with them, and that's a very sensitive form of intimacy."

ART AND COMMUNITY

In 2006, Theaster Gates started buying and renovating buildings in the South Side of Chicago intending to revitalize underprivileged neighborhoods. Gates is a multimedia artist from Chicago. He works in a variety of mediums including ceramics, paintings, sculpture, musical performance, and installation,

When Gates presented his revitalization plan to the local banks, they wouldn't finance it. They thought it was impossible to buy all these dilapidated buildings in the poorest neighborhoods of Chicago and turn them into art destinations to help communities at risk. Gates wasn't deterred; he purchased the buildings with his own money. He knew that eventually he'd find the support he needed for a collaborative partnership involving the local government, community organizers, and financial backers. The buildings he bought were then stripped down to their bare bones so they could be rebuilt. At the same time, Gates fabricated artworks out of the materials that would otherwise be discarded.

In time, art collectors and philanthropists got involved in Gates's project. Rahm Emanuel, then mayor of Chicago, took note and helped pave the way so Gates could benefit from tax credits and other fiscal incentives to keep reinvigorating the area. In the past fourteen years, a collaborative effort involving urban planners, government authorities, local communities, construction workers, and several artists have allowed Gates's real estate project and his aptly named Rebuild Foundation to buy and restore thirteen buildings that host libraries, performance spaces, artists in residence, reading rooms, exhibition galleries, and housing for low-income tenants.

BREAKING UP WITH TRADITION

A different type of collaboration happened when Damien Hirst partnered with Sotheby's. Hirst bypassed every conventional direct distribution channel that an artist has—dealers and galleries—and went straight to an auction house.

Hirst and Sotheby's joined forces in September 2008 and created an entire marketing plan around a sale. It brought more than twenty-one thousand visitors, who lined up to view the items that were going to be auctioned at Sotheby's in London. The first night, the sale was restricted to the most important collectors, with only 656 spots available for bidders. During the second day, there was a morning and an afternoon auction devoted to the remaining works. The sale, which Hirst titled *Beautiful Inside My Head Forever*, exceeded all expectations, grossing $200.75 million in the span of twenty-four hours. It became the most lucrative single-artist auction ever. On the cusp of a global recession, Hirst walked away with $172 million.

BETTER TOGETHER

Cobranding has become all the rage in the past fifteen years. When two (or more) companies collaborate in one or multiple products or services, they increase their customer base and bring something original to the marketplace.

In May 2015, Starbucks Coffee announced a partnership with Spotify. If you've ever been to a Starbucks, you will have noticed there's always music playing. Up until they partnered with Spotify, Starbucks sold CDs—music compilations that were part of the coffeehouse's culture.

The collaboration was structured so that every Starbucks employee in the United States received a Spotify Premium subscription (which lets users play music without ads and also skip and download songs). Starbucks employees could then generate playlists culled from twenty years of Starbucks music picks to play in their stores. They would also be available on the Starbucks rewards app.

Spotify would offer these playlists to all its users and brand them "Starbucks Playlists." Spotify users could buy streaming packages to earn "stars" exchangeable for currency using the Starbucks rewards programs app. The then 150,000 US-based Starbucks employees and 10 million members in its loyalty program would suddenly have access to Spotify's music packages. Spotify's 60 million users got access to a reward program they may not have even known existed.

In 2004, Swedish giant fast-fashion retailer H&M announced its first collaborative partnership with a luxury fashion designer. Then CEO Rolf Eriksen and his team had been asking themselves questions like these: How do we bring something cool and different to a consumer who spends $20 on a skirt? How do we keep ourselves relevant in a world that is drowning with options and constantly bombarded with information? The answer hit Eriksen—by partnering with other designers whose price points were aspirational for the H&M customer base. Eriksen would supply the manufacturing based on the other brand's designs and patterns. It would also provide worldwide distribution and a global marketing campaign.

Eriksen tapped Karl Lagerfeld to kick off what would become one of the most lucrative capsule collections that any fashion retailer has ever recorded. For the luxury labels, the collaboration opened a new consumer group, increased awareness, and expanded the reach of the brand by putting their names in over five thousand stores around the world. Following the successful Lagerfeld alliance, H&M continued expanding its collaborative partnerships, adding names such as Versace, Stella McCartney, Balmain, and Lanvin. Customers still line up to access the stores and crash H&M's website when it releases a new collaboration with a hot designer. After almost two decades, the model keeps working, generating immense revenues for H&M and insane exposure for the partner-designers.

In 2014, I was itching to play with products and saw an opportunity to design a capsule collection of limited-edition, luxury acrylic handbags with a trio of artists I love—Erik Parker, Kenny Scharf, and Carlos Rolón. I hadn't seen anything like what I wanted to do, and the risks were minimal.

Each artist agreed to license an artwork of my choice and to join in the marketing efforts. After weeks of painful trials with different acrylic manufacturers, I finally found the perfect solution. The manufacturing of the bags was done in parts. One factory made the bags, another printed the artwork, a third manufactured the suede linings. There was no manufacturer in the United States that could even understand what I was trying to do, let alone offer an integrated turnkey solution. I didn't want to produce two hundred units in China. I didn't even try to do it in Italy, where the costs would have skyrocketed. I bit the bullet and prayed that all three fabricators would do it right and on time. Not without hiccups, but my prayers were heard. Not only did I distribute the products through amazing concept stores in New York, Miami, Paris, Tokyo, and Hong Kong, but the capsule sold out everywhere. It was featured in magazines and newspapers ranging from the *Wall Street Journal* to *Vogue China*.

This initial success gave me some impetus to continue collaborating with other artists. In the three years that followed, I designed thirty more products. I expanded into scarves, leather bags, necklaces, and even ponchos. They, too, found similar success in sales and press. However, dealing with crazy manufacturers and retailers who didn't pay wasn't my cup of tea. In 2017, I decided not to sweat it anymore. I loved the experience and it was a win-win for everyone. We brought creative and original products to the marketplace. We did it at a time when artists' collaborations in the fashion space were either priced in the thousands of dollars or inexpensive, basic, and unoriginal, such as T-shirts that sold in volume but didn't really bring anything innovative for anyone.

Creative collaborations grow and expand in the right environment both for artists and entrepreneurs. They are an extraordinary way to expand into original offerings when each party has enough leverage. When you utilize the ideas and assistance of others and give your own, results take less time and significant dreams become obtainable. Whomever you partner with, make sure they have different skills and competencies from your own. That is what leveraging creative collaboration is all about. Your business or your practice may be small, but that isn't an excuse not to collaborate. You can hire freelancers and work with a variety of partners for distribution. You can also build connections with platforms that need what only you can offer. Big breakthroughs happen when people with a collective vision join together to share ideas, information, and work.

Be mindful that there needs to be lots of generosity and trust in creative collaborations. Make sure before signing any contract or agreeing to give away any of your ideas that everyone's roles, credits, contributions, and compensations are 100 percent clear. At the end of the day, collaborations multiply the human factor, and relationships can be messy. Keep in mind that your position of leadership is not about titles or flowcharts. It is about the influence you bring and the influence you receive. It is about how much bigger a creative collaboration can be as compared with the sum of its parts.

ALCHEMY LAB

- *Think about ideas that can bring about a creative collaboration:*

   Who can you partner with that is a completely unusual and
      unexpected choice?
   Where can you bring value that isn't obvious at first sight?
   Where can you sell or distribute your products or offer your services
      that isn't the norm? Think about places or spaces that aren't
      saturated with people who do the same things as you.

- *If you want to experiment and can bear the risk, could you collaborate with someone you trust so much that you could implement the Rauschenberg–Cunningham approach? If so:*

   1. Set the parameters of what the parties want to achieve
      collaboratively.

2. Have each party work independently on their part.

3. Meet again when each has something concrete to show. I wouldn't go so far as to recommend waiting until there's no chance to review or reverse course, but if you are daring, be my guest.

23

Connect the Dots:

Piecing the Puzzle Together

IT WAS DURING the blistering hot summer of 1991 that I visited Spain for the first time as my quinceañera gift. My friends and I had heard so much about Diego Velázquez and his masterpiece, *Las Meninas*, in school and during the trip that it seemed almost the sole reason for visiting Madrid. Since the 1970s, *Las Meninas* has been the most written-about and most researched painting in the world, as its not-so-apparent messages and interpretations keep bubbling up to the surface.

Why Las Meninas? *Didn't any other painter have similar skills to Velázquez? What did he do that is so special?* I wondered. When we got to the hexagonal gallery at the Prado Museum, where the painting has been exhibited continuously since 1990, the room was packed. Many people held pocket mirrors to see the painting from different angles, so it was almost impossible to appreciate the work. There were no phone cameras back then, but this was definitely worse than trying to take a selfie.

"What's going on?" we all asked Manolo, our guide. We were so puzzled by the mirrors. Manolo explained that all the secrets of *Las Meninas* resided in the mirror Velázquez painted in the background. It reflected two hazy figures representing King Philip IV of Spain and his wife, Mariana of Austria. *Las Meninas* was mystifying and alluring, but, for whatever reason, I couldn't figure out why. Manolo offered a series of explanations, but I was unable to follow his words. Maybe it was the heat inside the museum combined with my exhausted teenage mind and body that distracted me and made me move on. We had been traveling for a month. Sixteen years later and six months pregnant with my first child, I found myself again in front of *Las Meninas*. This time around, it was just me, my husband, and a curator, who told me of the many interpretations, symbols, and hidden connections that Velázquez left behind in his magnum opus.

HIDDEN SECRETS: PIECES OF THE PUZZLE

There are many reasons why *Las Meninas* has fascinated, puzzled, enamored, and obsessed people for more than 350 years. Yes, there's great execution and mastery in Velázquez's brushstrokes, light, shadows, and choice of colors, but mystery lies in connecting dots. These were the clues that were invisible to the viewer at the time but revealed through his work. Even the title seems like a riddle: *Meninas* is a word of Portuguese origin that was used to describe the young daughters of aides to the crown who were placed in the job of serving the infanta as ladies-in-waiting. Velázquez didn't name his masterpiece after the royals but after the underdogs.

It is worth understanding the context in which he painted *Las Meninas*. Velázquez was the court painter and a close friend of the king. He also was the private curator of the monarch's ever-growing art collection. Many of the paintings purchased under Velázquez's curatorship were incredible works by Raphael, Titian, and Rubens, which nowadays belong to the Prado. The king wanted Velázquez close to him and, in 1650, gave him a studio inside the Alcázar Palace in Madrid, located in an area that had become an art-display museum of sorts. The bottom line is that Velázquez was so intimate with the royals and had spent so much time hanging out with them that he observed and registered things not many were privy to, which he had to record.

In 1656, the king commissioned Velázquez a painting to memorialize his new family. His first wife and children had died, and he had married Mariana, with whom he had a child, the Infanta Margaret Theresa. She's the little five-year-old blonde girl, who's illuminated more than any other character in the painting. She's wearing an off-white, voluminous dress.

She is surrounded in the shadows by an entourage whose members include two young maids curtsying around the little princess. There are also two dwarves, a mastiff, a chaperone, and a female bodyguard. In the rear is the queen's chamberlain.

On the mirror on the back wall is the eerie reflection of the king and queen and, finally, Velázquez himself stands in front of his giant canvas looking straight on at us, the viewers, or, depending on the interpretation, at the king and queen, who may have been posing for him. This issue on perspective and who's looking at who is one of the debates that has occupied historians, writers, critics, and philosophers for two hundred years.

Some historians say that the reason Velázquez decided to paint the king and his wife in an opaque, shadowy, mirror reflection is because the king did not have a male heir. The succession of the throne had been settled in favor of John Joseph, an illegitimate son the king had with an actress. Maybe the painting contained a prediction on how the monarchy may cease to exist. The raison d'être for the inclusion of the royal couple continues to be a question centuries later for Spaniards and anyone who is interested in challenging arbitrary structures of power.

If Velázquez was indeed painting the king and queen as sitters reflected in the mirror, the size of the canvas in front of him makes no sense. Its enormous dimensions correspond proportionately to that of *Las Meninas*, which is ten feet tall. However, no single or double portrait at the time was ever made at such scale. Is Velázquez implying that the viewers, no matter how humble, can have the same perspective as the nobility? Does he want to equate the commoners and the royals?

The expression on Margaret's face is one of loneliness and responsibility. Although she is only five years old, Velázquez knew the rough life she had ahead of her—a life regimented by rules and controlled by others. Margaret is surrounded by much pomp and circumstance: people who kneel in front of her or are about to do so, and others who are looking to entertain her, catering to her needs and fulfill her every wish; however, she is just a child who wants to play.

History tells us that dwarves were kept as part of the court because of their astuteness and great intelligence. They were there as reminders to their masters of their own fleeting lives and that no crown or riches could change their fates at the time of their death. Interestingly, Velázquez includes them in the composition and dresses them magnificently. Their presence and that of the dog gives the impression that life for the royal family is a bit of a circus, a shallow façade.

Then there's Velázquez's self-portrait. He inserted himself in the scene for posterity. He didn't consider himself an artisan, as people in Spain tended to call painters. No, he was the king's friend, curator, and official painter. He wanted to elevate painting from a craft, as it was then considered, to a recognized art form and to immortalize himself with dignity. Velázquez was so confident about his role that the artworks hanging behind him show reproductions of two Rubens paintings of mythological scenes—Pallas and Arachne and Pan and Apollo. Both myths tell of jealous gods who couldn't stand the talents of mortals.

Velázquez's subtle message is that he wields the power of his brush with more strength, talent, and conviction than the king wields his own. Indeed, Velázquez continues to be more famous and more relevant than any previous Spanish monarch and will continue to be, long after the current ones have been forgotten.

CONNECT WHAT YOU SEE: AWARENESS IS EVERYTHING

That which is not apparent to the naked eye is a treasure trove for creative ideas. Innovative artists connect things that others miss. Being a great artist depends a lot on having novel ideas, researching and defending them, connecting dots that aren't obvious, and making them alive through art.

In the past thirteen years, I have observed that in order to connect ambiguities, innovative artists make use of three traits. First, they constantly sharpen their observation skills, seeing every detail in every story and in their surroundings. They look at the world, paying sharp attention to every level of detail. They use those observations and file them somewhere or write them down in their notebooks without overanalyzing them.

Second, once they have chosen which ideas to incorporate in a piece, or in a body of work, and often before creating anything physical, they take time to develop a significant point of view. Finally, they execute the connection of these ambiguous elements in a visually appealing way.

When I teach my creativity class, I ask my students to never disregard the first element: sharp observation skills. They ask me, "How do the artists develop those skills?" "By paying attention," I tell them, and look at their puzzled faces. They think my answer is too simple.

The truth is that most people are so distracted that even if they think they're paying attention, they aren't. What my students start to realize after the second or third week in the program is that many of the exercises in the class, which are also in this book, are aimed at making them pay more attention. This immediately increases their observation skills and their creativity. Additionally, I always tell them, "Spend more time looking at art." Actually, most artists constantly look at other artists' work. They either are studying and revisiting their idols or they go to galleries or museums to see current exhibitions.

Looking at art can polish observation skills in even the most improbable subjects. In 1998, Irwin Braverman, MD, professor emeritus of dermatology at Yale School of Medicine, realized that his medical students couldn't accurately describe what they were seeing in patients unless they had identified familiar patterns or seen similar cases before. In Braverman's words: "It occurred to me that if I were to ask them to describe some object that they were totally unfamiliar with—like a painting—they wouldn't know what was important or unimportant. They would describe everything in that object."

Braverman developed a course that is now mandatory for all first-year medical students. They have to look at each historical painting for fifteen minutes and extract the visual information and describe everything they see. They work mostly with eighteenth- and nineteenth-century paintings at the Yale Center for British Art.

The artworks recount historical events but contain ambiguous and contradictory information, just like a patient with unexpected symptoms. In a sense, the painting becomes the patient, and the students must figure out everything about it so they can form an accurate diagnosis. After taking the course, the students' ability to pick up on important details improves considerably. It also curbs their tendency to jump to conclusions and helps them look at their patients and the world in greater depth.

I have worked closely in many projects with Erik Parker, a Texas-born, New York–based artist, whose paintings are like visual hip-hop. They are filled with references about sociopolitics, contemporary culture, and history. His hieroglyphic series has the most loaded references that become obvious only when you come close and spend time with his work.

The pyramid-shaped paintings allude to both Ponzi schemes and the structure of society. He paints with acrylic and airbrush in the most wonderful vibrant neon colors, then adds small pieces of collage cutouts from underground magazines. These may include known or unknown characters that bring even more detail and meaning to each of his works. Parker knows that we live in an era of information overload. A painting is self-contained, so he hopes that viewers can look at it for a long time and find something new.

In his totems, which are canvases cut in the shape of a plank, he may paint the middle, leaving it as a hollow color block, adding all the collaged details on the edges. In this way, he nods to the value that the margins bring to the cultural conversation.

Parker tells me: "The idea of making art for me is being alive in this culture right here, right now, in this moment. My work of 1999 is very different from the work I do now." While he is fully engaged and present in the moment, he is gathering images from the internet, books, and his own past artworks. Everything is happening in real time. "I don't think about it too much. I try to have a lot of canvases around me that aren't finished, that's like a free flow. I pay attention to what's going on, but it's a highly intuitive process. I am also empathetic and connect with the viewer and what they are seeing or feeling. I want to communicate with people, but not trying to push an agenda. I try to find visual cues that bring people in so I can show them my world."

THE ROLE OF CREATIVE MINDFULNESS IN ENTREPRENEURSHIP

The act of paying attention to the now is intimately related to entrepreneurship. We serve a market that responds to the here and the now. We can choose to meet the needs of that market as is or to invent what they don't yet know they want. Pattern recognition is essential to coming up with creative ideas and opportunities that bring innovation to the marketplace. This is the phase where you need sharp observation skills. What undercurrents, movements, or circumstances are brewing under the surface that you could mine for gold? Changes in conditions, technology, and social, economic, and political circumstances are usually the places to start looking.

Actively and consistently paying attention and engaging with our world at large and with our specific industries also trains our eyes and minds to spot the opportunity for a creative service or product. You can do this by connecting independent events or trends that may not have an apparent relationship to one another. Taking notes of those events or trends, and allowing a couple of weeks or months to assess them, allows the brain to start thinking about them cohesively. Being nimble is crucial during this phase. Not fixating on one idea or another is key to the incubation of ideas. The most meaningful ones will stick to our minds. In the final step, you will connect these dots with a relevant offering.

During the phase of observation and pattern recognition, many entrepreneurs know there are elements worth connecting but also acknowledge that much refinement is needed. What's important is to gather the initial information that indicates where the opportunity may be.

That's what Brian Chesky and Joe Gebbia, two young graduates from the prestigious Rhode Island School of Design, did after moving in together as roommates in 2007 to an apartment on Rausch Street in San Francisco. Needing extra cash, they decided to rent their extra bedroom. Fully aware that the largest biannual world congress for the design community was coming up in San Francisco, they knew the hotel capacity was tight and the rates high. Why not rent the spare bedroom and offer breakfast for the conference? Maybe offer the living room too? After all, they had three air mattresses in the closet that they could blow up and fit with nice sheets.

The two men thought about all the ways they could offer this strange type of accommodation. For a couple of weeks they worked through their offer and how to promote it. They put together a rudimentary website and called the service AirBed and Breakfast. They promoted it as "two designers creating a new way to connect at the IDSA conference." The listing offered three air beds in their apartment for $80 each per night. Then they advertised it in design blogs and with the conference organizers.

They booked the three beds quickly and expected to receive some hippie backpackers. But the guests were professional designers who thought that Chesky and Gebbia's idea was useful in solving a problem. Chesky and Gebbia grilled their guests right there and then with questions about the experience. They learned that having the hosts around was helpful, having them prepare breakfast was great, being in that large apartment was more personal than being in a hotel, the price was unbeatable, and bonding with each other over design topics was a great bonus.

That's how the founders of Airbnb started connecting the dots. Over a two-year period, they kept experimenting and recruiting hosts and guests. They began recognizing patterns. They catered to people who didn't want to overspend, people who needed to go to places where the number of available rooms was very limited, homeowners or renters who wanted to make extra cash, and cash-strapped millennials with a desire for experience and adventure.

As they refined the concept and met with venture capitalists (most thought they were crazy), they also realized that the vacation rental business was up for grabs. Until then, they had focused on finding hosts in cities that were having conferences or large events. They hadn't thought of vacation travelers who might want to stay in someone else's house. As soon as vacation rentals entered the business plan, serious investor money started pouring in.

Connecting these dots led to the big launch of the Airbnb that we know today. It is a company that disrupted the hospitality industry, worldwide, by forging links between elements others missed: from designing a beautiful and easy-to-use website and app to making the process of browsing, booking, and paying a seamless one that never requires more than three clicks.

By the way, Chesky, Airbnb's CEO, spent a good part of his childhood and teenage years looking at art in museums. He wanted to become an artist. Gebbia, although a bit more partial to industrial design, is an art collector and enjoys visiting galleries in San Francisco or anywhere he may be. Whether through anecdotal experience or proven in medical school, it seems that looking at art does sharpen one's eyes and ability to connect invisible dots.

ALCHEMY LAB

Here are some ways to increase your observation skills:

- *Look at art often.* If you have an opportunity to visit a gallery or a museum once a week, great, but if not, choose a piece or two online—any figurative artwork, preferably from a museum's website or from Google Arts & Culture. This online platform offers high-resolution images and videos of artworks from cultural institutions around the world. Describe the painting—its details; textures; physical characteristics; facial expression(s); mood of the model(s); backgrounds, landscape, or interiors.

- *Pay attention to little details.* Go to a store and silently repeat to yourself for at least one minute the types of products and the brands you see on the shelves. Keep going until at least sixty seconds have elapsed.

- *Look for the oldest object around you, then find the newest thing.* Compare them, listing what they have in common as well as their differences. Write down which one will outlast the other and why.

In business, here are some ways to think about connecting the dots:

1. *Focus intently on developments in your industry.* Equally important, pay attention to the intersection of different industries, behaviors, cultures, disciplines, and beliefs. The more diverse and inclusive your perspective, the greater the opportunity for creativity.

2. *Generate a list of ideas you found in those seemingly disconnected areas.* Wait a few days to see which of those ideas are more appealing together.

3. *Recognize that opportunities emerge when shifts happen.* External conditions are adjusting all the time; noticing changing patterns in society, technological advances, and human behavior almost always will yield good results during a pattern-recognition hunt.

4. *Choose three or four ideas and come up with thoughtful ways to connect them.* This last step will require time. You must elaborate a cohesive and coherent way of associating and merging the elements.

24

Pivot: The Only

Constant Is Change

THE ANCIENT GREEK philosopher Heraclitus of Ephesus wrote, circa 500 BC, "The only thing that is constant in life is change." He couldn't have been more accurate. To be creative is to be willing to pivot. You may have found a formula that feels safe, but in the long run, safety equals stagnation. Your shifts don't need to be radical. They can come in many different shapes. They can progress at their own pace. Some call them "evolution," others "adjustment."

It's time to pivot if:

- you have too much competition to see a return,
- your efforts can't seem to pay off,
- you find it hard to differentiate yourself from others in the marketplace, or
- you are bored to tears, or feel stuck.

Artists have the luxury to change gears whenever they want. In the name of creativity and in order to nurture their own interests and desires, they may play with different mediums. Or they can cross from figuration to abstraction. They can start making paintings and then transition to sculptures. Maybe they stay with a gallery for a certain period, then decide to work on their own without any representation.

IF AT FIRST YOU DON'T SUCCEED, CHANGE COURSE

Piet Mondrian, the most famous Dutch abstract painter, and one of the greatest artists of the twentieth century, began painting human figures around 1893 without much success. Being intuitive enough not to stay in a place of failure, after 1901, Mondrian decided to take on landscapes, which had a better response from collectors and critics. Seven years later, he became interested in theosophy, an esoteric belief system that maintains that God can be known through spiritual ecstasy and intuition. This was a turning point for Mondrian, who experimented with ways to connect nature with the immaterial plane in his work. His paintings turned less representational and the objects more elusive. He moved to Paris in 1912. Influenced by cubism intermingled with his own theosophical beliefs, his first purely abstract paintings came to life.

But it wasn't until the outbreak of World War I that the Mondrian paintings he became famous for began to take shape. He was vacationing in the Netherlands and couldn't return to Paris. Forced to stay in his home country for the duration of the war, he found two other artists who were interested in new theories about art: Theo van Doesburg and Bart van der Leck. With them, Mondrian wrote and published a journal they called *De Stijl* (The Style) in 1917. This third shift was decisive. It pushed Mondrian in the direction he stayed in for the rest of his life—painting harmonious geometric compositions of vertical and horizontal lines, forming grids, and filling planes with an increasingly narrow color palette.

Upon his return to Paris in 1919, his new paintings started to get international attention for their novelty and simplicity. In the end, Mondrian gained international recognition and a spot in every art history book printed since. Mondrian's geometric paintings were, and continue to be, a major influence in art, design, fashion, and architectural movements including color field painting, abstract expressionism, and Bauhaus. Had Mondrian not pivoted, the modernist era would have looked vastly different.

WHEN THE MOOD CHANGES, GO WITH IT

Niki de Saint Phalle was one of those artists whose pivots gave her worldwide fame. In 1960, at the age of thirty, Saint Phalle was the only female member of a group of artists who lived in Paris and called themselves Les Nouveaux Realistes (The New Realists). They were looking to engage with the new realities of city life—industrialization, mass media, and consumption.

Saint Phalle was into radical performances using readymade objects and canvases. She attached bags of liquid paint to targets; then shot them with a rifle several times so the art started "bleeding." It was quite a violent spectacle. She performed in galleries and outdoor spaces as people watched while she demonstrated anger. It left spectators with a heavy feeling of despair and anxiety.

In 1963, Saint Phalle shifted—no more shooting, no more splats of bleeding paint. All the aggression subsided and she began working on colorful, life-size female dolls made of papier-mâché. These represented women in different roles—mothers, brides, prostitutes, and sometimes sorcerers. She called them *Nanas* (French slang for "chick"). They were curvy and buoyant, representing pure femininity and fertility. The colors and patterns with which she painted each doll started pale and with time became stronger and more whimsical.

This shift constituted what would become the trademark of Saint Phalle's practice for the following thirty-five years of her career. Fun, successful, and financially rewarding, the *Nanas* were shown and acquired by museums and collectors all over the world. Soon they became bigger in size and the medium changed to polyester resin and fiberglass, so they could live outdoors as well.

This change served Saint Phalle well, especially when it came to working with materials that were resistant to the elements. In 1979, her Italian friend Marella Agnelli and her brothers Carlo and Nicola Caracciolo invited Saint Phalle to build her own sculpture park in a fourteen-acre piece of land they owned in southern Tuscany.

For the next two decades, in parallel to large public art commissions, product design, and launches that included perfumes and inflatable toys, Saint Phalle worked tirelessly on her *Tarot Garden*. It opened in 1998 and is home to twenty-two monumental sculptures. Each represents the most important tarot cards such as the Magician, Lovers, Empress, and High Priestess.

Some of the sculptures are the size of a house, such as the Sphinx with mirrored blue hair. Saint Phalle lived inside it when she built the garden. This park represents her most important work. It is radically removed from the performances rooted in bitterness and dissatisfaction. In her own words, "provided you're open to it, life is full of the unexpected, relative to what can happen to you tomorrow."

NEW SITES, NEW INSIGHTS

Katherine Bernhardt is an artist with whom I've worked on product collaborations. I have also placed her paintings in the collections of many of my clients. She's fun, uncomplicated, and attuned to her surroundings and her own artistic voice. When she explores a subject, she mines it until she can get no more out of it. She's prolific and fast. Her canvases are gestural and full of vivid colors.

For many years, Katherine painted women, mostly inspired by fashion models and glossy magazines. Then she shifted and made giant paintings of Swatch watches. Following a trip to Morocco, she became obsessed with design patterns and the colors of the rugs sold in souks. She then produced a purely abstract series memorializing what her eyes had absorbed in her travels. One day, walking around Union Square in New York, she saw graffiti that depicted a popsicle, a smiley face, a watermelon, and a dollar sign. She took a picture and off she went.

That graffiti wall marked another significant shift for Bernhardt. It opened the door for her still lifes. In the beginning, they included exuberant tropical fruits, ice cream cones, tacos, parrots—anything that interested or inspired her. Soon she started combining the still lifes with Moroccan rug patterns or African textile shapes. That mélange constitutes some of the most important paintings of her career.

In the same vein, she continues to make amazing paintings tackling a vast range of subjects—from Pac-Man to the Pink Panther and anything in between. Nothing is off-limits, and as a wildly creative artist, she can't be pigeonholed.

ONE DECISION AWAY FROM STRIKING GOLD

Today, things get old really fast. Being nimble is paramount to creativity and allows for easier shifts. We are compelled to evolve because we have so much happening around us. Business pivots are necessary for survival. Even if a part of a company remains faithful to its original vision and holds on to its core, many other parts have to realign to serve the demands of an ever-changing marketplace. The closer you are to reality and the more you pay attention to the events and people in your world and beyond, the easier it is to pivot.

Sometimes a pivot is the last resort in saving a business. Sometimes it requires only repurposing what is already in place. In 1927, Cincinnati entrepreneurs Cleo and Noah McVicker bought Kutol Products, a cleaning products company. Kutol had a successful concoction that cleaned the surfaces of wallpaper inside homes, removing the residue from coal heating.

In the early 1950s, people began transitioning from coal to natural gas heaters, and Kutol's core product lagged on shelves. It wasn't needed anymore. The company was almost bankrupt, when the McVickers' adult sons were called to help. One of them recalled a magazine article that said children liked to play with wallpaper-cleaning putty. Prompted by this piece of information, Noah McVicker created a nontoxic, off-white version of the compound and added an almond scent to it. Red, blue, and yellow versions were soon in development and a new company called Rainbow Crafts was formed.

In 1955, after attending a manufacturing convention for school supplies and presenting their repurposed modeling compound, Play-Doh debuted in every elementary school in Cincinnati. The putty was so popular that soon after it became a part of every school in the United States. In 1965, the McVickers got a patent for Play-Doh and that same year they sold Rainbow Crafts to General Mills for $3 million. In 1971, Tonka bought the company; and in 1990, Hasbro acquired it and continues to manufacture Play-Doh today. From 1956 to 2018, more than three billion cans of Play-Doh have been sold all over the world.

In other cases, pivots are turns that stand on what already exists in a business to jump-start something different. When Michio Suzuki, a Japanese inventor who had dedicated thirty years of his life to the manufacturing and improvement of looming machines, felt that he was hitting a creative wall, he started experimenting with automotive technology. After all, pedals and engines were needed in both looms and cars. In 1952, the Suzuki Loom Works launched a motor-assisted bicycle. Two years later, embracing the success and demand for the new invention, the company changed its name to the Suzuki Motor Corporation, as it is known today.

KNOW WHEN TO HOLD 'EM; KNOW WHEN TO FOLD 'EM

The day I quit my law practice was the greatest and most important pivot of my professional life. It was very scary and very risky, but I couldn't betray myself and my creative instincts anymore. The pain of staying in that law firm was unbearable. That was a radical change of 180 degrees. But not every transition has to be like that.

Effective pivots come mostly from being present and aware of what's happening around us and knowing when to adjust our internal GPS. I stopped working with design clients because I discovered after several years that my mission was not to place rugs in people's homes. I also had more headaches than satisfactions, even though the money doing that job was really good.

I have left many things behind, but I have kept the core of my business— the inexhaustible exploration of art in all its forms—intact. I still decide what art to buy and how to display it in my clients' homes and offices and in galleries when I curate a show. I still have more outlets of expression than I ever dreamed of. If I ever want to do a one-off design project, I may.

How do I know when I want to pivot? When something doesn't give me any more joy. It is as simple as that. It is not a capricious and whimsical decision. Pivots should come after serious evaluation. And these transitions aren't about wanting a rosy path either. After all, owning a business and being an entrepreneur is filled with challenges. There are always problems to solve, things that go wrong, people who backstab. That comes with the territory. But since I know so well the feeling of being miserable from my lawyer days, I am incredibly truthful to myself in that regard.

Sometimes the market will tell you to shift when you see your balance sheet numbers going down month after month. Don't sit for too long on the information that is in front of you telling you it is time to make a change. But at the same time, don't adjust so often that you lose your essence.

Every pivot is another opportunity to become creative. That should be the main driver behind how you design the shift once it is in motion. The point of a business change is to bring something new and different that benefits a segment of the clients you serve or those you want to serve. Every pivot should be grounded on intuitive nudges and authenticity. Change creates growth and disruption and fuels the engine for the next step.

ALCHEMY LAB

- *You don't need to be radical.* When something in your business doesn't feel right, but your revenues are stable, think about gradual shifts. You can implement changes in stages until you reach an optimal point that balances profits and creativity. It is time for a progressive pivot if you are feeling the heat from investors, your numbers are going down, or your competitors are crushing you. Business shifts, adjustments, and evolutions demand a certain level of speed. As soon as you start feeling discomfort and hear your intuition's repeated messages, have the guts to lay out what a change or a new path would look like—and follow it.

- *Stand on what you've built.* Take inventory. Make a list of everything you have created to puzzle out the foundation for your next step.

- *Listen to your clients.* Watch the market's behavior closely. Most entrepreneurs, when they hit a plateau or a roadblock, try to solve the issue without first asking their clients how they feel, what they like, or what they are interested in. It isn't about having your clients dictate your business; it is about gauging their honest impressions to see what you can adjust.

- *It's time to pivot.* If you are repeatedly hitting the same or similar roadblocks, stop trying to solve the problem and finally consider taking a turn.

25

Inventing the Future:

Keeping Two Steps Ahead

Everything in this book should be a stepping-stone in your creative repertoire. It should lead you to the point where you can invent your own future
and profit from it. It is the combination of your vision, autonomy, authenticity, empathy, curiosity, intuition, risk-taking, daydreaming, improvisation,
and observation skills—along with your ability to use pockets of silence and
willingness to embrace your failures—that will help you come up with ideas
of value you can materialize.

Many artists have historically deployed new technologies and anticipated
cultural and societal changes in unexpected and often prescient ways. Artists are game changers, innovators, shakers, dreamers, and revolutionaries
who thrive on the quest for the new. Our modern-day entrepreneurs do the
same.

Throughout history, artists have been ahead of their time even when
they didn't know it. Being an artist and having to depend on their creativity
to execute their wildest ideas means they always live in a world of different
possibilities. When artists create new worlds, they are free to play with any
aspect of it—the timeline, the laws of physics, the places, and how people
feel and behave. For many artists, the future can be foreseen to a degree.
They think outside of what is possible and can be as far-reaching as they
want. Many artists move the aesthetic needle. Others are active in social

spheres and can effect profound changes in society. They aren't afraid of seeing everything as a work in progress and subject to change.

Part of the reason artists can predict societal changes, spot unseen trends, and connect invisible dots is because they can imagine new possibilities, different worlds, and alternative futures. They also possess adaptability of the mind and the spirit. They are always using their intuition and observing their surroundings in great detail. Artists are idea-generating people, and many times their ideas are prescient. Many artists also embrace diversity. They love traveling, learning about other disciplines, and connecting with different people of different backgrounds.

A "NEW AGE" VISIONARY

Hilma af Klint was the inventor of abstract art. You may have never heard of her. She was a classically trained Swedish artist. She also was interested in metaphysics. She was constantly writing in her journals—asking herself about her position in the universe, looking for cosmic perspective and its relationship to humanity. Her concerns were much bigger than just art. She wrote about how thoughts carried energy and how atoms change and affect matter. "A thought crystalizes the universe into geometric figures," reads one of her journal entries in the early 1900s.

In 1896, she was drawing freely scribbled shapes and spirals. That was exactly seventy years before Cy Twombly did the same type of work and became world-famous for his gestural, large-scale monochrome paintings. In 1906, at the age of forty-four, after twenty years of artistic practice, af Klint painted her first series of abstract paintings. She accepted a commission to produce paintings for an esoteric temple, which she created over the following nine years (with a four-year pause in the middle). During this time, she created 193 works. She allowed the spiritual to guide her creations. Her first series was *The WU/Rose Series*, a group of twenty-six compelling oil-on-canvas paintings of similar size (around twenty by fifteen inches each), in which abstract shapes resembling snails, math formulas, and planets in shades of blues, greens, and yellows collided with symbols, letters, and words. Nobody had seen anything like these paintings before. Nobody had ever done such a thing.

The following year, in 1907, af Klint produced some of the most spectacular works I have ever seen—a series she called *The Ten Largest*. Comprised of ten works on paper painted with tempera and mounted on canvas, each measures almost eleven feet in height by almost eight feet in width. Each painting describes a phase of life, from early childhood to old age. Each one possesses the most luminous, fresh colors ranging from a powdery lilac to a deep yellow, from a soft pink to a vibrant orange. The magnificent compositions include circles, helixes, calligraphy, symbols, and curves. Each color has a meaning—blue for the female spirit, yellow for the male, pink for love.

Nobody understood af Klint's paintings. Besides, she was a woman, and women at that time didn't write history. In 1908, Rudolf Steiner, the German founder of the Anthroposophical Society (another esoteric school that aimed to develop the spiritual faculties of its followers), traveled to Stockholm and met with af Klint. He persuaded her that her paintings were not for this world. He told her not to show them. Nobody would understand them, he said.

Af Klint deeply admired Steiner, so this was a huge blow. She stopped painting for four years. Oddly enough, Steiner kept some of her work for himself. He brought them to his office, which, the Russian artist Wassily Kandinsky, who lived in Munich, allegedly visited in 1908. He had read Steiner's text *How to Know Higher Worlds*. In 1911, five years after af Klint's original series of abstract paintings, Kandinsky exhibited *Komposition V*, an abstract canvas measuring nine feet in width by six feet in height, in a group show in Munich. It was regarded as the origin of abstraction—the future of art. Kandinsky stole the show as the pioneer of abstract art and became the one to make history.

Meanwhile on the island of Munsö in Lake Mälaren, eastern Sweden, af Klint went back to her *Paintings for the Temple* in 1912. Without the influence of any other artist, for the rest of her life she continued producing abstract work. It was avant-garde, unique, and extraordinary.

She died in 1944 at the age of eighty-one. She left a note in her notebooks bequeathing all 1,200 paintings and works on paper, plus 26,000 pages in her journals, to her nephew Erik af Klint. She also left a few instructions. Her work was not to be shown for twenty years after her death. The *Paintings for the Temple* were to be kept together. Nothing was to be sold.

It wasn't until the late 1980s that European and American museums started showing her work. In 2018, the Guggenheim Museum in New York opened af Klint's first retrospective in the United States, aptly named *Paintings for the Future*. It became the most visited exhibition in the eighty-two-year history of the museum, welcoming six hundred thousand people over a period of six months.

Af Klint had no ordinary perspective. She had a holistic view of the world that encompassed many different disciplines and realms. She formed and materialized these in her art. This was at least fifty years before the New Age movement, when spirituality would be popularized in books and on TV shows by people like Oprah Winfrey, Marianne Williamson, and Deepak Chopra.

How did af Klint invent the future? While it is impossible to elaborate exactly what crossed her mind and how she arrived at abstraction, af Klint left us many clues in her notes. (Her circle of friends and family also told her story for posterity.) What we can deduce is, first, she was very attuned to interests outside of art. She was curious and closely followed the latest scientific developments—the discovery of radioactivity by Henri Becquerel in France in 1896, the proof that atoms were divisible from British physicist J. J. Thomson in 1897, the theoretical framework for quantum physics proposed by German Max Planck in 1900, and Albert Einstein's theory of special relativity in 1905. These topics fascinated her and she studied them seriously.

Second, she traveled in Europe and got to know other cultures. She mingled with other people who opened up her mind and her perspective. Finally, she belonged to a mystical society, where she practiced meditation, prayer, and other rituals, which made her deeply intuitive. She often wrote and said that her abstract paintings "came to her" through energies outside of her body. In her journals, there is a note saying, "Only for those prepared to leave their familiar life behind, will life emerge in a new gown of continually expanding beauty and perfection. But in order to attain such a state, it is necessary to achieve stillness in both thought and feeling."

THE ART OF BEING PRESCIENT

Another future-making artist was Nam June Paik, an artist born in Seoul, who studied art in Tokyo. He later moved to Munich to study music and to collaborate with composers and musicians. He finally moved to New York in 1964 to work as an artist. Paik is considered the father of video art, but he also pioneered many technological advances. His installations, sculptures, and performances were a celebration of technology and its interactions with humans for the betterment of society.

He anticipated many of the technologies of our time by several decades. His 1963 work *Participation TV* was a TV set that lets the participant control the visuals on the screen by speaking or making sounds on a microphone. As people made a noise, the screen instantaneously translated the sounds into lines, graphs, and other forms. This was totally revolutionary at the time. Many people dismissed it, saying it wasn't even art. Today, when we look back at Paik's experiments, we can see how he anticipated twenty-first-century discussions about social interaction through multimedia platforms.

In 1971, he also created a famous piece called *TV Cello*. It featured a nude female cellist, his longtime collaborator Charlotte Moorman. She wore only modified sunglasses that operated as a video screen. It was the first time that an artist had played with the idea of wearable technology, forty years before the Google Glass or virtual-reality goggles hit the market.

Almost twenty years before the World Wide Web opened to the world in 1991, Paik wrote about his plans using the term *electronic superhighway* in a paper for the Rockefeller Foundation published in 1974. In that document he explained that "building of a new electronic superhighway will become a huge enterprise." He gave an example of connecting New York with Los Angeles by means of an electronic telecommunication network that operates by strong transmission, continental satellites, and wave guides. He later upgraded to laser beam fiber optics.

What Paik was doing, first, was creating a world of technology and human interaction, at a time where it didn't exist. He paid close attention to the movements of his time. For example, TV became mainstream in the 1950s—the big advancement of the moment—and he capitalized on it by adapting and incorporating screens in his work. His life had been informed by change and diversity, having lived in Asia, Europe, and the United States. He also was educated in visual arts and music. He was looking at the incipient trends and connecting the dots. He tried to humanize computers and, in some cases, also highlighted the dangers that excessive technology can bring to society at a time when technology wasn't within everyone's reach as it is now.

Andy Warhol also anticipated social change. He often insisted that popularizing art and making it for the masses was the way to go—both to fuel his own prolific practice as well as his burgeoning bank account. He explored every artistic medium that existed in his day—painting, sculpture, silkscreening, photography, and film. He completely transformed our perception of commercial imagery and our interpretation of what constitutes art.

In 1968, Warhol had an exhibition at the Moderna Museet in Stockholm. The program included Warhol's famous quote, "In the future everyone will be world-famous for fifteen minutes." That was forty years before reality TV, YouTube, and Instagram catapulted thousands of people to "fame" that lasted a season or two at most.

Warhol was a prescient artist who understood the power of photography and the importance of cultivating and maintaining a public persona—not only his own but that of others. He was infatuated with celebrities and had the ability to connect emotionally with people and make them feel important. Veiled under his inexpressive countenance, Warhol was empathetic enough to see people's needs, sense their insecurities, and feed their vanities, obsessions, and narcissism. He made millions of dollars making commissioned portraits of pop stars, socialites, politicians, and anyone who had the money to pay and the charm to convince him to do it.

He saw trends, felt human emotions, spotted people's needs, and combined them all together using the mediums he knew. He ultimately leveraged everything in the most successful branding and business enterprise of any artist to date.

THE RULE OF THREE

What are the three things that af Klint, Paik, and Warhol had in common? First, they were paying close attention to the world around them. Second, their interests were manifold, and they figured out ways to connect them in their work. Third, they invented their own worlds—one made abstract-mystical paintings, the other humanized technology as art, the third made pop culture an accessible space for all.

If these three elements were to be translated into today's world, they would pinpoint how to find undercurrent movements and how to set our own trends. That's the nest where the golden goose lays all her eggs.

These three elements are constantly running like software in the back of the minds and attitudes of some of the most innovative entrepreneurs in history such as Sergey Brin and Larry Page, aka the "Google Guys." When Brin and Page were students at Stanford in 1996, the internet was still a preschooler—a five-year-old novelty that had just started revolutionizing communications and the way people did business.

Both guys were fully immersed in learning the ins and outs of the most relevant invention of their time. Brin was very curious about data mining because he loved math and algorithms. He was also very interested in technology, consumer behavior, and understanding how all these elements interacted in the brand-new space of e-commerce. He forecasted that in a decade, people would have more access to electronics and to the internet—more than anyone in the world had ever dreamed.

Page was also into numbers and technology but had a different interest: digital libraries. He was convinced that books would become files rather than physical objects. One day, Page was browsing AltaVista, the leading search engine of the moment, when he saw that in addition to the list of websites, the results included something odd called "links." These links were pages that linked to the main site being searched, like footnotes in academic research connecting back to the main source of a quotation. That meant that the more mentions a site had, the more links showed up in the results. Therefore, Page concluded, a website with more links connected to it must then be the most important.

That's not how AltaVista worked. It wasn't very fast, and the searches were inaccurate. The ranking of websites wasn't properly organized. A lot of time was wasted trying to find the right information. By paying close attention to those links, Page left the digital library project behind and asked Brin for his data-mining expertise to see if they could build a better search engine.

In 1998, they applied for a patent for their improved invention—a faster, better, and more relevant search engine than AltaVista. They called it PageRank. Another friend nicknamed the project "googol" after the mathematical formula for 10^{100}. Brin and Page incorporated a company called Google, Inc. Even with seed money, later venture-capital funding, and improving the engine's capabilities month after month, there was a big problem to solve—how would Google make money?

It was Brin again who, by paying close attention to the landscape, started studying a company called GoTo.com. This engine was generating revenues by selling ads accompanying searches in simple lists intermingled with the results and not with distracting banners and pop-ups. Eureka! Page had found his own golden goose.

The Google Guys combined things that already existed—search engines, data mining, and ad sales. In the process they created their own world in which everything is data, everything is searchable. As a consequence, everything we think of can be retrieved even before we ask for it explicitly. You may have never bought anything on Amazon, opened a Facebook account, or owned an iPhone, but I'm 99.9 percent sure that you have used Google more than once.

Brin and Page invented a coherent product, paved with numerous additions along the way. They created a world with a clear set of rules, which they sometimes knowingly broke to expand and explore new territories. Google continues to evolve, using what they already have and combining things that already exist into new products—Gmail, Google Maps, Google Drive, Google Docs, and myriad of other add-ons and improvements that keep us going back for more. On a conversation organized by TED, Page was asked what state of mind had enabled him to think about the future and change the present. His answer was that "lots of companies don't succeed over time. What do they fundamentally do wrong? They miss the future. I try to focus on that: What is the future really going to be? And how do we create it?"

Developing a business world of your own enables you to define the rules. You can expand it, change it, and refine it later—it is yours to play with. That's why I opened my business. I wanted to let my creativity shape my world of art, artists, collectors, beauty, design, community, access, ideas, content, and products. I wanted the freedom to adjust the course when I feel off-track or to meet the market's new demands.

THE PRESENT IS PROLOGUE

The future is embedded in the present. Pay close attention. When you see small changes happening, look for other signs pointing in the same direction. Ask yourself, "What are the things in my industry that have changed dramatically in the past twenty years and have accelerated in the past five?" One change that directly pertains to my business is that the written word has been replaced by visual representation. Literary narrative has been displaced by visual arts, illustration, and the image, whether static or the moving one. The most effective form of communication nowadays is where there is a combination of words and visuals. That is a change that started with the emergence of mainstream TV in the 1950s. It continued growing with the heyday of the advertising industry in the 1970s. It exploded with the internet in the 1990s. It became the norm with the advent of social media in the twenty-first century. I keep following that thread because I know it will bring more changes in the next five, ten, and twenty years.

How you benefit is by employing the tools and methods in part III: deconstruction, aggregation, repetition, playing with dualities, and cross-pollination. Start looking for the invisible—things no one else has seen—and connect those dots with your narrative. And please, make sure to write it all down. Add some emotion to the story, if appropriate, to forge a direct connection with your customers or your audience; push their boundaries (or yours). Think of worlds that don't yet exist. Engage your mind by thinking about possibilities that are as far-reaching as you can envision.

I predict that in the next few years there will be a new leadership equation that will have a foot in the creative world at large. Traditionally, important decisions were made by political and corporate leaders. In the future, creative individuals like artists, architects, designers, entrepreneurs, and idea-makers with novel concepts will also have a seat at the table deciding how we shape our policies, our society, and our culture.

All ideas are critical for innovation. Without ideas and without executing them, we are just going backward. The point is to invent the future. That can be done only with creativity.

ALCHEMY LAB

- *The most accurate way to predict the future is to be deeply connected to the present.* It sounds contradictory, but it is the truth.

- *Identify a movement that you have seen in your industry or outside of your industry that is new and that you find interesting.* Record it, write it down, and see how to connect with and adapt it to other aspects of your business before it becomes mainstream.

- *To tell if a movement is worth exploring and not just a fad, use this formula:*

  Look at small, undercurrent events. These can't be too obvious; definitely not what everybody already knows. Look at the margins. Look at your kids. What are they playing with? What keeps them busy?

Do these events push people to take action, do things differently, or to try something new?

Do these events repeat and multiply so that they could live in the intersection of a variety of areas and industries?

Do they fulfill a human need?

If you answered yes to the last three questions, you may have discovered an incipient trend worth exploring.

- *Do you have an appetite for spotting the next big thing?* Take this test:

  Were you an early adopter of social media?

  Or even better, an early investor?

  Or did you feel skeptical, like a friend of mine who said "that ridiculosity of Facebook will be dead by 2010"?

  Why do you think social media has been such a revolutionary and popular way of communication and those who invented and invested in the platforms benefited beyond belief financially?

  Do you remember when Instagram was a simple photosharing app called Burbn and had one hundred users?

  Who spotted that opportunity? Those who saw that even though Burbn had one hundred users, with the proper name and interface, everyone would want to be a part of it. Why? Because it makes its users take action: posting, watching, commenting, giving likes. It also lives at the intersection of technology, business, communications, and culture. Finally, and most importantly, it satisfies the human needs of validation, connection, belonging, acceptance, and a sense of community that so many crave.

- *Invest in your own diversity.* Being diverse means that you have sufficient desire to spread your interests over a variety of fields.

Whatever your diverse interests are, invest in them with curiosity and intent. Applying the concept of diversity by design, with intentionality, is a critical aspect of being able to see the future and capitalize on those opportunities early on.

Epilogue

THAT NIGHT OF May 6, 2020, ater almost two months of lockdown, when I found that Reuters video of my grandfather being released from his kidnapping, I did three things: The first was that I posted an homage about him on Instagram—his picture, a snippet of the video, and a brief recount of his story in the caption. My second action item was that the next day, following an intuitive nudge, I started writing this book. The third is that when I couldn't figure out certain things in my business, felt stuck, or feared for the uncertainty of our times, I began to ask, "What would Enrique do?"

Those four words brought immense peace to my days, as the grave voice and image of my calm and ever-resourceful grandfather guided me. Sometimes I imagined him telling me that if he survived having a gun against his temple and being in the jungle with duct tape around his eyes and a straitjacket keeping his arms immobilized for almost a month without knowing if and when he'd be able to return to his home, I could also survive the pandemic and all of its consequences.

My grandfather always said that crises are great moments to pivot and to invent new things. He told me that even when he lost all his money paying for the ransom, he still had his health, his family, and his creativity: his most important and valuable resource. In my recent imaginary conversations with him, he reminded me that he bounced back and lived a full life, traveled with my grandmother, painted on his patio, went to every party he was invited to, started a new business, employed people, helped customers, and kept a positive outlook even in the face of the worst catastrophes, political upheavals, and personal losses.

Another night, he whispered in my ear and reminded me that our best ideas are worth sharing and that creativity without generosity isn't such.

He told me to keep going, to serve my clients with joy, and to keep my eyes wide open for clues, like the game we used to play when I was a child and he had hidden stuff around his house in a treasure hunt for me to find. When Enrique died in 2005 at the age of eighty, he had still been going to work every day and had useful and valuable ideas until the last day of his life.

Exactly six weeks after I posted that homage of him on Instagram, I was doing one-on-one consulting on Zoom with some of the students who had finished my four-week creativity program online. One of those sessions was with a woman, an attorney in her midthirties who worked at a large and prestigious law firm in Washington, DC. When our time was almost up, she told me something shocking: "I don't want to be creepy or anything, but I wanted to let you know that I was born in Venezuela, and when I saw that post on Instagram about your grandfather, I immediately connected the dots and asked my father if he knew Enrique Dao. And he did! He is related to some of the people who worked at the same bank as your grandfather did when he got kidnapped. My dad agrees with you—he also thinks Enrique was one of the best people he ever met."

I was so astonished with my student's revelation, and caught by complete surprise, that a heavy stream of tears flowed out of my eyes. Her words confirmed what had been in my heart the whole time. I then knew that Enrique had left all the clues for me to plow through and finish writing this book.

My banker-artist-physician-entrepreneur grandfather, my very own creative alchemist, exhibited all the attributes, practiced all the habits, and used all the tools I wrote about in these chapters. I hope that his story, and those of the others I have shared, have inspired you to take action in your own life. I trust you are now convinced that creativity is not an elusive trait meant for a select few. Creativity is the strongest, most powerful, and authentic amalgamation of qualities that any human can possess, so much so that no other species on our planet is equipped with creative thinking the way we are. Keep coming back to these pages when you need a boost of energy, feel short on motivation, or are looking to reinvigorate the alchemical faculties that allow you to turn your ideas into gold.

Acknowledgments

WRITING A BOOK is a long and arduous task. So many people are always involved, and thank God for that!

I want to thank my husband, Marcio, for his unwavering support when I needed it the most. You backed me and encouraged me in the pursuit of a new career at a moment when it was just a leap of faith. And to my sons, Daniel and Oliver—thank you for coming into my life to reinforce the idea that we are in this world to fulfill a creative purpose, where we can only be whole if we are happy doing what we love.

I also want to express my deep gratitude to:

Chelsey Saatkamp for being the best, and I mean it: early reader, editor, cheerleader, and the most efficient and reliable millennial I'll ever know.

Bhano Arbind—without your help, love, and dedication, I wouldn't have had the time to write this book.

Peter Koloff for helping me bring my vision to hundreds of thousands of people.

Steve Troha and Jan Baumer, my extraordinary agents and people who deeply believe that the written word can change the world for the better. Thank you for what you do.

Sara Kendrick, my acquisitions editor, who fiercely backed me up in this project and accommodated (almost) every one of my requests.

Sicily Axton, for coming up with so many interesting marketing solutions and for all the time dedicated to this.

Jennifer Joy, for helping me amplify the message in this book without diluting it.

Rita Black and Julie Trelstad, for being a sounding board throughout this process.

Jill Dearman, for your invaluable suggestions on the first version of my manuscript.

Allison Zuckerman, for your generosity in accepting my invitation to use your art for the cover of this book. There was no one better for it.

Ellen Coleman and Jeff Farr, for your incisive and sharp edits.

All my students at Jumpstart. Your breakthroughs and results thrill me and humble me every day.

All the many hundreds of artists I've worked with. Without all of you, this book would not exist.

All my clients, who have entrusted me with so much. I sometimes pinch myself when I get to look back at the extraordinary opportunities I have had serving you.

And to you, my reader. It is my sincere desire that, with what's written in these pages, you can turn your ideas into gold.

Sources and References

INTRODUCTION

IBM CEO survey

IBM Corporation. *Capitalizing on Complexity: Insights from the Global Chief Executive Officer Study*. Somers, NY: 2010. https://www.ibm.com/downloads /cas/1VZV5X8J.
Note: Every year, IBM changes the topic of their survey and the type of manager or employee they interview. The findings of the 2010 survey are still valid.

LinkedIn

Van Nuys, Amanda. "New LinkedIn Research: Upskill Your Employees with the Skills Companies Need Most in 2020." LinkedIn Learning Blog. December 28, 2019. https://www.linkedin.com/business/learning/blog /learning-and-development/most-in-demand-skills-2020.

World Economic Forum

Belsky, Scott. "How to Orepare for a Future in Which Creativity Is a Workforce Survival Skill." Quartz at Work. Last updated on April 12, 2021. https://qz.com /work/1929629/how-to-prepare-for-a-future-where-creativity-is-a-survival-skill/.
World Economic Forum. "This Is the One Skill That Will Future-Proof You for the Jobs Market." October 22, 2020. https://www.weforum.org/agenda/2020/10 /andria-zafirakou-teacher-jobs-skills-creativity/.

Adobe

Adobe. "Study Reveals Global Creativity Gap." Adobe News. April 23, 2012. https:// news.adobe.com/news/news-details/2012/Study-Reveals-Global-Creativity -Gap/default.aspx.
Adobe. *State of Create: 2016*. https://www.adobe.com/content/dam/acom/en/max /pdfs/AdobeStateofCreate_2016_Report_Final.pdf.

Study that equates creative process for artists and engineers

van Broekhoven, Kim, David Cropley, and Philipp Seegers. "Differences in creativity Across Art and STEM Students: We Are More Alike Than Unalike." *Thinking Skills and Creativity* 38 (December 2020). https://doi.org/10.1016/j .tsc.2020.100707.

1: CREATIVITY AND CRISIS

Blackboard Jungle

Golub, Adam. "A Transnational Tale of Teenage Terror: *The Blackboard Jungle* in Global Perspective." *Journal of Transnational American Studies* 6, no. 1 (2015). http://dx.doi.org/10.5070/T861025868.

"'Jungle' Appalls Critics in Britain." *New York Times*. September 18, 1955. https://timesmachine.nytimes.com/timesmachine/1955/09/18/91365575 .pdf?pdf_redirect=true&ip=0.

CIA financing abstract expressionism

Levine, Lucy. "Was Modern Art Really a CIA Psy-Op?" JSTOR Daily. April 1, 2020. https://daily.jstor.org/was-modern-art-really-a-cia-psy-op/.

Saunders, Frances Stonor. "Modern Art Was CIA 'Weapon.'" *Independent*. June 14, 2013.

Sooke, Alastair. "Was Modern Art a Weapon of the CIA?" BBC Culture. October 4, 2016. https://www.bbc.com/culture/article/20161004-was-modern-art-a-weapon-of-the-cia.

Study about creativity and crisis

Forgeard, M. J. C. "Perceiving Benefits After Adversity: The Relationship Between Self-Reported Posttraumatic Growth and Creativity." *Psychology of Aesthetics, Creativity, and the Arts* 7, no. 3 (2013): 245–64. https://doi.org/10.1037 /a0031223.

2: CREATIVITY AND ARTISTS

References about the Medicis

Hibbert, Christopher. *The House of Medici: Its Rise and Fall.* New York: William Morrow, 1999.

Evolution of creativity

Weiner, Robert Paul. *Creativity and Beyond: Cultures, Values, and Change.* Albany: State University of New York Press, 2000.

Prehistoric painting

Brumm, Adam, et al. "Oldest Cave Art Found in Sulawesi." *Science Advances* 7, no. 3 (January 13, 2021). https://advances.sciencemag.org/content/7/3/eabd4648.

Ferreira, Becky. "Mythical Beings May Be Earliest Imaginative Cave Art by Humans." *New York Times*. December 11, 2019. https://www.nytimes .com/2019/12/11/science/cave-art-indonesia.html.

3: DISPELLING MYTHS ABOUT CREATIVITY

Dr. Land and Dr. Jarman's findings

Land, George, and Beth Jarman. *Breakpoint and Beyond: Mastering the Future Today.* New York: HarperBusiness, 1992.

Georges Braque and collage

The Met. "Fruit Dish and Glass: Sorgues, Autumn 1912; Georges Braque." https://www.metmuseum.org/art/collection/search/490612.

Dom Pérignon

DeJean, Joan. *The Essence of Style: How the French Invented High Fashion, Fine Food, Chic Cafes, Style, Sophistication, and Glamour.* New York: Free Press, 2003.

Liem, Peter. *Champagne: The Essential Guide to the Wines, Producers, and Terroirs of the Iconic Region.* Emeryville, CA: Ten Speed Press, 2017.

Pablo Picasso

Brassaï, and Jane Marie Todd. *Conversations with Picasso.* Chicago: University of Chicago Press, 1999.

Esterow, Milton. "The Battle for Picasso's Multi-Billion-Dollar Empire." *Vanity Fair*, March 2016. https://www.vanityfair.com/culture/2016/03/picasso-multi-billion-dollar-empire-battle.

O'Brien, Patrick. *Picasso: A Biography.* New York: W. W. Norton, 1976.

Joan Miró

Cain, Abigail. "The Morning Routines of Famous Artists, from Andy Warhol to Louise Bourgeois." Artsy. August 15, 2018. https://www.artsy.net/article/artsy-editorial-morning-routines-famous-artists-andy-warhol-louise-bourgeois.

Miró, Joan, and Robert Lubar. *Joan Miró: I Work Like a Gardener* (Interview with Joan Miró on his creative process). New York: Princeton Architectural Press, 2017.

Is creativity inherited?

Barbot, Baptiste. "The Genetics of Creativity: The Generative and Receptive Sides of the Creativity Equation." In *The Neuroscience of Creativity*, edited by Oshin Vartanian, et al., 71–93. Cambridge, MA: MIT Press, 2013. https://doi.org/10.7551/mitpress/9780262019583.003.0004.

Goldberg, Elkhonon. *Creativity: The Human Brain in the Age of Innovation.* New York: Oxford University Press, 2018.

Eric Kandel

NobelPrize.org. "Eric Kandel Biographical." 2000. https://www.nobelprize.org/prizes/medicine/2000/kandel/biographical/.

Neuroplasticity

Merzenich, Michael. *Soft-Wired: How the New Science of Brain Plasticity Can Change Your Life*. San Francisco: Parnassus, 2013.

Study on how habits are formed

Lally, Phillippa, et al. "How Are Habits Formed: Modelling Habit Formation in the Real World." *European Journal of Social Psychology* 40, no. 6 (October 2010): 998–1009. https://onlinelibrary.wiley.com/doi/abs/10.1002/ejsp.674.

4: BEYOND 20/20

Michelangelo Buonarroti

Wallace, William E. *Michelangelo: The Artist, the Man and His Times*. Cambridge: Cambridge University Press, 2011.

Zöllner, Frank, and Christof Thoenes. *Michelangelo: The Complete Sculpture, Painting, Architecture*. Cologne, Germany: Taschen, 2009.

Christo and Jeanne-Claude

Austin, Tom. "He Dressed Miami's Islands in Pink, Changing the City Forever. Here's How He Pulled it Off." *Miami Herald,* October 12, 2018. https://www.miamiherald.com/entertainment/visual-arts/article219313155.html.

Hardymon, G. Felda, Josh Lerner, and Ann Leamon. "Christo and Jeanne-Claude: The Art of the Entrepreneur." Harvard Business School Case 806–14 (February 2006). https://www.hbs.edu/faculty/Pages/item.aspx?num=33013.

Steve Jobs

Isaacson, Walter. *Steve Jobs: The Exclusive Biography*. New York: Simon & Schuster, 2011.

5: DARING CONVENTION

Artemisia Gentileschi

Garrard, Mary D. *Artemisia Gentileschi*. Princeton University Press, 1991.

Ai Weiwei

Branigan, Tania. "Ai Weiwei Released from Detention." *The Guardian,* June 22, 2011. https://www.theguardian.com/artanddesign/2011/jun/22/ai-weiwei-released-from-detention.

Silver, Katie. "Ai Weiwei: Credit Suisse Closed Bank Account over China," BBC News, September 8, 2021. https://www.bbc.com/news/business-58484447.

Wee, Sui-Lee. "China Orders Ai Weiwei to Pay $2.4 Million for 'Tax Evasion.'" Reuters, October 31, 2011. https://www.reuters.com/article/us-china-artist-idUSTRE7A00NZ20111101.

Madame C. J. Walker

Bundles, A'Lelia. *Self Made: Inspired by the Life of Madam C. J. Walker.* New York: Scribner, 2020.

6: BRINGING THE INSIDE OUT

Frida Kahlo and Tina Modotti

Kahlo, Frida, and Tina Modotti. *Frida Kahlo and Tina Modotti.* London: Whitechapel Gallery, 1982.

Swoon at Brooklyn Museum

Brooklyn Museum. "Swoon: Submerged Motherlands; April 11–August 2, 2014." https://www.brooklynmuseum.org/exhibitions/swoon/?gclid=CjwK CAjwpMOIBhBAEiwAy5M6YOK7k7_C2CvMzJwXiJQhKjPg-8IMoqrTeIVS rWx7gQX4n4i01YYd8BoCJTUQAvD_BwE.

Serwan Baran

Chalabi, Tamara, Paolo Colombo, and Natasha Gasparian, ed. *Serwan Baran: Fatherland.* Milan: Mousse, 2019.

Study on creativity and emotions in business teams

Michael R. Parke et al. "The Creative and Cross-Functional Benefits of Wearing Hearts on Sleeves: Authentic Affect Climate, Information Elaboration, and Team Creativity." Organization Science, March 9, 2021. https://pubsonline .informs.org/doi/abs/10.1287/orsc.2021.1448.

7: TAKING THE OUTSIDE IN

Eugène Delacroix

Wellington, Hubert. *Journal of Delacroix (Arts & Letters).* New York: Phaidon, 1995.

Arnaldo Roche Rabell

García, Laura Tíscar. "Territory of the Soul: The Search for One's Self Through the Other." *Visión Doble,* December 15, 2018. https://revistas.upr.edu/images /visiondoble/2018/Ent1.pdf.

Walt Disney

Gabler, Neal. *Walt Disney: The Triumph of the American Imagination.* New York: Knopf, 2006.

Linetsky, Barry. *The Business of Walt Disney and the Nine Principles of His Success.* Edited by Bob McLain. Theme Park Press, 2017.

William, Pat. *How to Be Like Walt: Capturing the Disney Magic Every Day of Your Life.* Deerfield Beach, FL: Health Communications, 2004.

8: CURIOSITY

Leonardo da Vinci

Clark, Kenneth. *Civilisation*. London: John Murray, 1969.

Isaacson, Walter. *Leonardo da Vinci*. New York: Simon & Schuster, 2017.

Zöllner, Frank, and Johannes Nathan. *Leonardo. The Complete Paintings and Drawings*. Cologne, Germany: Taschen, 2019.

Mihaly Csikszentmihalyi art student study

Csikszentmihalyi, M., and J. W. Getzels. "Discovery-Oriented Behavior and the Originality of Creative Products: A Study with Artists." *Journal of Personality and Social Psychology* 19, no. 1 (1971): 47–52. https://doi.org/10.1037/h0031106.

Elon Musk

Musk, Elon. "Elon Musk: Founder, PayPal, SpaceX, Tesla Motors, & Solar City." Interview by Barry Hurd. The Henry Ford, June 26, 2008. https://www.thehenryford.org/explore/stories-of-innovation/visionaries/elon-musk/.

Musk, Maye. *A Woman Makes a Plan: Advice for a Lifetime of Adventure, Beauty, and Success*. New York: Penguin Life, 2019.

Vance, Ashlee. *Elon Musk: Tesla, SpaceX, and the Quest for a Fantastic Future*. New York: Ecco, 2015.

9: SILENCE AND SOLITUDE

Study about silence

Wilson, Timothy D., et al. "Just Think: The Challenges of a Disengaged Mind." *Science* 345, no. 6192 (July 2014): 75. https://wjh-www.harvard.edu/~dtg/WILSON%20ET%20AL%202014.pdf.

Georgia O'Keeffe

Lisle, Laurie. *Portrait of an Artist: A Biography of Georgia O'Keeffe*. New York: Washington Square Press, 1980.

Lynes, Barbara Buhler, et al. *Georgia O'Keeffe and New Mexico: A Sense of Place*. Princeton University Press, 2004.

O'Keeffe, Georgia. *Georgia O'Keeffe*. New York: Penguin, 1977.

Robinson, Roxana. *Georgia O'Keeffe: A Life*. Waltham, MA: Brandeis University Press, 2020.

"Settlement Is Granted over O'Keeffe Estate." *New York Times*, July 26, 1987. https://www.nytimes.com/1987/07/26/us/settlement-is-granted-over-o-keeffe-estate.html.

Steve Jobs

Isaacson, Walter. *Steve Jobs: The Exclusive Biography*. New York: Simon & Schuster, 2011.

Steve Wozniak

Wozniak, Steve, and Gina Smith. *iWoz: How I Invented the Personal Computer and Had Fun Along the Way*. New York: W. W. Norton, 2006.

Bill Gates's Think Weeks

Clifford, Catherine. "Bill Gates Took Solo 'Think Weeks' in a Cabin in the Woods—Why It's a Great Strategy." CNBC Make It. July 28, 2019. https://www.cnbc.com/2019/07/26/bill-gates-took-solo-think-weeks-in-a-cabin-in-the-woods.html.

10: INTUITION

Henri Matisse

Flam, Jack. *Matisse on Art*. Berkeley: University of California Press, 1995.

Intuition

Day, Laura. *Practical Intuition: How to Harness the Power of Your Instinct and Make It Work for You*. New York: Broadway Books, 1997.
Osho. *Intuition: Knowing Beyond Logic*. New York: Saint Martin's Griffin, 1997.

Estée Lauder

Israel, Lee. *Estée Lauder: Beyond the Magic (An Unauthorized Biography)*. New York: Macmillan, 1985.
Lauder, Estée. *Estée: A Success Story*. New York: Random House, 1985.

Measuring intuition

Lufityanto, Galang, Chris Donkin, and Joel Pearson. "Measuring Intuition: Nonconscious Emotional Information Boosts Decision Accuracy and Confidence." *Psychological Science* 25, no. 5 (2016): 622–34. https://journals.sagepub.com/doi/full/10.1177/0956797616629403.*Study about intuition and creativity*
Pétervári Judit, Osman Magda, and Bhattacharya Joydeep. "The Role of Intuition in the Generation and Evaluation Stages of Creativity." https://www.frontiersin.org/articles/10.3389/fpsyg.2016.01420/full.

11: DAYDREAMING

Hieronymus Bosch

Fischer, Stefan. *Hieronymus Bosch. Complete Works*. Cologne, Germany: Taschen, 2014.

Sigmund Freud's essay

Freud, Sigmund. "Creative Writers and Daydreaming." 1907. http://users.uoa
.gr/~cdokou/FreudCreativeWriters.pdf.

Salvador Dalí

Dalí, Salvador. *The Secret Life of Salvador Dalí*. New York: Dover, 1993.

Dalí, Salvador, and Haakon M. Chevalier. *50 Secrets of Magic Craftsmanship*. New
York: Dover, 2013.

Descharnes, Robert, and Gilles Néret. *Dalí. The Paintings*. Cologne, Germany:
Taschen, 2020.

Cirque du Soleil

Babinski, Tony. *Cirque du Soleil: 20 Years Under the Sun*. New York: Harry N.
Abrams, 2004.

Heward, Lyn, and John U. Bacon. *Cirque du Soleil: The Spark; Igniting the Creative
Fire That Lives Within Us All*. New York: Doubleday, 2006.

12: RISK-TAKING

Jacques-Louis David

Johnson, Dorothy. *Jacques-Louis David: The Farewell of Telemachus and Eucharis*.
Los Angeles: Getty Museum, 1997.

Roberts, Warren. *Jacques-Louis David, Revolutionary Artist: Art, Politics, and the
French Revolution*. Chapel Hill: University of North Carolina Press, 1992.

Damien Hirst

Colman, David. "Damien Hirst Will Take the Hate with the Love in Venice." *New
York* magazine, December 1, 2017. https://www.vulture.com/2017/12/damien
-hirst-on-treasures-of-the-wreck-of-the-unbelievable.html.

Hirst, Damien, et al. *Damien Hirst: Treasures from the Wreck of the Unbelievable*.
London: Other Criteria Books, 2017.

Nike

Knight, Phil. *Shoe Dog: A Memoir by the Creator of Nike*. New York: Scribner, 2016.

13: IMPROVISE

Jackson Pollock

Adams, Henry. "Decoding Jackson Pollock." *Smithsonian Magazine* (November 2009). https://www.smithsonianmag.com/arts-culture/decoding
-jackson-pollock-142492290/.

Harrison, Helen A. "Through a Glass Brightly: Jackson Pollock in His Own Words."
New York Times, November 15, 1988. https://www.nytimes.com/1998/11/15
/nyregion/through-a-glass-brightly-jackson-pollock-in-his-own-words.html.

Hentoff, Nat. "Jackson Pollock's Jazz." *Wall Street Journal*, February 19, 1999. https://www.wsj.com/articles/SB919391154127530500.

Naifeh, Steven, and Gregory Smith. *Jackson Pollock: An American Saga*. New York: Woodward/White, 1998.

The Phillips Collection. "When Pollock Embraced Spontaneity." Experiment Station (blog). March 8, 2018. https://blog.phillipscollection.org/2018/03/08/jackson-pollock-spontaneity/.

Shonda Rhimes

Rhimes, Shonda. *Year of Yes: How to Dance It Out, Stand in the Sun and Be Your Own Person*. New York: Simon & Schuster, 2015.

Bob Kulhan

Kulhan, Bob, and Chuck Crisafulli. *Getting to "Yes And": The Art of Business Improv*. Stanford Business Books, 2017.

14: EMBRACE FAILURE

Marcel Duchamp

"Explosion in a Shingle Factory." *New York Times*, August 3, 1975. https://www.nytimes.com/1975/08/03/archives/explosion-in-a-shingle-factory.html.

Folland, Thomas. "Marcel Duchamp, *Nude Descending a Staircase, No 2*." Smarthistory, January 9, 2017. https://smarthistory.org/duchamp-descending/.

Mancini, J. M. "'One Term Is as Fatuous as Another': Responses to the Armory Show Reconsidered." *American Quarterly* 51, no. 4 (December 1999): 833–70. https://www.jstor.org/stable/30041674.

Rosenberg, Harold. "The Armory Show: Revolution Reenacted." *New Yorker*, March 29, 1963. https://www.newyorker.com/magazine/1963/04/06/the-armory-show-revolution-reenacted.

Jeff Koons

Archer, Michael. *Jeff Koons: One Ball Total Equilibrium Tank*. London: Afterall Books, 2011.

Landi, Ann. "Top Ten ARTnews Stories: How Jeff Koons Became a Superstar." *ARTnews*, November 1, 2007. https://www.artnews.com/art-news/news/top-ten-artnews-stories-how-jeff-koons-became-a-superstar-188/.

Reyburn, Scott. "Jeff Koons 'Rabbit' Sets Auction Record for Most Expensive Work by Living Artist." *New York Times*, May 15, 2019. https://www.nytimes.com/2019/05/15/arts/jeff-koons-rabbit-auction.html.

Barbara Corcoran

Corcoran, Barbara, and Bruce Littlefield. *Shark Tales: How I Turned $1,000 into a Billion Dollar Business*. New York: Portfolio, 2011.

15: DECONSTRUCT

Pablo Picasso

Martin, Russell. *Picasso's War*. New York: Plume, 2003.

16: AGGREGATE

Gutai Group

Munroe, Alexandra, et al. *Gutai: Splendid Playground*. New York: Guggenheim Museum, 2013.

Allan Kaprow

Potts, Alex. *Allan Kaprow—Art as Life*. Los Angeles: Getty Research Institute, 2008.

Facebook

Levy, Steven. *Facebook: The Inside Story*. New York: Blue Rider Press, 2020.

17: REPEAT

Claude Monet

Wildenstein, Daniel. *Monet. The Triumph of Impressionism*. Cologne, Germany: Taschen, 2014.

Andy Warhol

Danto, Arthur, and Donna deSalvo. *Andy Warhol Prints: A Catalogue Raisonné 1962–1987*. Edited by Claudia Defendi, Frayda Feldman, and Jörg Schellmann. New York: D.A.P/Ronald Feldman Fine Arts/Andy Warhol Foundation for the Visual Arts, 2003.

Gopnik, Blake. "Andy Warhol Inc.: How He Made Business His Art." *New York Times,* November 1, 2018. https://www.nytimes.com/2018/11/01/arts/design /andy-warhol-inc-how-he-made-business-his-art.html.

Kamholz, Roger. "Andy Warhol and His Process." Sotheby's. *Contemporary Art.* November 10, 2013. https://www.sothebys.com/en/articles/andy-warhol -and-his-process.

Warhol, Andy. *The Philosophy of Andy Warhol: From A to B and Back Again*. San Diego, Harvest: 1977.

Warhol, Andy, and Pat Hackett. *The Andy Warhol Diaries*. New York: Warner Books, 1989.

Benetton

"Benetton Launches a New Ad Campaign—With No Clothes in Sight." Yahoo! News, August 2, 2008. https://news.yahoo.com/benetton-launches-ad-campaign -no-clothes-sight-155010144.html.

Povoledo, Elisabetta. "Benetton Severs Ties with Oliviero Toscani." *New York Times,* February 6, 2020. https://www.nytimes.com/2020/02/06/world /europe/benetton-oliviero-toscani.html.

Waxman, Sharon. "The True Colors of Luciano Benetton." *Washington Post,* February 17, 1993. https://www.washingtonpost.com/archive/lifestyle/1993/02 /17/the-true-colors-of-luciano-benetton/4a8bfcab-ed6a-42bd-80bf -27901ef9b9de/.

18: CREATIVE TENSION

Caravaggio

Schütze, Sebastian. *Caravaggio. The Complete Works.* Cologne, Germany: Taschen, 2015.

Scorsese, Martin. "Scorsese on Caravaggio." Interview with Andrew Graham Dixon. *The Culture Show.* BBC. June 21, 2011. https://www.bbc.co.uk/programmes /poohqprn.

Leonardo da Vinci

Isaacson, Walter. *Leonardo da Vinci.* New York: Simon & Schuster, 2017.

Zöllner, Frank, and Johannes Nathan. *Leonardo. The Complete Paintings and Drawings.* Cologne, Germany: Taschen, 2019.

Édouard Manet

Clark, T. J. *The Painting of Modern Life: Paris in the Art of Manet and His Followers.* Princeton University Press, 1999.

Roe, Sue. *The Private Lives of the Impressionists.* New York: Harper, 2006.

Coco Chanel

Charles-Roux, Edmonde. *Chanel and Her World.* New York: Vendome Press, 2005.

Mazzeo, Tilar J. *The Secret of Chanel No. 5: The Intimate History of the World's Most Famous Perfume.* New York: Harper, 2010.

Statista Research Department. "Perfume and Eau de Toilette for Women Brands of Chanel Ranked by Number of Users in Great Britain from 2015 to 2020." July 9, 2021. https://www.statista.com/statistics/305095 /leading-chanel-perfume-and-eau-de-toilette-brands-for-women-in-the-uk/.

19: CROSS-POLLINATION

Gustav Klimt

Kandel, Eric. *The Age of Insight: The Quest to Understand the Unconscious in Art, Mind, and Brain, from Vienna 1900 to the Present.* New York: Random House, 2012.

20: THE ANALOG METHOD

Leonardo da Vinci

da Vinci, Leonardo. *Leonardo's Notebooks.* Edited by H. Anna Suh. New York: Black Dog & Leventhal, 2005.

———. *The Notebooks of Leonardo Da Vinci: Complete & Illustrated.* Translated by Jean Paul Richter. Istanbul: E-Kitap Projesi & Cheapest Books, 2014.

Isaacson, Walter. *Leonardo da Vinci.* New York: Simon & Schuster, 2017.

Pablo Picasso's notebooks

Glimcher, Arnold, Marc Glimcher, and Mark Pollard. *Je Suis Le Cahier: The Sketchbooks of Picasso.* New York: Atlantic Monthly Press, 1986.

Ianco-Starrels, Josine. "Sketchbooks of a Genius." *Los Angeles Times,* December 14, 1986. https://www.latimes.com/archives/la-xpm-1986-12-14-ca-2795-story.html.

McGill, Douglas C. "Picasso Sketchbooks' Path to Gallery." *New York Times,* May 7, 1986. https://www.nytimes.com/1986/05/07/arts/picasso-sketchbooks-path-to-gallery.html.

Tully, Judd. "Master Strokes: New York's Picasso Coup." *Washington Post,* May 2, 1986. https://www.washingtonpost.com/archive/lifestyle/1986/05/02/master-strokes-new-yorks-picasso-coup/odf671e5-79a1-4648-a872-e138a2e9055b/.

Indiana University study

James, Karin H., and Laura Engelhardt. "The Effects of Handwriting Experience on Functional Brain Development in Pre-Literate Children." *Trends in Neuroscience and Education* 1, no. 1 (December 2012): 32–42. https://doi.org/10.1016/j.tine.2012.08.001.

Vinci-Booher, Sophia, and Karin H. James. "Visual Experiences During Letter Production Contribute to the Development of the Neural Systems Supporting Letter Perception." *Developmental Science* 23, no. 5 (September 2020): e12965. https://doi.org/10.1111/desc.12965.

University of Washington study

Berninger, Virginia W., Robert D. Abbott, and Amy Augsburger. "Comparison of Pen and Keyboard Transcription Modes in Children with and without Learning Disabilities." *Learning Disability Quarterly* 32, no. 3 (2009): 123–41. https://doi.org/10.2307/27740364.

Princeton University study

Mueller, Pam. A., and Daniel Oppenheimer. "The Pen Is Mightier Than the Keyboard: Advantages of Longhand over Laptop Note Taking." *Psychological Science* 25, no. 6 (2014): 1159–68. https://doi.org/10.1177/0945797614524581.

Richard Branson

Branson, Richard. "Why Everyone Should Take Notes." Virgin. *Richard Branson's Blog.* April 23, 2019. https://www.virgin.com/branson-family/richard-branson-blog/why-everyone-should-take-notes.

21: MIXING INTUITION AND RATIONALITY

Peter Paul Rubens

Lamster, Mark. *Master of Shadows: The Secret Diplomatic Career of the Painter Peter Paul Rubens*. New York: Anchor, 2010.

Nicholson, Louise. "How Rubens Made a Booming Business of His Art." *Apollo*, June 14, 2019. https://www.apollo-magazine.com/early-years-rubens-review/.

Otto Beisheim School of Management study

Kaufmann, Lutz, Claudia Maria Wagner, and Craig Carter. "Individual Modes and Patterns of Rational and Intuitive Decision-Making by Purchasing Managers." *Journal of Purchasing and Supply Management* 23, no. 2 (September 2016): https://www.researchgate.net/publication/309224846_Individual _modes_and_patterns_of_rational_and_intuitive_decision-making_by _purchasing_managers.

Ray Kroc

Kroc, Ray. *Grinding It Out: The Making of McDonald's*. New York: Griffin, 2016.

22: COLLABORATION

Donatello

Coonin, A. Victor. *Donatello and the Dawn of Renaissance Art*. London: Reaktion Books, 2019.

Elsa Schiaparelli and Salvador Dalí

Farra, Emily. "80 Years Later, Schiaparelli Brings Back Elsa's Famous Lobster Dress." *Vogue*, January 24, 2017. https://www.vogue.com/article /schiaparelli-behind-the-scenes-details-lobster-embroidered-dress-inspiration.

Rubenstein, Celestial. "1937–Elsa Schiaparelli, Lobster Dinner Dress." Fashion History Timeline. Last updated January 13, 2020. https://fashionhistory.fitnyc .edu/1937-schiaparelli-lobster/.

Robert Rauschenberg

Dickerman, Leah, and Achim Borchardt-Hume, eds. *Robert Rauschenberg*. New York: The Museum of Modern Art, 2016.

Sinclair, Sara, Peter Bearman, and Mary Marshall Clark, eds. *Robert Rauschenberg: An Oral History*. New York: Columbia University Press, 2019.

Damien Hirst and Sotheby's

Akbar, Arifa. "A formaldehyde frenzy as buyers snap up Hirst works." *Independent*, October 22, 2011. https://www.independent.co.uk/arts-entertainment/art /news/a-formaldehyde-frenzy-as-buyers-snap-up-hirst-works-931979.html.

Collett-White, Mike, and Soheil Afdjei. "Hirst Says Major Auction Comes from His Inner Punk." Reuters, September 8, 2008. https://www.reuters.com/article /slideshow/idUSL88593920080908.

Hirst, Damien. "Beautiful Inside My Head Forever." Damienhirst.com. https:// www.damienhirst.com/exhibitions/solo/2008/beautiful-auction.

Lewis, Dan. "Why I Was Banned from Damien Hirst's £120m Gamble." *London Evening Standard,* September 15, 2008. https://web.archive.org /web/20091201023820/http://www.thisislondon.co.uk/standard/article -23555605-why-i-was-banned-from-damien-hirsts-120m-gamble.do.

Sotheby's 2009 Annual Report. 2010. https://www.annualreports.com/HostedData /AnnualReportArchive/s/NYSE_BID_2009.pdf.

Starbucks and Spotify

Prins, Naomi. "The Spotify-Starbucks Partnership Is Digital Co-Branding Genius." *Forbes,* May 19, 2015. https://www.forbes.com/sites/nomiprins/2015/05/19 /the-spotify-starbucks-partnership-is-digital-co-branding-genius/.

Samuely, Alex. "Starbucks and Spotify Partnership Highlights Link Between Mobile Loyalty, Content." *Mobile Commerce Daily.* https://www.retaildive.com /ex/mobilecommercedaily/starbucks-and-spotify-partnership-highlights-link -between-mobile-loyalty-music#:~:text=Spotify's%20streaming%20will%20 now%20be,curate%20playlists%20for%20Starbucks%20stores.

"Starbucks and Spotify to Partner on Music Streaming Service." Starbucks Stories & News. May 18, 2015. https://stories.starbucks.com/stories/2015 /starbucks-spotify-partnership/.

23: CONNECT THE DOTS

Diego Velázquez

Jacobs, Michael. *Everything Is Happening: Journey into a Painting.* London: Granta, 2016.

López-Rey, José, and Odile Delenda. *Velázquez. The Complete Works.* Cologne, Germany: Taschen, 2020.

Sidey, Myoo. "Las Meninas—Interpretation Narratives Throughout Centuries." *Art Inquiry* XIX, no. XXVIII (2017): 73–87. http://cejsh.icm.edu.pl/cejsh/ele- ment/bwmeta1.element.desklight-5868668c-e993-4d11-b27b-597a148c8a18.

Underwood, Robert Milton Jr. "Critical Analysis of Diego Velázquez's *Las Meninas.*" Research paper, 2008. https://www.academia.edu/6928355 /Critical_Analysis_of_Diego_Vel%C3%A1zquezs_Las_Meninas.

Yale School of Medicine

Wheeling, Kate. "How Looking at Paintings Became a Required Course in Medical School." *Yale Medicine Magazine,* Spring 2014. https://medicine.yale.edu/news /yale-medicine-magazine/how-looking-at-paintings-became-a-required -course/.

Airbnb

"Airbnb Co-Founder Opens Up His Home." *Financial Times*, September 20, 2017. https://www.ft.com/content/cff96ef6-9872-11e7-8c5c-c8d8fa6961bb.

Gallagher, Leigh. *The Airbnb Story: How Three Ordinary Guys Disrupted an Industry, Made Billions . . . and Created Plenty of Controversy*. Boston: Mariner Books, 2017.

24: PIVOT

Piet Mondrian

de Jong, Cees W., ed. *Piet Mondrian: Life and Work*. New York: Abrams, 2015.

Niki de Saint Phalle

de Saint Phalle, Niki. *The Tarot Garden*. Salenstein, Switzerland: Benteli, 2006.

Pietromarchi, Guilio, et al. *Niki de Saint Phalle and the Tarot Garden*. Salenstein, Switzerland: Benteli, 2010.

Weidemann, Christiane. *Niki de Saint Phalle*. Munich: Prestel, 2014.

Suzuki

"Suzuki Motor Corporation." Reference for Business Company History Index. https://www.referenceforbusiness.com/history2/65/Suzuki-Motor-Corporation.html.

Play Doh

Kindy, David. "The Accidental Invention of Play-Doh." *Smithsonian Magazine*, November 12, 2019. https://www.smithsonianmag.com/innovation/accidental-invention-play-doh-180973527/.

25: INVENTING THE FUTURE

Hilma af Klint

Bashkoff, Tracey, ed. *Hilma af Klint: Paintings for the Future*. New York: Guggenheim Museum, 2018.

Dyrschka, Halina, dir. *Beyond the Visible: Hilma af Klint*. 2019. Zeitgeist Films. https://zeitgeistfilms.com/film/beyondthevisiblehilmaafklint.

Nam June Paik

Greenberger, Alex. "Nam June Paik's Pioneering Vision: How the Artist Predicted an Age of Digital Technology." *ARTnews*, July 20, 2020. https://www.artnews.com/feature/nam-june-paik-television-video-art-famous-works-1202694737/.

Hanhardt, John G., and Ken Hakuta. *Nam June Paik: Global Visionary*. Lewes, England: Giles, 2012.

Mellencamp, Patricia. "The Old and the New: Nam June Paik." *Art Journal* 54, no. 4 (Winter 1995): 41–47. https://www.jstor.org/stable/777693.

Tate. "Nam June Paik: 1932–2006; Artist Biography." https://www.tate.org.uk/art
/artists/nam-june-paik-6380.

"Video Visionary." *New Yorker*, May 5, 1975, 44. https://www.newyorker.com
/magazine/1975/05/05/video-visionary

Andy Warhol

Warhol, Andy. *The Philosophy of Andy Warhol: From A to B and Back Again*. San
Diego, Harvest: 1977.

Warhol, Andy, and Pat Hackett. *The Andy Warhol Diaries*. New York: Warner
Books, 1989.

Google

Galloway, Scott. *The Four: The Hidden DNA of Amazon, Apple, Facebook, and Google*.
New York: Portfolio, 2018.

Ha, Thu-Huong. "Computing is Still Too Clunky: Charlie Rose and Larry
Page in Conversation." *TED Blog*. March 19, 2014. https://blog.ted.com
/computing-is-still-too-clunky-charlie-rose-and-larry-page-in-conversation/.

Vise, David A., and Mark Malseed. *The Google Story: Inside the Hottest Business,
Media, and Technology Success of Our Time*. New York: Delacorte, 2005.

Index

About the Author

MARIA BRITO IS a New York–based contemporary art advisor, author, and curator. She is a Harvard Law School graduate, originally from Venezuela. Brito was selected by Complex as one of the "20 Art World Power Players," and she was named by *ARTnews* as "one of the innovators who gets to shape the art world."

She has written for *Entrepreneur*, HuffPost, *Elle*, Artnet, *Forbes*, *Cultured*, *Departures*, Goop, and the *Gulf Coast Journal of Literature and Fine Arts* from the University of Houston, Texas.

Maria has curated art exhibitions in three continents and also created and hosted *The "C" Files with Maria Brito*, a TV and streaming series for the PBS station ALL ARTS.

Maria has taught variations of her creativity class in companies for several years and has also designed and launched Jumpstart, a comprehensive online program on creativity for artists, freelancers, managers, and entrepreneurs. Jumpstart is based on her years of practical work, research, and observation in both the worlds of business and art.

She lives in New York City with her husband and two sons.

For more information visit mariabrito.com.